Dear IVP Author,

During my over forty years at InterVarsity Press, I was privileged to work with and get to know many of you. You gave so much to me by your friendship and by what I gained in heart and mind from your writing. You made it possible for me to pursue my aspiration of being a lifelong learner. Thank you.

Now, through the generosity of the folks at InterVarsity Press, I can give a gift to you in return. This special hardback edition of Write Better, which won't be available anywhere else, is for IVP authors only.

You can find many excellent books on writing. Some are memoirs of the writing life by well-known authors. Others offer wonderful help on grammar, punctuation, and style.

Write Better instead considers the larger issues of craft and art in writing, offering practical strategies on a wide range of topics— such as how to find openings, focus on readers, be persuasive, battle writer's block, increase your creativity, use metaphors, and say more by saying less. An additional section concerns the spirituality of writing. That is, how does the act of writing and publishing affect our life with God?

I would enjoy being in touch with you through my blog, andyunedited.com, which will continue to take up topics of the world of writing. I do wish I could greet each of you in person, hand this book to you, and wish you well. For the moment may this letter and book suffice.

Peace,

Andy Le Peau

"In what Richard J. Foster, author of *Celebration of Discipline*, has recently described as the new curse of our time, the 'age of distraction,' publishing professional Andy Le Peau has written the almost perfect book for Christian writers to help them overcome their own distractions and the distractions of their readers. He covers all of the creative writing topics, and he does it in a way that is compelling and accessible, wise and intelligent. This is now the important book on writing that every Christian writer (and many others) must own, both beginners and advanced professionals. Everyone can learn something from this amazingly well-constructed and well-written book—everyone."

Roy M. Carlisle, executive editor for Books, Independent Institute

"This book belongs on the reference shelf of every writer. It offers forty years' experience with words—giving readers the equivalent of multiple master's courses for the price of one volume. Le Peau invites, encourages, instructs, and inspires the writer who wants to develop the craft, communicate effectively, respect the reader, and provide a compelling reading experience."

Vinita Hampton Wright, author of *The Soul Tells a Story*

"To take Le Peau's reliable, witty advice is to find ways to get started and keep going, all the while staying sober about the responsibility of turning words out into the world. Gratefully, it's not at all like pulling a rabbit out of a hat."

Jen Pollock Michel, author of *Surprised by Paradox*

"Andy Le Peau's *Write Better*—witty, down-to-earth, and informed by a lifetime in publishing—combines a wealth of practical advice with a distinctively Christian perspective on the writer's craft. It will be useful to aspiring young writers just starting out and to seasoned academics who want to reach a larger audience."

John Wilson, *Englewood Review of Books*

"An invaluable treasure-trove of wisdom, counsel, humor, and practical suggestions and tips—as one of the poorer writers on whom Andy Le Peau has honed his legendary skills, I only wish I had read this book before I started writing."

Os Guinness, author of *Fool's Talk*

"Andy Le Peau has written a comprehensive book filled with wisdom, engaging illustrations, and practical tips for both beginning and seasoned writers. . . . This is a book that explores our spiritual formation as writers and calls us to steward the Word with integrity and precision, while providing tools to do so with excellence. What a gift!"

Sharon Garlough Brown, author of the Sensible Shoes series and *Shades of Light*

"Andrew T. Le Peau's *Write Better* is a gift to students and teachers of writing. Drawing upon his experience as an editor and author, Le Peau shares practical recommendations and specific strategies that will benefit all writers—novices and professionals alike. . . . The book is chock-full of examples of effective prose, and Le Peau's own writing is clear, memorable, and rooted in his Christian convictions. This is a well-written book about writing well."

James E. Beitler III, associate professor at Wheaton College, author of *Seasoned Speech*

ANDREW T. LE PEAU

WRITE

BETTER

A Lifelong
Editor on
Craft, Art,
and Spirituality

ivp

An imprint of InterVarsity Press
Downers Grove, Illinois

InterVarsity Press
P.O. Box 1400, Downers Grove, IL 60515-1426
ivpress.com
email@ivpress.com

InterVarsity Press® is the book-publishing division of InterVarsity Christian Fellowship/USA®, a movement of students and faculty active on campus at hundreds of universities, colleges, and schools of nursing in the United States of America, and a member movement of the International Fellowship of Evangelical Students. For information about local and regional activities, visit intervarsity.org.

While any stories in this book are true, some names and identifying information may have been changed to protect the privacy of individuals.

Grateful thanks to David Lamb for permission to tell the story about his book.

Cover design: Cindy Kiple
Interior design: Jeanna Wiggins
Images: ©Tolga TEZCAN/E+/Getty Images

Printed in the United States of America ∞

InterVarsity Press is committed to ecological stewardship and to the conservation of natural resources in all our operations. This book was printed using sustainably sourced paper.

FOR STEPHEN, SUSAN,
PHILIP, DAVID

The finest creations Phyllis and I
have sent into the world

CONTENTS

Preface 1

PART 1: THE CRAFT OF WRITING

1 Finding an Opening 9

2 Knowing Your Audience 25

3 Giving Structure 30

4 The Character of Persuasion 36

5 The Craft of Persuasion 48

6 Creating Dramatic Nonfiction 59

7 Cracking Our Writer's Block 72

8 The Nuts, Bolts, Hammers, and Saws
of Good Rewriting 81

9 We Remember Endings First 88

10 Titles That Work 99

PART 2: THE ART OF WRITING

11 Creativity, the Mysterious Muse 115

12 Breaking the Rules 128

13 The Key to Powerful Prose—Tone 135

14 For the Love of Metaphor 145

15 Less Is More 157

PART 3: THE SPIRITUALITY OF WRITING

16 Called to Write. 171

17 The Quest for Voice 180

18 The Spirituality of Writing About Yourself . . . 186

19 Spiritual Authority and Writing. 198

20 The Courage to Create and Let Go 209

21 Stewards with a Message 217

APPENDIX A: Get Thee to a Platform 227

APPENDIX B: Editors and Agents Do Make
Cowards of Us All. 233

APPENDIX C: The Coauthor Doth Protest
Too Much, Methinks 238

APPENDIX D: To Self-Publish or Not to Self-Publish 242

APPENDIX E: The Copyright's the Thing 247

Online Resources from Andrew T. Le Peau 253

Recommended Reading. 254

Notes. 256

Index. 268

PREFACE

Two of my sons, Phil and Dave, ran cross-country in high school. These grueling three-mile races were not on perfectly flat, machine-fabricated ovals but up hills, over ruts, through woods. In heat and cold, rain and wind I, like other parents, came to urge them and their teammates on.

Sometimes I'd run from one part of the course to another, taking a shortcut, so that several times during a race I could yell encouragement to press on, to not let down, to remember their training. Once when I was dashing from one place to another, a student cheering for another school almost slammed into me. As he flew by in another direction, he said, "Sorry, Coach." I've never felt prouder to be mistakenly identified.

For over forty years I've trained, guided, and cheered on hundreds of writers. I've made suggestions for what to write about, how to write, and how to revise. I've encouraged and praised, cajoled and critiqued. In every case I have been stimulated by a desire to help people express their ideas as clearly and powerfully as possible. That is the motivation behind this book.

I've also done a fair bit of my own writing, trying to follow my own advice as much as possible. What I have realized in the process is how hard it is to write. It requires work and determination. It means saying no to other things I want to do or fitting it around things I must do (like my job). I have to overcome discouragement when progress is slow and when I don't meet my own standards. As a result, I have great admiration for people who write, people like you.

In this book I offer some of the lessons I've learned in reading, writing, and editing nonfiction. If I can lighten your load as a writer of books, articles, blogs, newsletters, or manuals, and speed you on your way, I will be content.

Students and those who just want to write better may also find help in these pages. I hope you will feel free to take what is of value here and lay aside the rest till later.

I've divided my material into three parts. Part one on craft is about mastering certain skills such as finding strong openings and closings, staying focused on an audience, creating a clear structure, being persuasive, revising well, and developing good titles.

Part two is on art, which is notoriously difficult to define. I use the term a bit reluctantly because we can misapply it to writing pretentiously or can misunderstand it as being so subjective that nothing practical can be said about it. Rather than "high art" in the sense of historical or cultural artifacts, I mostly mean human creations that speak deeply to the full human experience (heart, soul, mind, body as well as our social and historical dimensions). Sentimentality and cliché need not apply. I seek to demystify some aspects of art in writing by considering strategies that can nudge us along the continuum toward fresher, more vital, and perhaps more beautiful expressions of our human condition.

Part three is on the spirituality of writing. Here I do not focus on the spiritual content of what we write so much as on our spirituality as writers. What affect does the act of writing have on my life in God?

While this book is about writing better and not about publishing or how to get published, in the appendixes I try to pull back the curtain of mystery a bit from this often unseen world. How do you find an agent? What is involved in promotion? How does coauthoring work? What about the self-publishing option? And is there any way to make sense of copyright? Also at the back are listed further online resources (found at ivpress.com/write-better), including questions and exercises for students. I like order, so I would tend to read a book like this straight through. But you can skip around if you wish, going from one chapter to another as your needs or interests lead you.

You will notice that throughout I include many examples from fiction. This may seem odd for a book about writing nonfiction, but the line between the genres of fiction and nonfiction is not as hard and fast as it might seem. Both fiction and nonfiction can speak truth—and both can lie. Both fiction and nonfiction use narrative. We can tell a true episode in a work of fiction, or we can tell a fictional tale in a work of nonfiction. Likewise, both forms can share discourse and reasoning. A fictional character might spin out a historical incident or a philosophical line of thinking that could just as well be found in a nonfiction book.

Obviously I don't deal with a lot of issues that are formally part of fiction writing—plotting, character development, dialogue, and so forth. But when a fiction writer offers a fine example of how to shape a narrative or use a metaphor, I'm happy to draw our attention to it. Indeed, fiction writers tend to use figures of speech, images, and allusion often and with great skill. We nonfiction writers have much to learn from our fiction-writing comrades.

In the pages that follow I emphasize the importance of gratitude in life and writing. Allow me to do the some of the same here.

For over a dozen years now I've been blogging at *Andy Unedited* (andyunedited.com), where I offer thoughts on writing, publishing, history, biblical studies, and more. Some of what is found in this book was originally posted there, though now in a much revised and expanded form. David Zimmerman once suggested that I could probably gather enough material from the blog on a topic to be the basis for a book. I was skeptical, but here it is. Thank you.

I know all too well that it takes a village to make a book. Cindy Bunch, Jeff Crosby, and the rest of the publishing committee at Inter-Varsity Press said yes, while ninety others handled fulfillment, sales, marketing, production, and the business side. The folks at IVP also long supported my blog and hosted it on their website. Thank you.

I also stress in this book the importance of getting input from others before your writing goes public, listening to them openly, and wherever possible doing what they say. I have tried to follow my own advice. As much as I could, I revised, cut, reorganized, and added to earlier drafts as friends, family, and colleagues suggested.

Those who generously helped me by reading some or all of the manuscript include Drew "Blue Pencil" Blankman, Cindy "Now the Boss" Bunch, Rebecca "Laser Scalpel" Carhart, Heath "Prolific Professor" Carter, Roy "The Editor's Editor" Carlisle, John "Wise Man" DeCostanza, Susan "Favorite Daughter" DeCostanza, Mark "Communication King" Fackler, Kathy "Super Agent" Helmers, Al "An Idea a Minute" Hsu, Ellen "Contract Queen" Hsu, Stephanie "What a Gem" Jewell, John "Doesn't Miss a Thing" Le Peau, Phyllis "My Love" Le Peau, Joel "Man of Passionate Ideas" Scandrett, Dan "Always Follow His Advice" Reid, Kate "Keep the Student in Mind" Rice, Elizabeth "The Intern" Williams, and Ev "Psychology Is My Superpower" Worthington. Thank you.

Most people can point to a handful of others who had a major influence on them. That is true for how I grew in my love for working with words. My older siblings, Mary and John, were avid readers when I was growing up. Reading for me was slow and agonizing in grade school. But reading was something they valued and modeled for me. Since I wanted to be as smart as they were, I kept at it. Thank you.

I also had a high school teacher who opened me to the beauty, power, and magic of words. Mr. James Ryan spent the whole first semester of my junior year taking us through *Hamlet* line by line. What at first seemed impossible to decode soon became a realm of wonder and truth. Thank you.

My first boss in publishing was James Sire. He became well-known as a speaker and author. People mostly know him for his classic book on worldviews, *The Universe Next Door*. For me, he was the one who taught me how to edit—how to work with words, structure, and ideas. His influence permeates the advice in this book.

Jim taught me more than craft and art, however. He taught the importance of integrity in relationships with authors. He taught me to respect their ideas, to not impose my style or viewpoints on their work. He taught the importance of staying true to yourself as a publisher and not trying to copy the success of others. Thank you.

PART 1

THE CRAFT
OF WRITING

1

FINDING AN OPENING

BEGINNINGS MATTER.

If on the first day of your diet you accidentally eat three jelly donuts—that is not a good beginning. If you are late for a job interview because you rear-end a beer truck—that is not a good beginning. If you trip and crash into your future mother-in-law the first time you meet her—that is not a good beginning.

But if in the spring you turn over the soil and add the right nutrients before you plant, your garden can be productive during the whole season. If you make good friends in your first weeks of college, that can make the difference in sticking with school and ultimately graduating. If the opening sentences of what you write are just right, they can be a balm to readers and a joy to you.

Strong beginnings arrest attention and alert readers for what is to come. With so many options for our time—pressures of work, school, or family; opportunities for relaxation or entertainment—readers need to be compelled to hear what we have to say and to keep going. They won't commit to reading a paragraph, a page, an article, or a book out of a generous spirit. No. We as writers must make it possible for them to draw away from other attractions and distractions. A writer in search of a way to pull readers in need look no further than a strong opening.

No single formula exists. Openings come in great variety. Here are some of my favorites.

THE THESIS OPENING

Having a clear statement of your main point is an obvious and legitimate way to begin. The danger is that it can become convoluted and abstract. One solution is to make it personal, punchy, or provocative.

Life is difficult.

M. Scott Peck, *The Road Less Traveled*

With only three words Peck flings a bucketful of cold realism into our overly optimistic faces, waking us from our self-help stupor. Part of the power of his opening comes from the contrast it presents to a society committed to the easy life. Losing weight should be as easy as taking a pill. Loving someone should be simple. Learning a language should as painless as listening to a recording. We just don't want to hear that all these take time and effort. But once we come to peace with that truth, says Peck, life becomes better.

Even fiction can begin strongly with a very nonfictiony proposition.

All happy families are alike; each unhappy family is unhappy in its own way.

Leo Tolstoy, *Anna Karenina*

Because no self-respecting novelist would write a story like a lot of others, we know this will be a story about one of those unique, unhappy families.

Were thesis openings the thing to do in the nineteenth century? I don't know, but they certainly knew how to do it well. Here's another:

It is a truth universally acknowledged, that a single man in possession of a good fortune must be in want of a wife.

Jane Austen, *Pride and Prejudice*

And we know just the woman for just such a man—or at least we will shortly!

THE PARTICULAR-TO-GENERAL OPENING

Rather than being broad and expansive, another option is to offer a specific, detailed opening that draws readers in. They become engaged as they place themselves in a particular scene.

> Air-conditioned, odorless, illuminated by buzzing fluorescent tubes, the American supermarket doesn't present itself as having very much to do with Nature.
>
> **Michael Pollan,** *The Omnivore's Dilemma*

Pollan engages all our senses by giving concrete facets of sight (fluorescent lighting), sound (buzzing), smell (sterile), and touch (the cool of the air-conditioning)—all in the service of taste. Because of these few details, we can picture the whole scene, even those things he doesn't mention—the fruit piled up in perfect pyramids, the polished floors, the trendy shelving. We are captured by immediacy.

Notice, though, that Pollan doesn't just pick any old details. The lighting is artificial, the buzzing is mechanical, the temperature is engineered, the smell is unnaturally void. They all deliberately point to one thing—his thesis. The food industry in America is ironically disconnected from nature. And that disconnect, when we stop to look at it, isn't really all that pretty. Pollan moves us effortlessly from the particular to the general in a single sentence.

Sometimes the more immense and complex the topic, the more important it is to bring things down to a human scale.

> At exactly fifteen minutes past eight in the morning, on August 6, 1945, Japanese time, at the moment when the atomic bomb flashed above Hiroshima, Miss Toshiko Sasaki, a clerk in the personnel department of the East Asia Tin Works, had just sat down at her place in the plant office and was turning her head to speak to the girl at the next desk.
>
> **John Hersey,** *Hiroshima*

A year after the first atomic bomb exploded over Japan, most people still had little idea what exactly it was or how it worked. Its sheer magnitude and unfathomable physics made it seem like something out of science fiction.

To overcome this barrier, John Hersey in his 1946 piece opens with a specific instant, with a specific person doing something very particular and very routine. A woman sitting at a desk in an office. Nothing could be more ordinary, except for what happened at that moment.

All his readers would know the bomb dropped. What they didn't know was what happened to Miss Toshiko Sasaki. An individual. Someone like you or me who might be about to talk to a colleague. In this way readers can begin to come to grips with a new era of warfare we will never be able to turn back from.

Picking the right details to include in an opening is key.

There is a housing project standing now where the house in which we grew up once stood, and one of those stunted city trees is snarling where our doorway used to be.

James Baldwin, "Fifth Avenue, Uptown" in *Nobody Knows My Name*

What do we know generally from this first sentence? We're reading (or at least we are starting with) memoir. It's a personal account of a moment that reflects on the author's past.

Baldwin does so much more, however, simply and powerfully. Just two words set the tone for the whole piece. With *stunted* and *snarling* he invokes a sense of lament. The home he grew up in, with all its intimate memories of joys and sadness, is now replaced with a massive, bureaucratic building. Like the tree "where our doorway used to be," the life in this new building is limited, confined, restricted. There is no room for growth. We do not have a tree happily wagging its branches in welcome. Instead, that tree, squat and unformed, stands guard at the door like a growling dog unwilling to let him in. Thus Baldwin begins his reflection on place, race, and loss.

THE HUMOROUS OPENING

It's hard to miss when you start with something funny.

I come from Des Moines. Somebody had to.

Bill Bryson, *The Lost Continent*

Bryson begins his travelogue through small-town America in his home state of Iowa. We join him as he travels thirteen thousand miles, east to west, smiling and chuckling all the way with his wit and droll observations.

Regarding his frequently intoxicated neighbor, he says, "Everywhere you went you encountered telephone poles and road signs leaning dangerously in testimony to Mr. Piper's driving habits." And while on his crisscross country tour he noticed a sign which read, "BUCKLE UP. ITS THE LAW IN ILLINOIS. Clearly, however, it was not an offense to be unable to punctuate."[1] But it was Bryson's opening line that prepared us for this whole enjoyable ride. As does this:

Had CC de Poitiers known she was going to be murdered she might have bought her husband, Richard, a Christmas gift.

Louise Penny, *A Fatal Grace*

With a fine comic touch we see immediately that our murder victim is so self-absorbed she couldn't be counted on to buy her own husband a Christmas present—even if her life depended on it.

THE DRAMATIC OPENING

If you've got a dramatic story to tell, don't shy away from it.

The French had collapsed. The Dutch had been overwhelmed. The Belgians had surrendered. The British army, trapped, fought free and fell back toward the Channel ports, converging on a fishing town whose name was then spelled Dunkerque.
Behind them lay the sea.

William Manchester, *The Last Lion: Visions of Glory*

The first short, rapid sentences pound away at us like German artillery that will not stop. Manchester then gives us a brief respite, breaking up the terseness with a long sentence before finishing us off with an ominous five-word image: "Behind them lay the sea." He uses no emotionally charged words like *disheartened*, *dazed*, or *desperate*. He doesn't have to. We feel it already.

Next we feel the heat.

It was a pleasure to burn.

Ray Bradbury, *Fahrenheit 451*

The sinister, almost sadistic, quality of this dystopia glows through this deceptively simple sentence. In grim irony, the firemen of the society Bradbury has created don't put out fires. They start fires. And they love to burn books.

THE INTRIGUING OPENING

We've become all too used to clickbait headlines we see on the web ("10 Surefire Ways to Lose Weight: You Won't Believe #7"). Creating intrigue is a valid approach, but we shouldn't follow the formula of being somewhat misleading and crassly provocative. Better options are available.

Making readers curious is the flipside of the thesis opening. Instead of being straightforward, we are oblique and mysterious. We rouse their interest, and in doing so encourage them to keep reading to find out what we mean, how what we say could be true, or what will happen next.

You may not believe me, but I have news about global warming: Good news, and better news.

Noah Smith, "The End of Global Warming," *The Atlantic*

Smith sets up a thesis that is contrary to much conventional wisdom, but he doesn't exactly tell us how this could be the case. We definitely want to read the next sentence.

The following one-page prologue offers us a gripping mystery.

It was predictable, in hindsight. Everything about the history of the Society of Jesus bespoke deft and efficient action, exploration and research. During what Europeans were pleased to call the Age of Discovery, Jesuit priests were never more than a year or two behind the men who made initial contact with previously unknown peoples; indeed, Jesuits were often the vanguard of exploration....

The mission to Rakhat was undertaken not so much secretly as privately—a fine distinction but one that the Society felt no compulsion to explain or justify when the news broke several years later.

The Jesuit scientists went to learn, not to proselytize. They went so that they might come to know and love God's other children. They went for the reason Jesuits have always gone to the farthest frontiers of human exploration. They went *ad majorem Dei gloriam*: for the greater glory of God.

They meant no harm.

Mary Doria Russell, *The Sparrow*

In this novel about making first contact with an unknown culture, the first line and the last line of the prologue set off a string of issues: What was predictable in hindsight? How could their good intentions go so horribly wrong? And what exactly did go wrong? These questions drive us to the end of the book to find out what happened and why.

THE UNDERSTATED OPENING

Sometimes when emotions are hot and debates are combative, trying to yell even louder won't work. Doing the opposite can make people listen. Sometimes, if you whisper, people will strain to hear what you are saying.

While confined here in the Birmingham City Jail, I came across your recent statement calling our present activities "unwise and untimely."

Martin Luther King Jr., "Letter from a Birmingham Jail"

As the civil rights movement was heating up in the early 1960s, Dr. King responded to eight fellow clergymen who wrote to urge an end to demonstrations and to instead use peaceful, orderly means to achieve a "better Birmingham." The rest of Dr. King's reasoned, orderly letter is in tune with his beginning. He sets forth a case for the protestors' actions that has become a classic of American public literature on par with Thoreau's essay on civil disobedience from a hundred years before.

THE LONG, POETIC OPENING

The rule: start with something short and punchy. So what's any self-respecting author going to do to surprise readers? Break the rules, of course.

> It was the best of times, it was the worst of times, it was the age of wisdom, it was the age of foolishness, it was the epoch of belief, it was the epoch of incredulity, it was the season of Light, it was the season of Darkness, it was the spring of hope, it was the winter of despair, we had everything before us, we had nothing before us, we were all going direct to Heaven, we were all going direct the other way–in short, the period was so far like the present period, that some of its noisiest authorities insisted on its being received, for good or for evil, in the superlative degree of comparison only.
>
> **Charles Dickens,** *A Tale of Two Cities*

With ill-advised attraction to the comma and dangerous indifference to the period, Dickens is one of the few who could get away with this.[2] Yes, short is usually better than long. Thus a word of caution to some of us: Professional Writer on Closed Course. Do Not Attempt.

The poetic nature of his prose makes this work. The paired contrasts set the theme for the tale of two contrasting cities and extremist viewpoints we are about to hear.

Something else subterranean gives his opening power. Dickens is echoing one of the most famous passages in literature.

There is a time for everything,
    and a season for every activity under the heavens:
    a time to be born and a time to die,
    a time to plant and a time to uproot,
    a time to kill and a time to heal,
    a time to tear down and a time to build,
    a time to weep and a time to laugh,
    a time to mourn and a time to dance,
    a time to scatter stones and a time to gather them,
    a time to embrace and a time to refrain from embracing,
    a time to search and a time to give up,
    a time to keep and a time to throw away,
    a time to tear and a time to mend,
    a time to be silent and a time to speak,
    a time to love and a time to hate,
    a time for war and a time for peace. (Ecclesiastes 3:1-8)

By recalling this passage for readers, even without their full awareness, he evokes the profound emotions of uncertainty we have about life—about its meaning, about why there is happiness and heartache, about the temptations of cynicism and the call of hope.

We may struggle to successfully generate an echo like this, but it can be worth the effort. The advantage of evoking a famous line is that doing so draws upon all the resonances of emotion and meaning that have accumulated with that passage over the years. It gives weight, depth, and substance to an opening. By building on a substantial existing foundation, our structure can go higher. We don't want to merely quote it but to give it our own twist or turn, fitting it to our task, as Dickens does.

John's Gospel does likewise. It opens with, "In the beginning was the Word," gaining immense traction by recalling the opening of Genesis, "In the beginning God." Here, John says, in Jesus is something as profound as the creation of the cosmos. And should we also think, perhaps, the Creator himself?

THE OPENING THAT FITS

My dear observant reader, I am sure you will have noticed that many of the examples above are stories. Usually a bit of drama is more likely to draw in readers than some abstract statement of the topic. The front-page feature articles of the *Wall Street Journal* have been masterful at this for decades. They have a topic or issue they want to cover, but they begin with a compelling story. Just look at any recent examples and you'll see.

It's hard to go wrong when you begin with a tale about yourself or someone else, comic or tragic, ordinary or dramatic. It's hard to go wrong. But it is possible.

The best-selling book *Blink* by Malcolm Gladwell begins in 1983 when Gianfranco Becchina offered to sell an ancient statue, a literally larger-than-life sculpture of a young male known as a kouros, to the Getty Museum for $10 million. To ensure its authenticity, the Getty conducted extensive (even microscopic) analysis. The conclusion of the expensive, time-consuming study was that the statue was genuine. Getty then made the purchase.

Later a few experts on viewing the statue had instantaneous misgivings, though they had a hard time articulating exactly why. After further analysis, the gut reactions proved to be correct. The statue was a fake.

With an extended version of this tale firmly planted in our minds, we carry with us throughout the book the idea that we (whether experts or shmucks) should rely on our intuition, our hunches, rather than detailed analysis. The problem? This is not the actual point Gladwell wants us to take from the book.

In fact, while Gladwell gives multiple examples of instant reactions that were right, he also gives many that were wrong, sometimes with deadly consequences. He explains how even the blink-of-an-eye conclusions of experts can be mistaken in many different situations. But the subtitle (*The Power of Thinking Without Thinking*) and the compelling opening story lead us to believe that the book is written merely to praise snap judgments rather than to partially bury them.

What does he actually want us to learn? One lesson is that we are often careless with our powers of rapid cognition. Experts make snap judgments but even they don't know why, and they are sometimes quite prejudiced in those decisions. A second lesson is that the problem can be remedied. Guards and guidelines can be put in place to protect even the most objective of us from biases that inevitably creep in.

By starting with the story of the statue, however, Gladwell conveyed the wrong message: everyone's intuition is better all the time in every circumstance; expertise, research, formulas don't matter. Gladwell doesn't end up with that view, however. He concludes with a helpful, balanced perspective, but the book is a bit muddy in how it gets there.

The lesson for nonfiction authors. While opening with a strong, compelling story is always a good option, be sure the story is consistent with your main point as well as your target audience.

If you are writing for parents, don't start with a sports story—start with a family story. If it is for teachers, don't start with a business story—start with an education story. If you are writing to affirm the value of exercise, don't start with a story about someone breaking a leg while running. If you want readers to know that intuition both works and doesn't work, don't start with a story that only shows a situation in which it works. The sports story, the business story, the broken-leg story, and the statue story can all come later. Just don't start there.

THE ANTI-OPENING OPENING

Going against expectations to capture attention is a theme found in many of the options already mentioned. We can also go even further by starting with something that isn't an opening at all.

And speaking of gifts, I should tell you a rule.

> **Robert Fulghum,** "Brass Rule," *All I Really Need to Know I Learned in Kindergarten*

Fulghum hadn't been speaking or writing of gifts at all in this essay. In fact, he hadn't been writing anything. He jumps right in, though, as if he had, catching us off-guard, pulling us in by making us ask, "Did I miss something here?" We look at the previous page. No, that's no help. We start again and keep reading to figure out what in the world is going on here. We've been caught.

Yet perhaps the ultimate in a nonopening opening is from Robert Farrar Capon's *An Offering of Uncles*, which goes like this:

AUCTOR: Well.

LECTOR: Well, what?

AUCTOR: Well, here we are.

LECTOR: But this is preposterous. An author is supposed to begin more surefootedly.

AUCTOR: Ah, but beginning is not that easy.

LECTOR: If you find it such a problem, why do you insist upon authoring?

AUCTOR: Because I have something to say.

LECTOR: Thank heaven for that. What is it?

AUCTOR: If I could tell you, I would have said it already.

LECTOR: Oh. And I suppose that since you have not said it, you cannot tell me?

AUCTOR: Precisely.

LECTOR: My congratulations. Your book is a model of brevity.

AUCTOR: Not quite. We are not yet ready to talk about a book, only a beginning.

And my beginning is a model not of brevity but of honesty. The start of a book, you see, can be written either before or after the book itself. If before, it will be an honest but shakily written piece of business during which the author struggles to get his feet under him, and from which he escapes the first chance he gets. If afterward, it will be a piece of Fine Writing in which he ticks off briefly and with utterly fake aplomb all the things he has spent months trying to keep himself glued together long enough to say. In the first case it is a beginning, but not worth reading, and in the second it is readable, but no beginning. There is, therefore, no way to begin a book both honestly and successfully.

Despite his protestations, Capon is definitely a surefooted author, beginning with immense confidence (and a touch of humor) under the guise of not knowing what he is doing.

With tongue firmly planted in cheek, he also hits upon the problem all writers face. How do you begin before you begin? He's right, of course. Prefaces and introductions are typically written last. That is often the case with the beginnings of chapters, blogs, articles, or newsletters. We only find our opening late in the process.

OPENING SALVO

In the musical *1776* there's a classic scene in which Thomas Jefferson starts his solitary work of drafting the Declaration of Independence. Quill in hand, he scribbles down a line, looks at it, then crumples up the paper and throws it on the floor. He sits a moment, thinking, and then scribbles another line. Again, dissatisfied, he wads it up and throws that on the floor as well. He thinks once more. Then as he's about to make a third attempt, but before he even writes one word, he looks at the blank paper, crumples it up, and throws it down.

Logically enough, most people start by trying to think up and then write down various openings. But, as Jefferson displays, that is almost always the wrong approach. It is very difficult to come up with something strong and memorable without a context. So how do we craft one? How do we come up with a line or story that is powerful, substantive, and shows our readers clearly where we are going?

Here's a simple technique that I have found helpful in my own writing and in working with many authors.

First, just start writing. Don't worry about the opening line. Begin wherever you want and get your thoughts down on paper. You may write several pages or even complete the whole draft—or a second or third draft—all without a strong beginning.

Once you've done that, throw away your first three paragraphs. Your piece probably begins with the fourth. Why? We almost all need some time to get going, to figure out what we want to say. Once we build up a little momentum, things begin to flow. But no one wants to watch us change the oil, check the tire pressure, wash the windows. They just want to get on the road with us. So don't make your readers watch you try to get a car started that is out of gas.

You may only need to throw away one paragraph or it may be ten. Get rid of anything that looks like preliminaries. Background information about your topic or about yourself is probably unnecessary. If it does matter, put it in later.

One likely place things get rolling is when you begin telling a story. After relating the tale, then you can step back and explain how that episode connects to your topic and why it is important. But all that leads up to the story? Make it go away.

STARTS AND FITS

If dumping your first few paragraphs doesn't result in a good opening, look over what you've written with the sole purpose of finding the strongest sentence in the whole piece. If you have trouble, maybe ask a well-read friend or two to help find some candidates. (Or they might be able to see how many paragraphs could be cut at the start.)

Once you've identified the sentence, make that your opening and rework the rest of the piece to fit that new beginning. You may only need to redo the next few sentences or paragraphs to make it flow well. Sometimes it may require more extensive reorganization of the whole. Work hard at your opening, but don't obsess about it. It doesn't have to be great. Good can be good enough. In fact, you've probably already written it—somewhere in the middle.

Looking to the middle could have helped even as accomplished a writer as Malcolm Gladwell. Later in *Blink*, Gladwell offers an equally compelling story of Abbie Conant, who in 1980 auditioned as a trombonist for the Munich Philharmonic Orchestra. She and the others all performed behind a screen so the decision-making committee would focus on the music and not be distracted by appearances. During Abbie's turn she cracked a note and thought, *It's over for me*. After she finished playing she immediately began to pack up to leave, knowing she wouldn't be selected. But after her solo, the music director cried out, "That's who we want," and sent everyone else away who was waiting to audition. When she walked out in front of the committee, they were shocked. They didn't expect a woman to play a "masculine" instrument like the trombone with such confidence and authority.[3]

The story made Gladwell's point. Amateurs like you and me would have no idea which of the trombonists would have been best. They would have all sounded equally good. Experts can tell the difference. But even experts have blind spots. Their intuition and expertise are not enough. We all need help overcoming our biases. Using a screen to hide age, gender, and ethnicity has revolutionized the makeup of orchestras in recent decades. Now they truly have the best in the world available to them, and they are more diverse.

If Gladwell had looked for the most fitting story for *Blink* (even if it wasn't quite as powerful as a story about $10 million and the elite, world-famous Getty Museum getting hoodwinked by a fake statue), he might have pulled this account of the musical audition to the front. The story would have been a better one for Gladwell to begin with because its conclusions more closely fit the overall theme he wanted to convey in the book. Expertise and intuition are still important and valuable, but they need to be guarded with procedures that take bias out of the equation.

Beginnings matter. But when crafting a beginning, look to the middle.

2

KNOWING
YOUR AUDIENCE

WHEN PEOPLE HAND ME A PROPOSAL or manuscript for a nonfiction book or article and ask me for an editorial opinion, we'll talk about several issues, but I have one chief diagnostic question. Almost anything and everything an author has to say flows from the answer. It tells writers what kind of vocabulary and images to use, how long the piece should be, how to organize the material, what to leave in, what to take out, and even where to try to publish it.

This is the question: *Who is your audience?*

If we don't know clearly who we are writing for or who we want to reach, we are writing with a pen that has no ink, with a laptop that has a dead battery.

The immediate instinctive (and wrong) response is to say we are writing for everyone. A book that is for everyone is for no one. It will be too broad and general to interest any particular readers. We shouldn't even say we are writing for all parents or all voters or all pastors or all women or all business people. We have to be much more focused than that.

When thinking about our audience, we should try to be as specific as possible—age range, economic status, religious background, ethnicity, geographic location, life experiences, and so forth. In fact, I encourage writers to pick out one person they know that they would love to have read their work. Then write for that one person.

Say you want to write about teaching. Maybe you've narrowed it down to high school. You have important things to say to high school teachers, to parents of high school students, as well as to professors of high school teachers. That is too much. Focus on high school teachers. Then think of one high school teacher you know and write for her.

Obviously, we hope many people from a wide range of backgrounds and circumstances will read our book or article. But it is best to think of all these others as reading over the shoulder of the one person or group you have in mind. That in fact is what happens all the time. You no doubt read many pieces not primarily intended for you. Unexpectedly, the concreteness and particularity of such pieces give them a more universal appeal.

Suzanne Collins wrote *The Hunger Games* for young adults, and she successfully reached those readers—and millions more who read over their shoulders.

Michael Crichton wrote *Jurassic Park* for sci-fi readers but managed to pull in hordes of others who found the premise of the book and the cast of characters fascinating.

At the same time, some books don't gain such extra readers. They simply go deeply into a narrow market. Richard Bolles's *What Color Is Your Parachute?* for job hunters is one example. I can't imagine that many people read it who are happy and secure in their jobs. And he didn't write for them. They were excluded. The genius of the book, of course, is that at one time or another most of us do look for a different job.

All these books illustrate the same principle—stay focused on a narrow audience.

WHAT ABOUT ME?

The book I most often recommend to writers is William Zinsser's *On Writing Well*. It is wise, practical, and enjoyable to read. Friends have even heard me talk about Zinsserizing a manuscript—a mischievously ironic term since Zinsser abhors such neologisms.

In *On Writing Well*, however, Zinsser self-consciously makes an apparent contradiction. On the one hand he tells writers not to worry about the audience, what people will like or understand or agree with. Don't write for an audience. Write for yourself, he tells us confidently. Write about what interests you. If you think something is funny, put it in. If you like a word, say *neologism*, don't fret over whether most people will know what it means. If it fits you, use it.

If you find cockroaches to be fascinating, then don't let your fear of squeamish readers deter you. Do chess-playing bronco riders give you a kick? Then make the move. If the atonal music of Arnold Schoenberg sends your heart into rhapsodic palpitations, then strike that chord in your prose. Don't be concerned if Aunt Henrietta doesn't know the difference between a twelve-tone scale and the twelve apostles. Just have fun.

As I write, podcasts are widely enjoyed. Of course, true crime stories have been a popular genre for generations; no surprise then that podcasts should enjoy success there too. But many other types abound. No topic is too specialized for *How Stuff Works*, which has episodes like "How Lion Taming Works" and "How Commercial Jingles Work." Neither life nor death nor my pocketbook depend on being informed on such subjects. But the producers and reporters do a fascinating job, and we listen.

I personally enjoy *This American Life* and *Radiolab*. They lean on telling stories about what otherwise might be considered an arcane subject. Where did the legal phrase "We can neither confirm nor deny" come from? Why are US cities opposed to fighting crime using successful techniques developed by US companies for places like Mexico and Iraq? Why did badminton players try to lose in order to win a tournament? When *Radiolab* puts together stories like these, they keep our interest. They tell stories with drama, with compelling narrative questions as we learn something new. They don't give a second thought to what others may or may not like. If they alone think it's a good story, they tell it.

DON'T WORRY ABOUT AUDIENCE, BUT DO WORRY ABOUT AUDIENCE

But here's the contradiction. While Zinsser tells writers not to worry about what readers might think, he also advises writers to work hard to keep readers' attention, to not let them get distracted in the middle of a paragraph. "The reader is an impatient bird, perched on the thin edge of distraction or sleep."[1] So we must also be aware of and concerned about readers.

How can we do both at once? How can we not worry about readers and worry about readers at the same time? By realizing that two different issues are involved. One, he says, is a matter of attitude. The other a matter of craft.[2]

Be willing to express your opinions or interests or personality regardless of what others may think (attitude). And do so in a way that engages and compels them to read on even if they disagree with you or may not have a natural interest in the topic (craft).

The best podcasters think a lot about audience. While their choice of topic may be their own, the audience influences how they cover the subject. They make assumptions about what their audience knows and doesn't know, what may need to be explained and what doesn't. They consider what might motivate their listeners and what might seem boring.

Likewise, the best writing comes when authors follow Zinsser's apparently paradoxical advice. How do we keep our audience in mind *and* not keep our audience in mind? We do it at different times. When we are first picking a topic, researching, drafting, and smashing down ideas on the page, we need not give one thought to the audience. We just do our best to get into a flow.

But later, after we've got the semblance of a draft together and go back to rework, refine, and edit our own material, then we keep our audience in mind. Zinsser himself hints at this. When talking about whether to put in humor, he writes, "If it amuses you in the act of writing, put it in. (It can always be taken out, but only you can put it in.)"[3] That's the key—we can always take it out later. We just shouldn't take it out early in the process.

When we revise, we need a guide, a grid, a set of criteria for what to leave in and what to take out. Sometimes too much of a good thing can make a piece fail. We may think all the illustrations are spot-on, but too many of them (or the wrong ones or even too many good ones) can put readers off.

How do we determine what may work for our audience and what may not? We will have a hard time figuring that out with a big amorphous readership in mind, thus the earlier suggestion to make it specific. Having one person in mind is a great way to do that—someone who is not on the fringes of the kind of people you want to reach but someone at the center.

Who should that person be? How do we choose? Another way to phrase the question, Who is your audience? is this: *Who do you want to reach and why?* That is, What is motivating you to write? What have you learned that you want others to know? Who could benefit from it? A friend? A coworker? Someone you worship with? A customer? A family member?

Write for that person, and let it be your gift to them.

3

GIVING STRUCTURE

A LWAYS MAKE AN OUTLINE before you start writing."
Isn't that what your fifth-grade teacher told you? Well, I'm sorry to break this to you, but Miss Whitebread was wrong. This is one of those "stupid things we were taught in school," so let me deconstruct this bad boy.

To begin, it is impossible to make an outline before we start. How can we outline something when we don't even know what we want to say, haven't started thinking about what we want to say, or don't have any research or notes on what we want to say? We can't. Plain and simple.

Thinking is a messy business. We start with random, maybe disconnected ideas, facts, opinions, and, yes, feelings. Perhaps we have a general notion, but that's about it.

Maybe we are the sort of person who can work things out in our head before we write, but even then our first step is not outlining. It's thinking. Step one, then, is definitely not to create an outline.

Step one may be to just start writing. We take one idea and see where that takes us. If it goes nowhere, we abandon it and try another idea. If it goes somewhere, we keep writing.

That, however, is not the only possible first step. Another step one could be to collect scraps and bits of information and stories and guesses and quotes. We store these in our memory or write these down on a sheet of paper or put them in a word processing document or even (if we are old school) on 3" x 5" cards. We then follow up some of these notions by talking to friends, reading, reflecting, remembering, and taking more notes.

After that, while shampooing in the shower, a related idea pops to mind, and we write that down (after we get out of the shower). More reading. More note taking. More musing.

Along the way we may start writing random, disconnected paragraphs about stuff we've collected, playing with some of the things we've written down, trying to develop them a bit. Eventually we gain some momentum and paragraphs begin to link to each other, pages follow, and we're on a roll.

After a while we see what we've got and start revising, adding, and organizing—yes, organizing (maybe into an outline, maybe not yet) after we've written. We begin to see what facts and guesses and stories fit and which don't.

We may discover that the anecdote that triggered the whole thing suddenly doesn't fit at all, and with deep sadness we must exile it to the land of "To Be Used Later." Or it may fit and make a beautiful opening or a grand conclusion.

We may have collected seventeen points and realize that's crazy, so we pare it down and work with three or four or five. More rearranging, more revising, more adding, more subtracting. We do this in light of the specific audience we've identified (chapter 2), all the while looking for a good opening (chapter 1). At some point an outline may emerge, and then we fill in gaps and round it out.

When did we outline? Maybe in the middle, maybe at the end, maybe (if we're writing a blog) never. But when we do create an outline, it's not primarily for us and certainly not for a teacher. It's for our readers.

OUTLINE OPTIONS

Why are outlines for readers instead of us? The human brain yearns for structure, for organization. It's a survival instinct.

With all the stimulus in the world, prehistoric people could lose track of what was truly dangerous. If they didn't have categories in their minds of things that weren't dangerous (butterflies) and things that were (lightning-swift predatory mammals with razor-sharp teeth), they'd have to stop and think each time they came across something, by which time they might already be someone's lunch.

Over the millennia, we've all learned that lesson. Our brains thrive on the known, on predictability, on organization. With that in place we can then take the time to learn from, appreciate, or sometimes enjoy the unknown, the unpredictable—those things that break the rules. So, yes, structure brings joy to your readers.

We don't want to overwhelm readers with where we are going and how we are getting there, but we want to give enough so they can benefit from what we are saying and don't become confused. Here's a baker's dozen of some of the possible structures you might use for a nonfiction piece.

Question and answer. Each chapter, section, or paragraph leads with a question and follows with one or more answers. This has the virtue of clarity, but it can get tedious for readers after a while. And the questions may not represent those your audience really has. One way to overcome the tedium is with humor.

Letters. Actual or fictitious letters are collected, either offering one side of the correspondence or both. This form is much harder to pull off successfully than it seems. The niceties of greeting each other and keeping up on the incidentals of life can become tiresome letter after letter when such elements keep readers from getting to the main topic of the correspondence. And if you skip all those details, why bother with the letter format at all?

Story. A narrative dominates the book or article. This is common in biography, autobiography, and memoir but can also be found in general interest writing. In a culture dominated by narrative, primarily through movies, this can be an effective way to keep readers' attention. Episodes may be interspersed with commentary or reflection as each part of the story is told.

Beads on a string. A series of independent but related topics are discussed one by one. A book on habits might devote successive chapters to different behaviors. As an alternative, each chapter could be a different strategy for breaking or forming any number of habits.

Shish kebab. Like "beads on a string," each chapter is of equal weight and related to an overall theme. But the theme skewering each chapter together is much stronger, making each chapter much more similar to the others than in the beads structure. The overall topic could be having a positive mental attitude. Instead of covering many approaches, one approach is proposed. Each chapter shows how this one idea plays out in a different group—teachers, students, athletes, parents, businesspeople, and so forth.

Pie. The whole of a topic is divided into logical parts. Thus we can make some attempt to be comprehensive, with the parts being much more integrated. Areas or disciplines that already have standard categories (like world history or world religions) often provide their own structure.

Concentric circles. Start with the core idea and move out. For example, (1) food and me, (2) food and my friends and family, and (3) food and the world. (Or you can go in reverse order.)

General to particular (or vice versa). Broad concerns or issues are addressed before individual examples are considered in more detail. Often practical application is reserved for the end. A piece on technology might begin with broad cultural trends and then consider specific issues of the day. Or the order could be reversed—beginning with specific pressing felt needs readers have and then considering the larger social influences that created these concerns.

Theory to practice. This can be a subcategory of "general to particular." It can work for a specialized or professional readership, or as an academic book. But for general readers it is best to avoid this structure. People tend to get bogged down if the first half is theory with no application. Impatient, they want to know sooner than later what the payoff is for them. An alternative is to spread application throughout. Instead of first explaining the theory of brain science and considering how this applies to, say, relationships, include some of the science and some practical implications in each chapter or section.

Chronological. The primary structure is past to present to future. The topic could be a scientific discovery, the development of an idea or a person, or how to make a meal. But often it is best not to start right at the beginning and go straight through to the end. Starting in the middle or end (how friends raved about your butternut squash soup) can make for more interesting reading (more on this in chap. 6).

Biblical. The canon of Scripture or particular books of the Bible provide the overall structure. This is used in commentaries as well as studies that trace a topic from the Old Testament to the New.

Persuasive case. In chapter five I discuss in more detail the classic rhetorical three-part structure for a persuasive argument—*ethos* (making a personal connection with your audience), *logos* (offering facts and reasons), and *pathos* (using emotion to make a plea for action).

Sandwich. This structure can overlap any of the outline options. A book or article opens with general concerns, closes with general concerns and has specific topics in the middle. This could also be reversed: specifics—general—specifics.

Books or longer articles have the space to combine some of these structures. For example, the first half might be historical and the second half topical. Or key episodes might be arranged chronologically with each being a springboard to discuss one main topic.

If you don't like one of these outlines, many others are possible. Remember though: don't start with one but do end with one. Miss Whitebread meant well, you see. It's just too bad she believed what she was taught in school.

4

THE CHARACTER
OF PERSUASION

IN ROGER RUEFF'S *The Big Kahuna*, two veteran salesmen, Phil and Larry, are at a convention trying to sell industrial lubricants. Along for the ride is a young new hire, Bob, who has joined them for training. Unexpectedly Bob has the opportunity to talk at length with a major potential customer, Mr. Fuller. This could be the big break Larry and Phil are looking for.

When Bob debriefs with Phil and Larry after the conversation, he confesses that lubricants never came up. But Jesus did. Larry is angry. In an intense cross-examination by Larry, Bob admits that he was the one who first brought up Jesus because it was that important to him, even though their purpose for being at the convention was to sell lubricants. Larry eventually storms out, and Phil remains who tells Bob,

> You preaching Jesus is no different . . . than Larry or anybody else preaching lubricants. It doesn't matter whether you're selling Jesus or Buddha . . . or civil rights . . . or how to make money in real estate with no money down. That doesn't make you a

human being. It makes you a marketing rep. If you wanna talk to somebody honestly, as a human being, ask him about his kids. Find out what his dreams are, just to find out. For no other reason. Because as soon as you lay your hands on a conversation, to steer it, it's not a conversation anymore. It's a pitch, and you're not a human being. You're a marketing rep.

The conversation raises many worthwhile questions. Was Bob being manipulative with Mr. Fuller? What is the role of honesty in relationships? Are all attempts at persuasion mere salesmanship? If so, is that a bad thing? If in conversation you intentionally bring up a topic you care about, are you automatically being unnatural and insincere? In fact, is any kind of persuasion good?

Answering such questions about conversations is a bit trickier than about something you've written. Personal relationships can be very complex. With a book, however, people can choose to pick it up or not. They can see an article online and read it, or they can click on the next thing. Usually, people can tell up front how the writer wants to persuade them and what the topic is.

Let's face it. Persuasion is part of almost every piece of nonfiction. Something as innocent as a travelogue wants to expand your view of the world, get you thinking about taking a trip yourself, or perhaps just entertain you (and so persuade you to finish the article). A biography of an athlete may want you to gain a deeper appreciation of a sport. Or the author might hope you will see the value of a life, whether as a positive role model, a cautionary tale, or both. Often the element of persuasion is right out front—diet books, political commentary, parenting advice, books on how to write better, and more.

We pick a topic, research it, settle on an audience, and start drafting. As we structure the piece and look for an opening, we also need to think about the what, why, and how of persuading our readers.

THE NATURE OF PERSUASION

Before turning to the craft of persuasion in chapter five, let's look at the topic in a broader context. Consider this continuum: persuasion, manipulation, coercion. First is persuasion itself—the honest attempt to influence others for a good purpose. (I'll say more about what that means in a moment.)

Second is manipulation—which can range from nudging to tricking to haranguing until someone does what they may not want to do or perhaps shouldn't do. Manipulation is possible because we don't always think or act rationally. Often our implicit mental processes come into play. This often-hidden part of our minds performs many valuable functions by rapidly processing our environment and applying worthwhile rules of thumb. But it can also be taken advantage of.

For decades retailers have known that products with red labels sell better than those with other colors. So in a grocery store we see lots and lots of red. Or consider these two signs for a soup display: Limit of 12 per Person and No Limit per Person. Counterintuitively, testing showed that the first sold more, about twice as much as the second. The impression of scarcity or of giving a concrete target to shoot for has a powerful effect.[1] Similarly, a ninety-dollar coffee maker may seem expensive next to a lot of thirty-dollar coffee makers. But if the store groups it with three-hundred-dollar coffee makers, ninety dollars seems quite reasonable.[2]

Political attack ads are much crasser in their attempts to manipulate, appealing directly to our base fears while often playing fast and loose with the truth. Many seem to be following the tongue-in-cheek advice credited to Carl Sandburg: "If the facts are against you, argue the law. If the law is against you, argue the facts. If the law and the facts are against you, pound the table and yell like hell." As a result of being inundated with such abuses, we have grown suspicious of any attempt to influence. Even honest persuasion is sometimes considered impolite at best and morally wrong at worst.

Relativism has only added gasoline to this blaze. If our inevitable subjectivity means we can't prove that our viewpoints correspond to reality, if it doesn't matter whether ideas show coherence and consistency, then we should not be in the business of persuading, much less manipulating.

But if both persuasion and manipulation are banned, what is left? Some think the result would be peace and tranquility, with everyone tolerantly leaving everyone else alone. But that is not how the world works. Rather, if we feel strongly that others should think the way we do—for their own good—and we can't persuade them or manipulate them, then only the third option is left: coercion.

If society rejects influence, only power remains. If we want our fellow citizens to care about the homeless, the elderly, teen pregnancy, the disadvantaged, drug abuse, abortion, the environment, education, crime, debt, families, or whatever, raw political force to compel compliance is our only tool. Only the power of the state is left to enforce our own agenda without regard for those who disagree or who may be harmed. When even this fails to yield satisfactory results, coercion's close cousin, violence, is there to get things done.

To avoid being locked into such a pattern, we need to rehabilitate persuasion and once again give it an honored place in our society and, of course, in our writing. As a starting point, I commend principled persuasion (a phrase many others have used) to help separate persuasion from its unfortunate associations with manipulation and coercion. Principled persuasion is essentially how I defined persuasion earlier: the honest attempt to influence others for a good purpose. Let's break down this definition into its key parts. To begin, we can understand "honest attempts" in five ways.

HONESTY IN PERSUASION

First, honesty in our writing means we respect the truth as best we can know it and speak in a way that reflects this. As a result, we check facts from multiple sources. The more reliable the source, the more reliable the facts. But how do we tell if a source is reliable? Here are some general guidelines. While these may not always hold and exceptions exist, in general they are a good place to start.

Reliable sources

- Have been recognized as trustworthy by a broad range of people—not just a narrow group

- Have been recognized as trustworthy for a long time, for decades or centuries—not just years

- Are accountable to others for their work—rather than being independent

Many major universities have been around for centuries and recognized widely for their excellence. Professors are accountable to their institutions and to their professions, which regularly review their work publicly. These tend to be good sources.

Joe or Josephine Blogger, who are not accountable to an organization, who have only been writing and speaking for a few years, and who are endorsed only by likeminded people (even if by thousands) are usually less reliable sources—no matter how compelling they seem to be.

A book published by an established publisher tends to be more reliable than a self-published book. That may not always be the case, but a publisher has a reputation in the market that it wants to maintain and so usually puts books through an editing or vetting process.

When fake news is regularly generated by bloggers and politicians alike, we must be extra cautious. It used to be said, "Figures don't lie, but liars figure." Now we might say, "Whether or not figures lie isn't the point, since liars make up their own figures."

Even established sources can be biased, even those that call themselves objective. So here's a tip on how to tell which is which. If a source almost always confirms your own opinions and never challenges them, it is probably biased. Likewise, if it almost always challenges your views and never confirms them, it is probably biased.

If a source usually makes you mad at certain political, ethnic, or religious groups and not others, it's probably biased. The solution: gather opinions and information from a variety of sources that aren't in the same narrow group.

Be honest with statistics. If we say a study showed that 80 percent of all depressed people are men, that may sound significant. But if the researchers who came up with that figure only studied seventy-four people, it is not statistically valid since the sample size is too small. Not all data or surveys are created equal, and we shouldn't pretend they are.

Second, in addition to respecting the truth as best we can know it, honesty in persuasion means we are truthful about contrary viewpoints. Otherwise, we set up a straw man. We have made something flimsy, so we can easily knock it down. If politician A supports improving public highways or schools, it's a straw man to respond, "Why do you want to make this a communist country?" This is misrepresenting the other side so we can easily win an argument. Rather, we are obligated to investigate the actual costs and benefits to see what impact they might have. Then we need to respond to those. Every story has two sides. Tell both sides.

The state I live in, Illinois, is not known for its political honesty. But it does one thing well. Whenever an amendment to the state constitution is on the ballot, I receive in the mail a brochure from the state. Briefly but completely it first outlines the meaning and purpose of the amendment. Then the brochure gives several arguments for and several against passing it. I am always impressed by its clarity and evenhandedness. If only more political discussion followed this example.

The advantage of presenting the strongest case against our viewpoint is that when we show the opposing view is still wrong, we have made our case even more convincing. The disadvantage is that doing so takes longer and requires us to work harder than offering a snappy sound bite. That also creates more demands on those we want to influence, perhaps making it harder for us to convince them. But honesty requires us to take that approach.

I have often heard from friends and the media something like, "Religion is the major cause of wars in the world." That sounds like it could be right since we hear so much about religious-motivated violence today and know about religious wars in the past. Once when I heard the comment I wondered about it but let it go for the moment. Instead I did a little research.

Later, when I heard Helen (who has a graduate degree in history) repeat this claim I responded, "Well, actually that's not so." All conversation stopped and every head turned.

Surprised, Helen asked, "What facts do you have to support that?"

"Well," I said, "take the twentieth century. Over 150 million people died for political reasons. There were 50 million who died in World War II. Another 20 million in World War I. Stalin took another 20 million at least. Mao another 20 or 30 million. Pol Pot 2 million. A million in Rwanda. A million Armenians. Now there may have been 10 million violent deaths in the twentieth century primarily provoked by religion, and that is 10 million too many. But the vast majority of violent deaths in the last century were motivated by political and atheistic ideological reasons."

"Hmm," Helen replied, "I guess so." It was a complex question, but I tried to deal with it briefly by using facts and recognizing that there was some truth in the opposing viewpoint.

Third, honesty means you give credit where credit is due. I'm a bit dismayed I have to say something about plagiarism since it is so universally recognized to be wrong. Yet every few months we hear of people, even highly respected authors and public figures, continuing to do it. The internet makes it incredibly easy to copy and paste material into your work without acknowledgment. Busyness and laziness also conspire against our better intentions.

Plagiarism is, simply, presenting someone else's words as your own. It is a form of stealing. Just to be absolutely clear:

1. When quoting exactly, you must use quotations marks or a blocked quote, and you must cite a source in a note or directly reference it in the text. Both are needed. A note without accurate quotation marks is not enough.

2. Putting someone else's thoughts into your own words can be okay if you note or reference the source in the text. But if in the process you quote several words in a row, you must use quotation marks each time.

3. Sources of specific information or examples should be noted unless they are common knowledge. You don't need to cite a source for Paris being the capital of France. But you can't use all or part of a definition word for word from, for example, Wikipedia without using quotation marks and giving a reference, even if what is being dealt with is common knowledge. Admittedly, this rule is a bit mushier than the other two. It can be irritating to readers and just unnecessary to note every sentence. Still in general, it is better to err on the side of caution and do it too much. Let an editor or teacher decide if you have too many notes.

Ideas can't be copyrighted. You are free to assert the existence of gravity without citing a source. But the particular expression of ideas is legally protected. If you quote Newton, say so.[3]

Fourth, honesty in persuasion means we are careful in our use of logic. One of the most common fallacies is assuming that because something happens before another event, the first event caused the second. Formally this is called the *post hoc ergo propter hoc* fallacy.

Often we hear or read that studies show that married people are happier than the nonmarried population. The explicit or unspoken implication is that marriage helps people be happy. What the surveys (or those reporting on the surveys) fail to note, however, is that correlation does not mean causation. Just because two things are linked (correlated) doesn't necessarily mean one caused the other. In fact some research suggests that happiness causes marriage rather than the other way around. That is, happier people tend to get married more often than unhappy ones. Which makes sense. Who wants to marry a grump?[4]

In 2013 a televangelist told his audience, "From a prophetic standpoint, every time the United States gets involved in some kind of a pressure on Israel to split their land, there's some natural disaster that happens here in America."[5] So what was the cause of all the disasters that hit the United States before the modern state of Israel existed? Or what about natural disasters following political scandals, or increases in gambling, or reductions in charitable giving, or release of movies starring Ben Affleck? It would be possible to find any number of events that regularly preceded such actions by the United States. But they would be completely unconnected.

Books like *Thank You for Arguing* by Jay Heinrichs and *Why Good Arguments Often Fail* by James W. Sire offer excellent summaries of several logical fallacies we commonly fall into. These and other such books are worth our time. If we want to be honest persuaders, we will be on the lookout for and stay away from hasty generalizations, false analogies, demonizing opponents, avoiding or sidelining the central issue (that is, using red herrings), and more.

Honesty means respecting the truth as best we can know it, respecting contrary viewpoints, giving due credit, and using logic.

Fifth, honesty means showing humility. Despite our carefully researched evidence and excellent use of logic, we still might be wrong. As finite, fallible human beings, all of us should always be willing to learn, to have our minds changed, and to have our most cherished beliefs challenged. We need to be careful, then, not to overstate our conclusions. We should be confident but not cocky.

THE PURPOSE OF PERSUASION

That's the first half of the definition of principled persuasion—it is an *honest* attempt to influence others. But why are we making this attempt? I suggest it should be *for a good purpose.* Intuitively almost all of us recognize that if honesty and truth break down, not much is left to hold together the fabric of society. Can we go further than that to define "a good purpose" in a culture that has mostly lost its Judeo-Christian consensus?

Given the diversity of the world and the widespread disbelief in absolutes, little agreement exists regarding what is good, what is moral, or even whether such things can exist. But we need some guidelines because the tools of persuasion work for con men and for Mother Teresa. To train people in the principles of rhetoric can be like acting as an arms dealer who sells weapons to both sides of a conflict. Con men can still be mostly honest in the ways I've described (though usually they are not) but for a nefarious purpose. In my mind principled persuasion means we are not persuading for immoral ends. What then is moral?

This question requires far more time and space than is possible here. All I can suggest for the moment are a few questions to guide us: Does what I propose enhance the common good? How might my ideas injure certain groups of people or individuals? Is my goal to help people flourish? Are my aims consistent with those of justice? These are huge questions. The answers we offer regarding particular courses of action may not guide us perfectly in an imperfect world. But they can help move us toward a fuller and more ethical conclusion.

From a Judeo-Christian perspective, we might say morality is learning to live out the image of God. We fulfill the purposes for which

ANCIENT WISDOM ON PRINCIPLED PERSUASION

Western ideas about persuasion are rooted in Greek and Roman principles of rhetoric. These were intended not only to improve public speaking but also to protect society from unscrupulous persuaders. Os Guinness writes:

> The common safeguard for the Greeks, as well as for Romans who followed them, such as Cicero, was that the speaker should be a person of good sense, good character and good will. Or put differently, the dangerous gap between truth and virtue should be filled in by means of three principles: first, the reminder that truth and virtue are more powerful than falsehood and vice; second, the reminder that a speaker should be a person of character and virtue; and third, the reminder that the speaker should always address the public good and not only his or her own interest. Together, it was thought, these three principles would close the door against the wiles of the Sophists and all the dangers implicit in the gap between truth and persuasion.*

The ancients thought that what is good and virtuous would be innately attractive. Those who followed these principles would therefore be more successful persuaders. History and experience sadly show, however, that some people can be very persuasive who do not follow any of these three worthwhile guidelines.

---

*Os Guinness, *Fool's Talk* (Downers Grove, IL: InterVarsity Press, 2015), 173.

he made us when we act as good stewards of the world we inhabit. That is why all kinds of injustice—slavery, racism, lying, stealing, gross material inequities—are so problematic. They prevent people from becoming who God intends them to be.[6]

Based on research from a wide variety of fields and perspectives, David Brooks argues that some sort of understanding like this is consistently found in human beings. "Nobody," he writes, "has to teach a child to demand fair treatment; children protest unfairness vigorously as soon as they can communicate. Nobody has to teach us to admire a person who sacrifices for a group; the admiration for duty is universal. Nobody has to teach us to disdain someone who betrays a friend or is disloyal to a family or tribe. . . . There is no society on earth where people are praised for running away in battle."[7]

Values of fairness, duty, loyalty, and the like can, however, erode. Our own selfish desires, trauma from our past, or influences from society can twist these ideals. Thus we need to deliberately encourage ourselves and others to be consistent with our own values—whether when seeking to lose weight, reform the prison system, find God, or use industrial lubricants.

In *The Big Kahuna*, Phil was right that seeking to convince others about such issues is persuasion. He was wrong that doing so makes us less than human if we are making an honest attempt to influence others for a good purpose.

Have I persuaded you?

5

THE CRAFT OF PERSUASION

WHAT MAKES SOME WRITING more compelling than others? What brings your audience with you and leads them to positive action? What are the best ways to put a case together?

In a sense, this whole book is about helping you write persuasively by, for example, communicating more clearly (chap. 8 on rewriting) and more imaginatively (part 2 on artful writing). If you have a laserlike focus on your audience (chap. 2), you'll be more likely to bring them around to your way of thinking.

Some other straightforward approaches can make writing more persuasive. Let's look at a few.

BE SIMPLE

First, be simple. We often think that sophisticated vocabulary makes us seem more impressive and intelligent. It's a way, we think, of making ourselves credible, giving us an air of authority. The opposite is true.

Daniel Oppenheimer, a professor of psychology at Carnegie Mellon, published a serious academic article with the tongue-in-cheek title,

"Consequences of Erudite Vernacular Utilized Irrespective of Necessity: Problems with Using Long Words Needlessly."[1] The upshot of his study: fancy vocabulary was not more persuasive than simple words even in scholarly writing. KISS (Keep It Simple, Stupid) is more than an acronym. It is just plain good advice.

Don't follow Mr. Burns of *The Simpsons* down the path of bureaucratic gobbledygook. He once said, "Oh, meltdown. It's one of those annoying buzzwords. We prefer to call it an unrequested fission surplus."[2] Too much highfalutin language may not just confuse, it may make it look like we are trying to hide something.

The inclination to be complex can, however, be an honest one. As writers, we have two forces pulling us in opposite directions. First, we have learned something (maybe quite a lot). Second, we want others to benefit from that. But the more we know, the harder it can be to communicate that effectively.

I am all for learning as much as we can. We want to offer solid nourishment to our audiences, not junk food that goes down easy yet has no value or may even be harmful. But often with much learning comes complex concepts and a specialized vocabulary otherwise known as jargon.

I appreciated Oppenheimer's title because psychology is itself often laden with five-dollar words like *dysfunctional, holistic, self-actualization*, or even deceptively simple words like *act out*, which have technical meanings. Such overuse has even garnered its own label—*psychobabble*. But something as seemingly ordinary as coffee tasting can also get out of control. Remember friends: not all of us know what animal-like, earthy, or woody aromas are—not to mention tastes that are astringent, phenolic, or nippy.

If you only want to connect with other experts and specialists, fine. Go ahead and sound pretentious. Otherwise, KISS. And if you must introduce a technical term, then clearly define it.

Part of the problem is that when we know a subject well, we lose track of what is specialized vocabulary and what isn't. We are so familiar with such words, we forget that others don't know them. Solution: give your work a test drive with your intended audience. Ask one or two (usually nonexperts) from that group to read it and note any words they are unfamiliar with.

Simplicity extends beyond vocabulary to the overall ideas you want to communicate. If you can't explain the main concept of your piece in thirty seconds, you are probably in trouble. This means you may need to limit the range of topics covered or keep working till you can express your key thought in a sentence or two.

When I was writing a Bible commentary called *Mark Through Old Testament Eyes*, I tried all kinds of ways of explaining what this three-hundred-page book was about. It was a rather complex and nonintuitive idea. I'd read thousands of pages in academic books, taught hundreds of students, and heard dozens of lectures.

As a result, I had a rather complicated and detailed idea in my head. Those who wrote the New Testament weren't making a clean break from the past. In fact, their minds and lives were so full of Old Testament images and ideas, stories and symbols, that they couldn't help using them to explain who Jesus was. Because of this, we could misunderstand what seems plainer (the New Testament) when what seems more distant and baffling (the Old Testament) actually makes things clearer. Both the strange and the familiar in the New Testament make much more sense in light of the Old.

Finally, after talking about the book dozens of times and writing thousands of words, I found myself writing this: "The New Testament writers were Old Testament people."[3] There it was. Just eight words. Simple. Better than that, it was memorable.

BE MEMORABLE

Being memorable is inseparable from being persuasive. If we can't recall what we read or heard, it probably didn't influence us very much.

Rhyme makes it easy to bring things to mind. Alcoholics Anonymous uses a slogan to help people realize they don't have to be perfect, that it is okay to be in process. They tell each other, "Fake it till you make it." Even if you don't feel emotionally healthy, you can grow in emotional health by acting as if you are. This is like Aristotle's notion that we acquire virtues by first putting them into action.[4]

When someone is struggling with sobriety and the opportunity comes to join friends at a bar or sneak a trip to the liquor store, trying to recall mounds of scientific evidence on the destructiveness of alcohol will not do the trick. When years of habitual self-justification arise ("I've been under a lot of pressure; I deserve a break"), remembering the complex effects of alcoholism on your family may get blocked out. But with enough repetition, a six-word rhyme may be able to surface. Such a phrase can crack open a door for us into a much deeper network of memories, emotions, relationships, and beliefs that can pull us back from the brink.

Not only are sayings that rhyme more memorable, they also seem truer than those that don't. In one experiment, a group of people was given several aphorisms like these:

Woes unite foes.

Little strokes will tumble great oaks.

A fault confessed is half redressed.

Another group was given their nonrhyming counterparts to consider.

Woes unite enemies.

Little strokes will tumble great trees.

A fault admitted is half redressed.

The sayings in the second group were judged to be far less perceptive than the rhyming maxims.[5]

How many parents have had to deal with children complaining that they got too many carrots for dinner or a smaller cookie? In response

I've heard my adult children calmly tell my grandchildren, "You get what you get, and you don't get upset." Wow, I wish I had known that one when they were kids!

Persuading someone can be quite a climb. Make it easier by using a rhyme. But please don't do it all of the time. Rhyme can seem corny or forced, especially in prose. Watch out, then, for overuse, which can reduce the effectiveness of any technique.

Though my one-sentence summary regarding the Gospel of Mark doesn't have end rhyme, the parallel structure and rhythm of the two halves and the repetition of *Testament* makes it easy to recall. "The New Testament writers" pairs nicely with "were Old Testament people."

Alliteration can also help us remember ideas. Preachers producing three points, each beginning with the same letter, is a proverbial practice. Principled persuasion can lock in the idea more effectively than ethical influencing. Other ways to be memorable include metaphors, analogies, and giving a twist to a cliché (which are discussed in chap. 14).

Made to Stick by Chip and Dan Heath is an excellent book on how to make our message memorable. Their six principles are:

- Simplicity
- Unexpectedness
- Concreteness
- Credibility
- Emotions
- Stories

And, to help us remember the six, the first letter of each word coincidentally spells out SUCCESs. I've already mentioned simplicity. Briefly here's what each of the others can offer to memorability and so to persuasion.

- *Unexpectedness* offers the element of surprise, like telling people that they have a 50 percent chance of dying from cancer or heart disease but one ten-thousandth of a percent chance of dying from a terror attack.

- *Concreteness* means giving specific examples. A general principle about not seeking revenge comes down to earth with "If anyone slaps you on the right cheek, turn to them the other cheek also" (Matthew 5:39).

- *Credibility* concerns your credentials as a writer, the sources you cite, and the facts you marshal.

- *Emotions* engage the whole person, which are important for motivation. In particular, emotions engage implicit mental processes, which are important for decision making. We are not merely logic machines.

- *Stories*, as we'll see in chapter six, show ideas in action and give us a holistic setting in which to understand them.

The entire book by the Heath brothers is worth the time and effort of every writer and speaker.

Rhyme, parallelism, alliteration, acronyms—these are just a few of the tools in your toolbox you can use to sharpen the memory of your audience.

REPEAT

In addition to making your points simple and memorable, make them over and over again. Repetition makes things more familiar, and familiarity sets our minds at ease, which makes us more open to perceive them as true. We return to the same ideas, but usually in slightly different ways each time—perhaps from the perspective of a different time period or from within a different culture or from accounting's viewpoint as well as sales's or from a child's as well as a parent's.

Rhetorically, word-for-word repetition is far more effective in speaking than writing. In speaking, repetition can drive home points and implant them firmly in our memories. Repetition in writing must be done carefully and subtly. Too much direct repetition in writing is usually boring, tedious, and boring.

Dr. Martin Luther King Jr's "I Have a Dream" speech offers a prime example of the power of repetition in speaking. If he had written and published this as a magazine article, it would probably not have the lofty position it holds in history.

A few paragraphs back I wrote, "In addition to making your points simple and memorable, make them over and over again." I was subtly reviewing what had come before while introducing a new topic. But notice how I just now got away with word-for-word repetition by quoting my own summary as an example. Very subtle indeed!

Repetition does have a dark side, however. As Daniel Kahneman reminds us, "A reliable way to make people believe falsehoods is frequent repetition, because familiarity is not easily distinguished from truth. Authoritarian institutions and marketers have long known this fact."[6] As emphasized in chapter four, therefore, while we seek to persuade, we need to be sure we do so with honesty and for the sake of the common good.

PUTTING IT TOGETHER

Those are three ways you can be persuasive. But how do you put it all together into a cohesive package? Chapter three, "Giving Structure," offers some options for organizing your writing. We can also overlay simplicity, memorability, and repetition on almost any of those. In addition, we can make direct use of a persuasive structure.

For centuries up to the present, speakers have been using a simple, three-part organization employing the classical rhetorical categories of ethos, logos, and pathos.[7]

We start with ethos, argument by character. In the introductory section, our goal is to win our audience by getting them to like us, identify with us, respect us as trustworthy and authoritative, or perhaps all of these. Essentially, we're saying, because of who I am and what I have done, you should listen to what I have to say.

Giving our credentials and listing our relevant experiences can help establish our reliability as an authority, but we don't want to merely recite our résumé. Telling a story about how we struggled to learn or grow or finally experience some success can be a better approach.

Finding points in common with our audience is another option. Shared background experiences can do this. Getting stuck in traffic, having a health scare, studying all night for a test—these may be the kinds of things those in our audience can relate to.

One counterintuitive way to help my audience identify with me is by saying that I am a person with flaws and foibles just like them. ("Once I lost my wallet, and . . .") This disarming self-deprecation can set our audience at ease and help them listen to us better as "one of them."

Say I want to do a piece about how to overcome fears and insecurities in writing. If I tell a story of how I was afraid my writing stunk when I was writing a book about how to write better, you are more likely to listen to my advice than if I said I never had any problems.

Next is logos, argument by logic and facts. Usually we begin the next section by briefly outlining the problem and possible solutions. Then we show the inadequacy of the other options. But we do so, as noted in chapter four, by presenting the arguments for these other viewpoints in as strong a form as possible before showing their weaknesses.

Here we can also increase our credibility and trustworthiness by admitting when our opponents are right. It shows our honesty, objectivity, and appreciation for the truth.[8]

After considering opposing views, we present our own solution and the arguments supporting it. This is also where we present objections to our viewpoint and show why they don't hold up.

Pathos comes last, argument by emotion. Pathos means appealing to our emotions as we call our audience to action, to apply our conclusions. An emotional appeal can become manipulative, of course, so we need to be careful we don't fall into the kinds of traps mentioned in chapter four. Exaggerating causes for fear or for opportunities for gain at the expense of others is not appropriate.

At the same time emotions are part of what it means to be human, and we want to legitimately appeal to the whole person. After all, just appealing to the mind can often be ineffective. Many alcoholics and other addicts know the facts about how they are hurting others and killing themselves, but that rarely changes behavior. Facts and logic alone are often inadequate.

In politics, the conclusion is usually an appeal to patriotism. In self-help literature, the final pitch is an optimistic image of a better you. In matters of faith and religion, we remind each other that we are part of something that is larger than ourselves giving meaning and hope to our lives.

As an example of the ethos-logos-pathos format, I thought I would pick something that many writers could identify with—being an introvert. We love time alone to think, to read, to play with words. Susan Cain's Ted Talk on her book *Quiet: The Power of Introverts in a World That Can't Stop Talking* seems just right.[9]

She starts her *ethos* section with a story of going to summer camp at age nine. While not all of us may have gone to camp as children, we all know what it was like as kids to join some activity for a day or a weekend with others we didn't know beforehand. Will we fit in? Will it be fun? Will we like it?

As it turns out, every time Susan pulled out a book, she got clear signals from her counselors and campmates that this was not cool. So she sadly closed her suitcase of books and didn't open it again till she got home. Later in life she made other changes to help her fit in, like becoming a lawyer to prove she could be assertive. In this way she draws in both introverts and extroverts because we all have given in to pressures to do what would make us accepted and liked, even if it wasn't what we wanted.

Cain then moves into her *logos* section by first identifying the main problem. Our colleagues, our communities, and our world are poorer when introverts aren't valued for the creativity and leadership they can bring to the table.

She offers facts ("A third to a half of the population are introverts.") and definitions ("Shyness is about fear of social judgment. Introversion is more about, how do you respond to stimulation, including social stimulation."). While extroverts work best in loud, active, stimulating environments, introverts are their most productive, creative, and energized "in quieter, more low-key environments."

Cain continues by naming specific problems that arise from a largely extroverted culture: Most of our institutions, like schools and the workplace, are designed for extroverts. Classrooms are arranged with pods of desks, so students are constantly working in groups and are rarely alone even for math or creative writing. Open-plan offices have the same problem.

More specifics come by way of examples of transformative leaders who were introverts: Eleanor Roosevelt, Rosa Parks, Gandhi. Many of our most creative people are also introverts like Dr. Seuss who worked alone and was afraid to be in public with children. "Steve Wozniak invented the first Apple computer sitting alone in his cubicle in Hewlett-Packard where he was working at the time."

Several times Cain anticipates objections and so clarifies that she is not saying that all environments should be quiet all the time and that we should stop collaborating. After all, Wozniak needed Steve Jobs to start Apple. The solution to the problem is to restore balance. The goal is to gain the best from both types of people.

Finally, in her *pathos* section, she leaves us "with three calls for action for those who share this vision. Number one: Stop the madness for constant group work. Just stop it." Here is passion we can all share. In a world gone mad in so many ways, we long for, we yearn for sanity, to stop obsessively doing crazy things that keep causing harm. She has touched on the deep human craving for order, balance, and a deep, multilayered sense of well-being called shalom.

"Number two: go to the wilderness." Again, she qualifies that we need not become hermits. Rather we need to follow the example of Jesus and others who went "alone to the wilderness, where they then [had] profound epiphanies and revelations that they then bring back to the rest of the community." Cain's appeal to ancient rootedness and permanence in our speed-of-light culture is subtle but very real.

Number three returns to where she began, with a suitcase full of books, wondering if she can be herself or not. Cain urges us all to look inside our own suitcases, whether we be introverts or extroverts, to use what we have to grace others with the gifts we've been given. She touches our desire to matter in the world. Writers, computer nerds, truck drivers, pastors, scientists, waiters, parents, teachers—any who are introverts, for the sake of others, need to "open up your suitcases for other people to see, because the world needs you and it needs the things you carry."

6

CREATING DRAMATIC NONFICTION

BOB HARVEY, MY FORMER PASTOR, told the congregation in a sermon about the time he was on vacation at a lake, sitting in a giant inner tube when suddenly and unexpectedly he lost his balance and found himself upside down in the water—still stuck in the tube. As a man with a few extra pounds on his frame, he was unable to get out and right himself immediately. While he was underwater trying to figure out what to do, he told us that he thought to himself, *You know, this will make a good sermon illustration.*

Perhaps the first rule of public speaking and writing is to tell stories. Facts touch our minds. Stories touch our whole person—our emotions, our desires, what we remember from the past, and what we hope for the future. Stories tell us who we were, who we are, and who we can be.

Facts, information, knowledge—these are all important and valuable. Yet while data can help us understand, stories help us act.[1] In a way, stories bypass our rational minds constructively. That was a surprising sentence for me to write since I am passionate about ideas and the importance of thinking well. Our rational faculties are necessary and important. Nonetheless, reason is not the totality of life. It is limited. And sometimes it can backfire.

When we put forward an argument, we can trigger the rational, judging, and evaluative faculties in our audience. As a result, they may respond (at least in their own minds) with arguments of their own. They may start considering what is wrong with what we are saying. Stories can bypass objections and settled conclusions (including our prejudices) by going to the heart, to our emotions. But notice I just said, "stories bypass our rational minds constructively." How is that constructive?

I once heard author and English professor Dan Taylor talk about reading *The Lord of the Rings* when he was in high school. While he hadn't read it since, he still carried with him one main impression that had shaped his perspective on the world ever since—evil is real. This didn't come from philosophical debate or deep reading of the great minds of past and present. It came from a story. The story not only shaped how he thought but how he interacted with the world, how he determined what was important and what wasn't. It shaped how he lived.

Fiction writers shouldn't have all the good stories. Nonfiction writers can tell them too. In chapter five I noted that stories are one of the keys to making ideas stick. Here we will look more closely at the how and why of narrative in nonfiction.

EMBRACING NARRATIVE

Stories aren't just window dressing. They are every bit as much part of your content as the information or advice you might include. They are bound to stick with us long after the information has been forgotten. In fact, stories can be better than mere data because they are richer, embracing more depth, detail, and dimensions than a statement can. A story can tell us more (and in many ways it tells us more accurately) than a series of propositional statements, which inevitably must leave out much.

Those of us from the Western world usually begin with an idea and then illustrate it with a story. For us the story is merely an aid to memory or a way to engage emotions. In much of the rest of the world, they tell a story first and then illustrate it with concrete application. They think first in terms of a narrative that offers a wider, deeper, more multidimensional understanding. Ideas, principles, and procedures are limited. They may not tell us who we are, so we know how to act when new situations arise. We should never underestimate the power of stories to shape our beliefs and to move us to action.

Be careful, however, with canned stories that you might find in a collection of tales about people who succeed or fail greatly. These often-recycled yarns can come off as just too good (or too bad) to be true, that is, as pat and artificial. The best stories are those that you discover yourself or ones that come from your own life or from those you know. That's part of what made Bob Harvey's inner tube story so effective. It was *his* story.

So, what can you do to develop your storytelling? Here are some options.

Collect stories. Keep a file of stories from your childhood and stories your parents told you about their lives. Include anything funny or dramatic or unexpected, even if you are not sure you will ever use the stories. You may find that stories can have more than one point and be used for several purposes.

You can jot down one sentence per story to remind you what it is with the option to fill it out later, or you can write a draft of the story in a few paragraphs or pages. The intent is not to publish—at least not yet. The idea is to deposit your stories in a bank, so you can withdraw them later when the need arises.

Practice telling stories. Be alert to funny or interesting things, situations, happenings during the day or week. Try telling them to friends at meals. See how people react. Write down and file the good ones.

BAILEY ON STORY

Kenneth Bailey, who spent decades living, studying, and teaching in the Middle East, considers the relationship of stories and ideas. He writes:

> Middle Eastern creators of meaning do not offer a concept and then illustrate (or choose not to illustrate) with a metaphor or parable. For them the equation is reversed. . . . The Middle Eastern mind creates meaning by the use of simile, metaphor, proverb, parable, and dramatic action. The person involved is not *illustrating* a concept but is rather creating meaning by reference to something concrete. The primary language is that of the metaphor/parable and the secondary language is the conceptual interpretation of the metaphor that in Biblical literature is often given with it. . . .

> In the book *Speaking in Parables*, Sallie McFague TeSelle discusses the parable of the prodigal son. She writes,

> > One could paraphrase this parable in the theological assertion "God's love knows no bounds," but to do that would be to miss what the parable can do for our insight into such love. For what *counts* here is not extricating an abstract concept but precisely the opposite, delving into the details of the story itself, letting the metaphor do its job of revealing the new setting for ordinary life. It is the play of the radical images that does the job.*

---

*Kenneth E. Bailey, *Finding the Lost* (St. Louis, MO: Concordia Publishing House, 1992), 16, 18.

Listen to stories. Mack is one of the best, funniest storytellers I have ever met. Not only do wild and crazy things happen to him, but he also has an amazing ability to wring out the most laughter and tears from any episode he tells—whether to a small group of friends or to hundreds of listeners. "How did you learn to do that?" I asked him once.

"I go to the National Storytelling Festival.[2] Over three days you sit and listen to the most skilled and dynamic storytellers you will ever hear. I go from speaker to speaker and listen, absorb, learn, take notes, and am enraptured."

Build the drama. Think about how to increase intrigue and tension in listeners as you tell a story, whether at an informal meal or while giving a talk. Try arranging the events in different ways, organizing the material first one way and then another to see which is more dramatic. In any case . . .

Don't give away the ending. One of the best ways to kill drama is to tell too early how a story ends. By holding off, you keep people reading or listening. Usually (though there are exceptions), giving the conclusion at the beginning tends to take the tension out of the story and make it less gripping. Allowing people to hang in suspense will keep them more attentive throughout. (See also "Other Dramatic Structures" later.)

Show, don't tell. Don't tell us that Rose was mad. Say that she threw her plate across the room. Don't say Javier was sad. Say that tears silently fell down his cheeks or that he sat silently at his meal without eating anything.

That is, don't spell out emotions or intentions but rather show actions and trust readers to understand. By allowing them to interpret what is going on, you involve them at a deeper level (galvanizing their interest) and allow your story to become richer. Ironically, your story takes on three dimensions by virtue of what you do not say. This happens because your audience become active participants (filling in the gaps you leave) rather than passive observers (who mindlessly allow your words to splash over them).

Be vulnerable. Personal stories that show your own weakness or mistakes will help your audience identify with you, appreciate you, and open themselves up to what you have to say. Often when I speak, I try to use self-deprecating humor, putting myself in a poor light compared to others.

Once I was giving a talk to 150 college students, whose supersaturated, hormonal fugue state became quite focused on my every word when I started talking about marriage. I told them that when thinking about a future spouse, what's important is not finding a mate who has a similar personality but someone who has similar values. With the same attitudes toward money, time, relationships, and faith, you could be as different as—well, as different as my wife, Phyllis, and me. I told them that

Phyllis is an extrovert. I am an introvert. *[silence]*

Phyllis cares passionately about the world. I love *to think* about the world. *[a few chuckles]*

Phyllis is full of life and energy. My mom said I was born tired. *[some laughs]*

When we were first married, Phyllis was a morning person and I was a night person. Now Phyllis is a morning *and* a night person, and I am neither. *[louder laughter]*

Phyllis thinks everyone she meets is fascinating. I think the dictionary is fascinating. *[lots of laughter]*

Phyllis has a heart as wide as the horizon. I have the emotional range of a turnip. *[uproarious laughter]*

Phyllis is a wonderful conversationalist who can make a fence post talk. *[pause]* I *am* the fence post. *[the room exploded]*

The audience got the point. In fact, one of the staff got the point so well that he decided to ask out a woman he had been interested in. Before that, he thought she was not right for him because they were so different. A year later they married.

Even if you have the most profound truths, you can still be profoundly boring. I was once on the pastoral search committee for our church and heard a sermon from a prospective candidate who delivered fourteen points. Yes, count 'em, fourteen points! There must be a better way, and there is. We didn't hire our fourteen-point candidate. We hired the one who preached a sermon with solid content and who told a story, simple, personal, and vulnerable. That made all the difference.

USING A NARRATIVE QUESTION

Telling one or more isolated stories within a larger piece is always an option. But it is also possible to structure the whole using a dramatic frame.

Using a narrative question to maintain interest throughout a book or short story is an effective and time-honored technique in fiction. Will Ahab kill the great white whale? Will Red Riding Hood escape the Big Bad Wolf?

The narrative question is established early, and readers keep going because they want to find out how the narrative question will be answered. Curiosity motivates readers to stick with it till the end. In an age of short attention spans spawned by distractions from smartphones, social media, and our own to-do lists, this is no small achievement.

But what about nonfiction? Narrative questions can be used effectively in this genre as well. For example, you begin by setting up an issue (say difficulty in finding new customers or problems getting along with mothers-in-law) but don't give the answer right away. Instead, you reveal the solution step by step throughout the book or article. In a book, the setup may even take a chapter or two before the remedy is slowly laid out, piece by piece.

A narrative question can be effectively deployed within a chapter as well. Maybe the question is, How can we lose weight when we are constantly surrounded by reminders of food in the media, in our homes, and at work? Here's one possible structure.

After describing the problem people face, discuss solution A, showing why it seems logical and helpful, then explain why it ultimately doesn't work. Then do the same with solution B, which also turns out to be ineffective. Likewise solution C. It fails.

By this point, readers are really ready for an answer that solves the problem. They are thinking, *If those three seemingly reasonable solutions don't work, then what does?* They are motivated to know.

This is how murder mysteries are constructed. We are provided with a dead body and then a catalog of potential suspects. Clues are offered why each might be guilty and why each might be innocent. The best writing gives us the information we need to identify the murderer but camouflages it with details. This keeps our attention focused as we try to solve the crime, try to pick out the relevant detail and cast aside the rest. Then the novelist reveals the answer. A tried-and-true formula, yes—but effective.

When setting up the problem, it's important therefore that we not set up a straw man that's easy to knock down. As said earlier, we should give the very best, the most convincing arguments for the solutions that we think will ultimately fail. Our audience will feel the tension and yearn more keenly for an answer, which will make your solution all the more satisfying.

TURNING FACTS INTO STORIES

If you have somewhat dry information to impart to your readers or listeners, another narrative approach can help you convey those facts in a memorable way. This strategy has gained popularity in recent years. Why? Because it has become fashionable to note that we all have biases no matter how well trained we might be in science or law or history. We all come from somewhere that affects how we think about a subject. This would seem to be a rather difficult problem to overcome. How do we say something is true when it will inevitably be colored by our own perspectives?

Rather than trying to eliminate the problem, many writers are making a virtue out of a vice. They exploit or magnify their personal involvement with a subject—and it can make for some dandy reading. How does this work?

Writers tell the story of how they became interested in a topic, what motivated their investigation, the mistakes they made in the process, who helped guide their work, what obstacles they overcame to get the information, a conversation that gave them an aha moment, how what they discovered was not what they expected, how they reacted when they finally had a breakthrough, and what difference all this made to them personally. In short, they tell the story of how they gained the information or insights they want to impart to you.

Several nonfiction narratives have used this method successfully. Journalist Lee Strobel used this technique to good effect in his best-selling book *The Case for Christ*. He told the story of his search for the facts behind some of the most challenging claims of Christianity.

Rebecca Skloot's *The Immortal Life of Henrietta Lacks* offers two (well, actually three—okay, four) interweaving stories for the price of one. The first story line is the remarkable history of how the cells from Henrietta Lacks's cancer (known in science as HeLa cells) have been growing and duplicating in laboratories (and biological factories) for over sixty years. It is a fascinating scientific history of a cell line that has been instrumental in developing the polio vaccine, mapping the human genome, and many other medical breakthroughs.

This leads to a further story line of the legal history of and ramifications of using human biological material without the knowledge or consent of the people it came from. Finding out how our courts have ruled on these matters is perhaps the most shocking aspect of the book.

The third story is of Henrietta Lacks herself and her family, a story of rural and urban cultures sometimes colliding with the medical industry. Skloot takes us back to Henrietta's birth, her hometown, as well as to her siblings, children, and grandchildren who lived well beyond her. Where did Henrietta come from? What effect did her death and the research spawned by her cells have on her family?

The fourth story line is the author's own quest to uncover who Henrietta Lacks was, a quest that stretched out over decades of discoveries and setbacks, of crossing barriers with courage and grit. Skloot weaves these four stories together skillfully into a seamless whole. And the result is a fascinating true tale.

David Grann's *The Lost City of Z* uses a similar but simpler approach, going back and forth between just two story lines. The first is the tale of British adventurer Percy Fawcett (an inspiration for the explorer Charles Muntz in the movie *Up*) and his early twentieth-century quest for the remains of a hidden civilization in the Amazon. When Fawcett disappeared, many searched for him, never to return themselves. The second is the story of Grann's own efforts to research Fawcett, even to the point of retracing Fawcett's trail through swamp and overgrown wilderness.

OTHER DRAMATIC STRUCTURES

The narrative question and the story of your own research are not the only possible frames for building drama into your nonfiction. Several other long-established options can keep your audience with you every word of the way.

Loop back to the beginning. Even if you tell all or most of a story at the beginning, as you conclude go back to the story you opened with and use it to tie things together and bring home your main idea.

I was working with one writer, Orlando Crespo, on his book *Being Latino in Christ*. I suggested his first chapter tell his own story of growing up as second-generation Puerto Rican. And he did. Then after his opening tale of confusion, anger, and rejection, he transitioned into an overview of the topics readers would find in the book. Without my telling him to do so, however, he concluded the chapter with this:

> Sometimes, though, I wish there were a way to go back to that little Puerto Rican boy raking crabapples and playing stickball, that seven-year-old boy who was me. I would take him by the hand and walk him through his new neighborhood. I would tell him, "Don't be afraid. You're going to be OK. One day you will know who you are and to whom you belong."[3]

Even this time as I copied out this paragraph, just as the first time I heard him read this to me, my eyes fill with tears for the pain he experienced and the hope he expresses.

Start with the first half of a story and leave it hanging. Tell a story but stop at a particularly dramatic point without revealing how it was resolved. Then transition to your main content. At the end of the chapter, article, or talk, tell the rest of the tale. Holding the end of the story in suspense builds drama and keeps people attentive while you go through somewhat less interesting material.

Use **in medias res.** This Latin phrase *in medias res* ("into the middle of things") refers to starting in the middle of a story instead of at the beginning. Often this is a climactic moment, such as right before a championship game or when the doctor is about to give a diagnosis. As with starting with the first half of a story, we do not give the resolution. Rather, we stop and go back to the beginning to explain how things built up to this midpoint. When we get back to the part of the story where we left off originally, we can finish it from that point or do so later.

Movies often use this technique with much of the narrative being an extended flashback after an opening scene. *Gandhi*, the Oscar-winning best picture, begins with the day the title character is assassinated in 1948. After the funeral, the movie flashes back to the seminal moment in 1893 when Gandhi is thrown off a train in South Africa, which launched his life of activism. We then follow the rest of his life chronologically up to the point of his death.

Gandhi may sound like the opposite of what I said above, "Don't give away the ending." The difference is that Gandhi is a historical figure, so most of us will already know the broad outlines of his life. There's not much of a secret here. The drama comes in finding out more details about how he got from being thrown off the train to becoming an international icon.

Another way to use *in medias res* successfully is to tell part of how the story ends, but not all of it. In chapter one I quoted the opening of Mary Doria Russell's *The Sparrow* where we learn that something terrible has gone wrong with an expedition. But we don't know exactly what or how it went wrong. Thus the drama is sustained throughout the novel as the author then goes back to the beginning and unfolds the tale.

Tell a story within a story. One of the many things Shakespeare's *Hamlet* is famous for is the play within a play. Hamlet believes that his Uncle Claudius has killed his own brother, Hamlet's father, so he can marry Hamlet's mother and claim Denmark's throne. But the prince can't quite prove it.

He decides then to work with a drama troupe to perform a play for the royal pair that will be very similar to what Hamlet suspects Claudius did. He hopes the play will evoke an intense response of anger, shock, or remorse from Claudius. He concludes, "The play's the thing wherein I'll catch the conscience of the king."

The Gospel writers did the same thing. Within their story of Jesus, we hear this miracle worker himself tell stories. Indeed, on one occasion he does so to catch the conscience of those plotting against him. Jesus recounts the tale of a vineyard owner who rents out the land to some farmers. He sends a series of servants to collect what is due him, but the tenants abuse them and send the servants away empty-handed. Finally, the owner sends his own son, but the tenants kill him.

How do the Jewish leaders respond? The Gospel of Mark tells us, "Then the chief priests, the teachers of the law and the elders looked for a way to arrest him because they knew he had spoken the parable against them" (Mark 12:12).

Stories within stories add drama to drama. By comparing and contrasting the two, we gain new insight and deeper understanding of the characters, the themes, the emotions involved. We add layers of complexity while maintaining the interest of readers.

Jesus, one of the great storytellers of all time, would even let some of his parables just hang in space with no clarification of what exactly he might have had in mind. He trusted his listeners enough to let them work it out for themselves. And if they couldn't, he trusted them to come and ask him for more explanation. That's what stories do. They pull us in. Jesus wanted to reach the whole person, so he sought to touch not just minds with propositions or doctrinal statements. He wanted more. He wanted hearts. So he told stories.

After Bob Harvey told us what he thought while stuck upside down in the inner tube, we all howled. As is typical, however, I don't remember what that sermon was about. I remember the story. And I do remember that Bob (who died some years later) was a humble, self-effacing man whose unpretentious character had an impact on everyone he touched, including me. His story was not mere decoration. It *was* the point. And I got it.

7

CRACKING OUR WRITER'S BLOCK

OUR PRODUCTION MANAGER Jock (yes, that was his name) worked with printers to produce our books, since, like most publishers, we didn't have printing presses. He knew the processes intimately and was fond of telling me, "With all the things that can go wrong in printing a book, it's amazing the ink ever hits the page."

What's true for printers is true in spades for writers. With so many reasons for writer's block, it's a miracle anyone writes anything.

Fear and perfectionism, two of the most common obstacles, are an accomplished dance pair. They reinforce one another in seamless motion. Our desire to get things just right does a do-si-do with our fear of what others will think about what we've written. Then our fear spins our perfectionism even faster. Dread that readers will discover what we already know—that we are ignorant and that our writing is bland, boring, and bad—keeps us refining, reediting, revising without end, until exhaustion sucks all the ink out of our pens.

Failure to get published, failure to meet one's own standards, failure to finish, or failure to get many readers once published can, unsurprisingly, be debilitating. So can the failure we feel when criticism comes in response to what we have produced.

Success, ironically, can be failure's evil twin. One writer I know unexpectedly received critical acclaim and a prestigious book award for his first novel. But he became paralyzed as he wondered how he could possibly meet the expectations this created for a second book. Despite a generous contract in hand for his next work along with active support and encouragement from his editor and agent, he had a terrible time getting unstuck.

Some well-known authors have suffered from such maladies. Harper Lee never wrote another book after her hugely successful *To Kill a Mockingbird*. Even her sequel, *Go Set a Watchman*, was written beforehand but sat unpublished for decades. Ralph Ellison was never able to follow up his landmark book *Invisible Man*, despite writing thousands of pages of notes that he could never turn into a book.

SIMPLE IDEAS TO CRACK A COMPLEX PROBLEM

How do we break through these barriers? If your problem is a dry well, if you just don't seem to have any ideas for what to write next, here are a few possibilities to get you going.

Read lots of stuff. To get unstuck, read—especially in the area you want to write about. But also read broadly outside your target topic or your area of expertise. You might be surprised how stimulating this will be. Write down relevant ideas or quotes, even if they seem only loosely related to your work.

Keep an idea file. Always carry a small notebook or a smartphone with a note-taking app so you can put things down right away. Taking a picture can help too. Ideas can come to mind at any time—while talking to someone, watching a movie, taking a walk. Record anything that could be developed later—a character's name or a piece of her backstory, an illustration for a point in an article, a news item, or a vivid descriptive phrase. I use my phone to write myself quick emails with ideas I don't want to lose.

I also have an idea file for potential blog posts. Each idea is just a sentence, a phrase, or a question. When I'm not sure what to do next, I go back to it and look for something that I might be ready to develop.

Take notes on anything and everything. Just to get words flowing again, pay attention to what you see, hear, and smell as you travel, commute, go to the store, or work in the yard. Stop and write down every detail you can. Go to a park, a mall, a busy street, or a college campus to people watch. Write snatches of conversation, what people are wearing, odors you notice, architectural details, everything. Again, just write, even if it's not related to the project you are working on, to get you in the pattern of once more putting words down.

Copy the greats. If all else fails, pull out Shakespeare or Steinbeck, Austen or Achebe, or any other favorite, and literally start writing or typing their words exactly as you read them. The act of writing itself (even if the words are someone else's) can stimulate your own work. By being attentive to style and vocabulary, you can even improve your own writing.

Like many composers, Beethoven kept a sketchbook of musical themes and ideas. In one he copied a portion of Mozart's Symphony No. 40, which he used as inspiration in the third movement of his Fifth Symphony. If the exercise of copying is good enough for Beethoven, it should be good enough for us.

Get some rest. Take a break. Do something different than the routine. Take a vacation. Or at least take a week or month away from writing or research. If you normally sit at a desk, do something physical or vice versa. Get in a totally different environment like the countryside if you are a city dweller or the reverse. Even if only for a weekend.

Why? Because turning our attention to other topics or resting from any concentrated rational thought gives other parts of our brain time to work. New ideas or solutions to problems come when we give our minds a chance to change direction. When we are so locked into one kind of task, the rest of our brain doesn't have freedom to contribute. But when we stop, new ways of thinking can emerge.

PLAYING BALDERDASH

Sometimes our writing is stuck because we don't know where to start. For some of us, we feel that we must know where we are going to end up before we can begin. And if we don't, it is like our ink has run out, our pencil is down to a nub, our muse is silent, and our laptop has crashed.

Just starting to write without knowing where you are going is hard. Yet I often find that the act of beginning to write stimulates further ideas and clarifies my thinking as I go. I didn't think I had anything to say, but by starting blind, suddenly I can see. I don't worry about where to begin. What I'm putting down is likely something that will end up in the middle or even get deleted. But it primes my pump, gets my juices going, and stimulates all manner of clichés and occasionally some fresh prose. If I know that it doesn't have to be perfect at the beginning, I have greater freedom. Later I can reorganize and rewrite.

A fun exercise that can give you good practice at writing from a standing start is the game Balderdash, otherwise known as dictionary. One person gives everyone else playing an unusual word. Each person then creates an imaginary definition with the intent of fooling the rest of the players into believing it is the real definition. The person handing out the word also writes down the real definition, collects what everyone has written, and reads them to the group. Everyone then votes on which they think is correct.

Playing the game trains us to just start writing because the game goes fast, and you don't want to keep everyone else waiting. I was once given the word *burgonet*. I started writing, "In fencing," because it was the first thing that came to my mind. The word seemed vaguely French and somehow I associate fencing with France.

Then what? After a moment, I continued, "a movement in which . . ." knowing that now I had to come up with some tactic that could fit a fencing match, though I had no idea what that would be. I thought a second more and concluded, "one feigns a retreat as a prelude to an attack." It took me all of thirty seconds. I didn't evaluate or second-guess myself as I went along. I just wrote.

In the end I thought it might fool a couple people. The actual definition was, "A sixteenth century army helmet with a retractable visor." But by just starting somewhere, even though I had no idea where I was going, I could move forward.

Another Balderdash variation involves obscure movie titles for which players are to come up with a bogus plot summary. Consider *Blond Crazy*. Start with something slightly offbeat like, "a golden retriever." But what does the dog do in the movie? "falls for an Irish setter . . ." Now we need conflict or drama. "and will do anything to attract her attention." And for a wrap-up? An old standby is just fine. "Hilarity ensues."

What is this 1931 James Cagney movie (in which he utters the famous line, "You dirty, double-crossin' rat") actually about? In this romantic comedy, a bellboy enlists a maid to help him con people out of their money.

Want to get started? Here are a few words to try out on your own. Don't take more than one minute for each:

padishan

icekhana

swallet

The game is a lot more fun in a group when players may come up with riotous definitions. As a bonus, it gives you practice at putting words down on paper before you have any idea of where they are going. Just what you may need to crack your writer's block.

DON'T BE THE JUDGE—YET

Betty Flowers offers a practical four-word rubric for freeing ourselves from writing quagmires—Madman, Architect, Carpenter, Judge.[1]

We start with an idea or maybe many ideas. It may be an idea for a whole piece or for a sentence. We write something down and immediately see how inadequate it is. So we throw it out. We try something else, which is worse, and hit the delete key.

This scenario, Flowers says, reflects two conflicting forces at work in us. One is the Madman full of crazy ideas and crazy wonderful ways of expressing them. But before the Madman can get going, the Judge intervenes and squelches everything outlandish or ordinary. It's too flashy or too boring or too confusing or too personal. So out it goes.

The problem is, nothing gets written or at least not finished. The solution, however, is not to get rid of the Judge. Rather, we should promise the Judge a turn later. But first, we give the Madman full reign to write anything and everything.

After the Madman has finished, at least a day later invite the Architect to look at what the Madman wrote to start giving it some structure. The Architect deals with large chunks (paragraphs or key points), not details, and may point out big items that are missing, like walls or windows.

After that, again perhaps the next day, the Carpenter goes to work, fixing things on a sentence-by-sentence level and adding in the missing items the Architect pointed out. Now the work is ready for the Judge. Spelling, grammar, and punctuation get full attention at this last stage. Getting caught up in those details at the very beginning can derail any project.

Holding off the determined Judge at the first stage can be difficult. But with practice, it can be done. The Judge can learn to trust you for a turn, letting the other participants do their jobs.

LIFE ISSUES

Ron Brackin tells us, writer's "block occurs when a writer has nothing to say. Unfortunately, not all writers experience it."

You are not like that since you obviously have something to say (even if you are not quite sure right now what that is). But sometimes we are challenged by something deeper than not having any good ideas at the moment.[2]

If your problem is a life event. If you are moving to a new city, getting a new job, dealing with a death in the family, managing a crisis at work, or having a new baby, you just need to be patient with yourself until things settle down. But set a date, like six months or a year afterward. Decide that's when you are going to start writing again, and then make the changes necessary in your schedule or commitments to get started.

If you are an extrovert. If you love people and love talking to people, you may find, ironically, that whenever you start to write, the words just evaporate. Even though you care passionately about an idea or a story, you have no idea how to get going.

What to do? Here's an option. Find a friend who is willing to sit down with you and listen to your ideas, paragraph by paragraph, chapter by chapter, or scene by scene. Then, with your friend still there (such a good friend), start writing. If you get stuck while writing, say it aloud to your friend again, and then write down what you just said. In an extreme case, you may need to ask your friend to take notes as you talk, then give those back to you so you can start writing.

Obviously, this will be in very rough form, but at least you will have broken through. From there you can revise and edit. You can take the disorganized material you have and rearrange it into key ideas or plot elements that become your after-the-fact outline. (Or if you are stuck again, ask your friend for suggestions for an outline based on what you've said.) Likely you will also find you've got some unnecessary or redundant material. When that happens, just do what you know needs to be done—delete it.

Rachel is an extroverted author and powerful speaker who is constantly in demand. She desperately wanted to write a book, but each time she started, nothing happened. Finally, a friend, Esther, told Rachel to come and meet at Esther's office for two hours every other week. She did. Rachel would talk to Esther for an hour about one topic in the book. Then, while Esther still sat there, Rachel would write for an hour about what she had just talked about. What a gift of time and listening Esther gave! The happy ending? The book eventually was finished and published.

If you are someone who likes details. If you like details, researching can be a great way to get unstuck. Start taking notes on information you find. Writing down the data and ideas others have developed can be much less intimidating than trying to create your own work ex nihilo. And the notes you take may trigger ideas of your own that you can put into a sentence or two.

One problem could arise, however. You enjoy researching so much that you never stop and never start writing. Again, you might try setting a deadline for yourself or find an accountability partner who can keep you disciplined. Once you've amassed enough notes, start organizing and expanding. You will have started writing and rewriting without even realizing it.

Maybe you've written a lot but just can't finish. You can't get it organized or can't draw it to a close. You keep finding new ideas and plot elements to include. You find yourself polishing and polishing over and over, never quite satisfied. The drafting process never ends.

At this point you may need an accountability partner who is not a peer. It needs to be someone you respect and will listen to, who has some authority in your life. Give that person permission to be tough with you and to call you on it when you make excuses or are defensive. Together come up with a series of intermediate deadlines, such as when each chapter will be completed. Meet or call regularly to monitor progress. Then listen to your accountability partner and do what he or she says. Otherwise, you have no right to complain to anyone about your unfinished project.

Finally, don't expect writing to be easy. It is hard work. The more we are willing to commit ourselves to any and all strategies to write, the sooner we will. The goal is not to effortlessly write a bestseller, make buckets of money, become famous, get rave reviews, or win a prestigious award. The goal is to look at every project as an opportunity to grow and learn. We can always succeed at that.

8

THE NUTS, BOLTS, HAMMERS, AND SAWS OF GOOD REWRITING

AS MY FRIEND GARY LIKES to tell the story, his ninth-grade English teacher was the perfect stereotype. Glasses, stern face, hair in a bun, outdated dress that came up in a tight collar around her neck, leaning over her desk and in a crackly voice exhorting her students, "There's no such thing as good writing." *(dramatic pause)* "There's only good rewriting."

That was the last thing Gary and his classmates wanted to hear. But he remembered. It's the last thing you and I want to hear. But we know it's true. So we rewrite. Even geniuses rewrite. Contrary to myth, Mozart and Beethoven regularly reworked their compositions.

What made artists like them and athletes like Michael Jordan, Mia Hamm, and Tom Brady the absolute best in their fields was not their supreme talent. It was their talent combined with a driving work ethic.

Long before they stepped onto the court or the field, in practice and in the film room, they outworked and outthought their opponents.

William Zinsser famously begins his classic *On Writing Well* with a story about a time he and "Dr. Brock" were on a panel about writing:

> Dr. Brock was asked if it was important to rewrite. Absolutely not, he said, "Let it all hang out," he told us, and whatever form the sentences take will reflect the writer at his most natural. I then said that rewriting is the essence of writing. I pointed out that professional writers rewrite their sentences over and over and then rewrite what they have rewritten.[1]

Zinsser generously suggests that there is a range of writers and writing patterns. His way may not be the only way. Not everyone is alike and whatever helps you write is for the good. But since his whole book is essentially about how to rewrite, clearly Zinsser thinks a piece that required no rewriting would be as rare as a hole in one by a first-time golfer. (That he revised and updated his book eight times also bears witness to his belief in redoing his material.)

My personal guess based on four decades of editing is that an editor and copyeditor (with maybe a ghostwriter) picked up the pieces of Dr. Brock's fragmentary, rough-hewn manuscript and cut, shaped, sanded, glued, stained, and varnished it into serviceable form—all of which he was oblivious to. Editors know when writers have been lazy.

Rewriting is not the message we want to hear. We have already researched, drafted, organized, powered through writer's block, and plucked a dandy opening from the middle of our work. We don't want to be told more work, time, and hard thinking are needed. Rewriting means trying several variations to see which works best. It means listening to objective voices from the outside who point out problems. It means paying attention to word choice and taking time to find the best one. It means being brutally honest with yourself about those phrases (and pages) you are in love with and being willing to mercilessly consign them to the eternal destruction of the recycle bin.

TRUTH REQUIRES CLARITY

How do we go about rewriting? George Orwell sends us in the right direction in his famous essay "Politics and the English Language." He published it in 1946 about the time he began working on his dystopian novel *1984*. Both essay and novel deal with the way bureaucracies hide their agendas with convoluted grammar, pretentious word choice, and intentional ambiguity. In this way, they conceal the fact that "pacification" of the population actually means "defenseless villages are bombarded from the air, the inhabitants driven out into the countryside, the cattle machine-gunned, the huts set on fire with incendiary bullets."[2]

The rest of us may not hide what we really mean for such nefarious purposes. We may not be tyrants bent on enriching ourselves at the expense of our countrymen. But without a rigorous commitment to clarity, we, too, fail in an important way. We fail to tell the truth straightforwardly.

So for social and ethical reasons, but also to help us all write better, Orwell offers six simple guidelines. Keep them in mind as you review and revise what you've written, and you can resolve most problems. Here they are with a bit of comment from me:

1. "Never use a metaphor, simile or other figure of speech which you are used to seeing in print."[3] If you spot a cliché, take it out and replace it with a fresh metaphor of your own or with plain language. For example:

Not "It cost an arm and a leg" *but* "It cost a lot."

Not "Dead as a doornail" *but* "Completely ineffective."

Not "She went ballistic" *but* "She was furious."

2. "Never use a long word where a short one will do." Writers often use long words to sound more authoritative or convincing. The opposite is the case.

Not commence *but* begin

Not currently *but* now

Not assistance *but* help

Not implement *but* do

Not utilize *but* use

3. "If it is possible to cut a word out, always cut it out." Don't use six words where two will do.

Long-winded: the fact that he did not succeed. *Better*: his failure

Not such a variety *but* these

Not two or three different *but* several

Not tall skyscraper *but* skyscraper

Not due to the fact that *but* because

Not build up *but* build

4. "Never use the passive where you can use the active." Give the main noun of the sentence some action. When you see a sentence begin with "There was" or "It is" you should almost always rewrite it.

Passive: The race was won by John.
Active: John won the race.

Passive: There were a great number of dead leaves lying on the ground.
Active: Dead leaves covered the ground.

Passive: The passive voice is to be avoided.
Active: Avoid passive voice.

5. "Never use a foreign phrase, a scientific word or jargon word if you can think of an everyday English equivalent." Some foreign words and phrases have worked their way into common English usage. Words such as *avant garde, graffiti, guerilla, gulag, per capita, prima donna*, and *status quo* are fine to use in most writing. However, many others are not common such as *bête noir, pater familias*, and *sturm und drang*. If you are in doubt, cut it out.

6. "Break any of these rules sooner than say anything outright barbarous." For example, to avoid repeating a single-syllable word you may want to occasionally substitute a two- or three-syllable equivalent. Or sometimes (we hope rarely) you may need to use passive voice to convey drama or if you really don't know who was responsible for the action in question. We might say, "*Beowulf* was written in the eighth or ninth century," because we don't know who wrote it.

PRO TIPS FOR BEING YOUR OWN COPYEDITOR

By regularly rewriting with Orwell's guidelines in mind, you will be able to use them even as you write first drafts. But even experienced writers slip from time to time, so reworking will still be essential.

Ready for more? If you want to delight your editor and please your readers, go through your piece a second time with the following guidelines in view.

1. *Read aloud*. Many writers are wise to read their work aloud to themselves as part of the rewriting process. That way we engage our hearing, which can reveal grammatical errors, repetition of words, awkward phrasing, or unintentional rhyme. It also forces us to slow down so we can notice problems more easily.

2. *Maintain parallelism*. When elements are compared or contrasted, be sure your sentence structure treats them equally. Otherwise the result can be awkward or confusing.

Unparallel: We went to Paris to study French, but in Rome we had fun.

Parallel: We went to Paris to study French, but we went to Rome to have fun.

3. *Replace generalities with specifics.* Without concrete details our writing will lack vividness and sound abstract. Specifics bring life.

General: The weather turned bad.

Specific: The gray clouds began pelting us with bits of ice and snow.

Even though the sentence about gray clouds is longer, it is much stronger. So while shorter is generally better, here's a case where we apply Orwell's sixth rule to break any rule rather than say something badly (or to say something better).

General: The student should do one hour of homework each weeknight.

Specific: Students should do one hour of homework each weeknight.

Though "the student" sounds more specific than "students," it is actually an abstraction. We know what "students" look like. No one, after all, has ever met "the student."

4. *Put the longest item at the end of a series.* Reading aloud can particularly alert us to problems with rhythm. When we put the longest element at the end, the pacing of a sentence is almost always better.

Awkward: The car was packed with the fishing gear, enough food to last a week, and the tent.

Better: The car was packed with the tent, the fishing gear, and enough food to last a week.

5. *Vary sentence length.* When all sentences are the same length, our writing can become tedious. Sometimes very short sentences set off by long ones can be powerful. It's true.

Gary's ninth-grade teacher may have had a tight face and had her hair in a bun, but she was on to something. Good writing requires the hard work of rewriting. And rewriting often involves cutting out what's unnecessary, drab, or confusing. She summed it up well for Gary's class by quoting Ernest Hemingway: "The test of a book is how much good stuff you can throw away."[4]

9

WE REMEMBER
ENDINGS FIRST

OPENINGS MOTIVATE READERS TO KEEP GOING. Strong endings stay with people after they finish.

The end can be more than just the last line. It can be a strong final story that embodies the heart of your piece. Here, though, I want to focus on closing lines or the very last line.

First, a couple don'ts. Summaries are not strong endings. You don't want your last line to merely say in slightly different words what has already been said. Sure, it can be fine to review key ideas by way of reminder in your last paragraph or so, but don't end there.

It's also usually a bad idea to end with a quotation, even a strong quote from someone famous. Readers want *you*. If they wanted someone else, that's who they'd be reading. An exception can be a quote from someone in a story you've told. In such a case you can use a final quote you've not included before that pulls things together in a fresh, compelling way. But using something you might find in *Bartlett's Familiar Quotations*? Never.

UNEXPECTED BUT JUST RIGHT

What should we aim for in an ending? "The perfect ending," William Zinsser tells us, "should take your readers slightly by surprise and yet seem exactly right. They didn't expect the article to end so soon, or so abruptly, or to say what it said. But they know it when they see it."[1]

While you want something new at the end, it can't be totally different. The trick is for the end to be intrinsically related to the topic at hand while also being fresh.

Zinsser practices what he preaches in *On Writing Well*. He regularly ends his chapters in just this fashion. At the end of his opening chapter, "The Transaction," he writes:

> Good writing has an aliveness that keeps the reader reading from one paragraph to the next, and it's not a question of gimmicks to "personalize" the author. It's a question of using the English language in a way that will achieve the greatest clarity and strength.
>
> Can such principles be taught? Maybe not. But most of them can be learned.[2]

With good-humored self-deprecation, he suggests that maybe he won't do a great job teaching such things in his book. But he reverses that negative by closing with the hope that readers will be able to catch on anyway.

In George Orwell's *1984*, we find the sort of abrupt, unexpected but perfect ending that Zinsser recommends. The dystopian novel tells the story of Winston Smith, a functionary in the ironically named Ministry of Truth. Slowly Smith becomes disillusioned with the deceptive, oppressive government headed by Big Brother, who finds his way into every crevice of life and thought. When Smith is found to have sympathies with the resistance, he is arrested and tortured until he breaks. As Smith walks to his execution, he sees a portrait of the dictator:

He gazed up at the enormous face. Forty years it had taken him to learn what kind of smile was hidden beneath the dark mustache. O cruel, needless misunderstanding! O stubborn, self-willed exile from the loving breast! Two gin-scented tears trickled down the sides of his nose. But it was all right, everything was all right, the struggle was finished. He had won the victory over himself. He loved Big Brother.[3]

Here is one of the most haunting and shocking last lines in all literature. After following Smith's slow, agonizing recognition of the evil in Big Brother's regime, we are stunned by this ironic reversal. Nonetheless, it captures the insidious power of the dictatorship and how thoroughly Smith had been brainwashed.

Nora Ephron offers another example. She wrote "The Assassination Reporters" on Hugh Aynesworth and Bob Dudney, who worked for the *Dallas Times Herald* when President Kennedy was shot in 1963. She follows their work on that day and in the years following that dramatic week, which included the capture of accused assassin Lee Harvey Oswald and his murder by Jack Ruby on live television. At the end, Ephron considers their perspective after many years. How do they see it all now?

"The other night I was at a party," Bob Dudney said, "and we were talking about certain great events that shaped the lives of people my age. The emergence of the Beatles and the Vietnam war were obvious influences. And I said that I thought the assassination of Kennedy was a big influence—and as soon as I said it I corrected myself. Oswald's death was more an influence than Kennedy's. Had he lived, so much more would have come out. His death left us a legacy of suspicion and doubt that's turned in on everybody. It's unusual. Such a neurotic little man, who was really such a loser, you know, and he's left a very profound influence. The country would have recovered from the death of John Kennedy, but it hasn't recovered yet from the death of Lee Harvey Oswald and probably never will."[4]

We are given a provocative reversal of conventional wisdom—Oswald's death had more lasting effects than Kennedy's. The unexpected is just right.

ENDING WITH A TWIST

Similar to "Unexpected but Just Right" is ending with a twist. In *It Could Be Worse, You Could Be Me*, Ariel Leve writes a short piece on how energizing it can be to have something to look forward to. She gives various examples of this in the lives of others while lamenting her lack of anything to anticipate, closing this way:

> I think that the whole idea of looking forward to something might be the problem. That's when I decided: from now on, I'll look forward to nothing. That way, I won't feel let down. I have nothing to look forward to.
>
> I'm feeling better already.[5]

She gives us a nice wry twist here. After arguing the whole piece that we need to have something positive lined up, she flips it by saying that looking ahead to nothing gives her a lift. She knows, and we know, and she knows that we know, that she is kidding herself, and us. And we're all happy about it.

In one essay Maya Angelou reflects on aging, noticing that "at sixty my body, which had never displayed a mind of its own, turned obstreperous, opinionated and deliberately treacherous." She then closes by expressing a shift in attitude as she neared seventy:

> Mostly, what I have learned so far about aging, despite the creakiness of one's bones and the cragginess of one's once-silken skin, is this: do it. By all means, do it.[6]

While the piece chronicles problems with the aging process, she ends with an unexpected but welcome upbeat finale. We feel her energy and are energized ourselves.

Angelou pulls off the same feat in a story about vacationing in Mexico. She was amazed that people on a beach were sucked in by a vendor selling vases, figurines, and other knickknacks that the tourists could paint themselves there by the surf. The vendor was clever. He let them do all the labor while he sat there relaxing. Why would people spend time on their vacations working like that?

> I was amazed at how they were squandering their free time, so what did I do? I rushed to my room, unpacked my yellow pads, got out my pen, dictionary and thesaurus, and sat down and took three days of my vacation to write this essay.[7]

CIRCLING BACK

Another model ending comes from Zinsser's *On Writing Well* in his chapter, "The Audience."

> "Who am I writing for?" The question that begins this chapter has irked some readers. They want me to say "Whom am I writing for?" But I can't bring myself to say it. It's just not me.[8]

Zinsser doesn't summarize by saying something like, "Don't worry about your audience. Just be yourself." He's already said that in various ways several times in the chapter. Instead, he stops not with a conclusion but with a specific example. Of course, it is also a conclusion, but not in a trite, expected way.

Zinsser also circles back to the beginning, an option suggested in chapter six. As he says, he started off the chapter with the question, "Who am I writing for?" Now he concludes with it as well.

In a blog I tell a story that was legendary in my family as I was growing up.

> Once my mom went to have lunch with my dad, who worked as an executive at a company in downtown Minneapolis. When she got to his office she saw him behind his desk with his back turned to the door, looking out the window. She was so impressed by how hard he was working that she immediately elevated him to "Vice President of Looking Out of the Window."

My dad would always get this wry, sheepish smile on his face whenever we told the story. He never defended or justified himself. He just enjoyed the story along with the rest of us.

It wasn't until many years later that it dawned on me what he was doing when my mom got to his office. He was thinking. I know because I found myself doing the same thing at the office when I was editorial director—looking out the window ruminating over a problem or an opportunity, a question or a strategic issue. He wasn't daydreaming or taking a break. This was his work.

I went on in the blog to extol the benefits of taking time to think, the pressures that squeeze it out, and practical things I did to build reflection into my schedule. I would occasionally close my door, get a couple hours at a coffee shop or library, or even go away by myself for a couple days. I ended with this:

> Sometimes, of course, I just sit in my office with my back to the door and catch myself looking out of the window. When I do, I think of my dad.[9]

In this ending, I circle back to the beginning but with a bit of a twist. The blog was written to encourage and justify leaders taking time to slow down and think about important matters even when it looks like we are doing nothing. When I say that I catch myself looking out the window, readers may be expecting me to reinforce that valid point. But I reinforce another point hidden in the blog. I end by affirming the importance of reflecting on family and our past. After all, that's where this lesson for leaders came from.

THE BIG DISCLOSURE

We can also reveal something at the end that we've been holding back. This can give an air of intrigue that keeps readers with us or wake them up with a surprise. Here's one:

"The Curriculum"

The last class of my old professor's life took place once a week in his house, by a window in the study where he could watch a small hibiscus plant shed its pink leaves. The class met on Tuesdays. It began after breakfast. The subject was The Meaning of Life. It was taught from experience.

No grades were given, but there were oral exams each week. You were expected to respond to questions, and you were expected to pose questions of your own. You were also required to perform physical tasks now and then, such as lifting the professor's head to a comfortable spot on the pillow or placing his glasses on the bridge of his nose. Kissing him good-bye earned you extra credit.

No books were required, yet many topics were covered, including love, work, community, family, aging, forgiveness, and, finally, death. The last lecture was brief, only a few words.

A funeral was held in lieu of graduation.

Although no final exam was given, you were expected to produce one long paper on what was learned. That paper is presented here.

The last class of my old professor's life had only one student.

I was the student.[10]

Mitch Albom begins his book *Tuesdays with Morrie* with this apt analogy. A professor holding class. Soon we see, however, that this is no ordinary course. Physical tasks like lifting a pillow for the professor are involved. Albom keeps everything at a distance. He effectively employs some passive voice and second-person point of view to keep the account at arm's length, as if it is too sensitive to deal with directly. Then, suddenly switching to active voice and first person, his last, deceptively simple, four-word sentence jolts us.

Ending with a story (like beginning with a story) is always a possibility, but we can do more. We can provide a strong finish by not revealing the actual identity of our main character until the end. Or we might withhold information about some other feature of the story that is key to our point—perhaps the locale, the time period, or the exact nature of the activity involved. After all, mystery writers aren't the only ones who can benefit from using mystery.[11]

A STRONG CLOSING IMAGE

Another way to conclude with freshness while still maintaining continuity is to introduce a new image or metaphor that vividly encapsulates your piece. Maya Angelou concludes an essay on the importance of African American art (music, painting, sculpting, writing, acting) for strengthening the black community, with this:

> We need art to live fully and to grow healthy. Without it we are dry husks drifting aimlessly on every ill wind, our futures are without promise and our present without grace.[12]

While it is a dark image, she nonetheless powerfully conveys the sense of permanence art can provide for those who have otherwise felt rootless.

Likewise, F. Scott Fitzgerald memorably ends *The Great Gatsby* with a compelling image, as Nick Carraway reflects on Gatsby's life and death.

> So we beat on, boats against the current, borne back ceaselessly into the past.[13]

I've been in a boat fruitlessly trying to fight the tide moving against us. Just so, the past had an inexorable hold on Gatsby even as he reached for the future. This is Fitzgerald's powerful picture of us all.

THE SO-WHAT ENDING

While I do not recommend offering a formal summary of our points, which can be stiff and deadly, we can find ways to review what we've written, remind readers of where they've been, in a fresh and moving way. One option is to invite readers to take what has been said and act on the main idea. Here are two examples.

Novelist and social critic James Baldwin, in a 1950s essay about William Faulkner's views on race, takes on the white novelist's contention that civil rights should "go slow." While conceding how wrong the South is, Faulkner wants to allow white folks to change, grow, and improve at their own pace since "it is not wise to keep an emotional people off balance." Baldwin critiques Faulkner's concern about the South's feelings for their Civil War history of ruin, gallantry, and death. After all, "Negroes and Northerners were also blown to bits," and the situation of blacks at the time of the essay was not due to the war but to Jim Crow laws that followed the war.[14]

Faulkner says he is trying to save "whatever good remains in those white people." Baldwin contends that Faulkner is wrong to plead for "the time in which the Southerner will come to terms with himself." He ends this way:

> The time Faulkner asks for does not exist—and he is not the only Southerner who knows it. There is never time in the future in which we will work out our salvation. The challenge is in the moment, the time is always now.[15]

Baldwin does not review the topics covered or his arguments. Rather, he clearly, simply, powerfully states the upshot of all he has said.

In "How Doctors Die" physician Ken Murray begins with the story of his mentor Charlie, an orthopedist, who refused chemotherapy and surgery to treat his cancer so he could enjoy the time he had left. Doctors tend to do this at a far higher rate than the rest of the population. They also sign documents making it clear they reject CPR, not wanting extraordinary efforts to revive them as their cancer takes hold because they know firsthand the terrible effect these types of measures have on patients and families, effects which Murray describes in some detail.

He then ends with the story of his cousin Torch, who made the same decision, enjoying his last eight months before dying quietly. Murray concludes:

> Torch was no doctor, but he knew he wanted a life of quality, not just quantity. Don't most of us? If there is a state of the art of end-of-life care, it is this: death with dignity. As for me, my physician has my choices. They were easy to make, as they are for most physicians. There will be no heroics, and I will go gentle into that good night. Like my mentor Charlie. Like my cousin Torch. Like my fellow doctors.[16]

Murray recalls his two main stories about Charlie and Torch without beating us over the head with summaries of their situations, but he doesn't leave us just with them. He adds a new character at the end—himself. Until the end he hasn't directly discussed what he would choose. The three clear, very human sentence fragments at the end offer quiet confirmation of his decision.

Murray combines the so-what with another approach we can use—getting personal. If we haven't covered it so far, we can answer, How did I grow or change? What affected or still affects me? What is the takeaway for me?

Neither Baldwin nor Murray gets preachy. Neither says "you ought" or "you should." As straightforward as both are, they don't lecture or harangue. While referencing the essay's main topic, they clearly and powerfully suggest a direction readers can take.

THE LIGHT AT THE END

If you're having trouble coming up with an ending, you can use the same strategies mentioned in chapter one for finding an opening. First, delete the last two or three paragraphs, which may be just a bland summary. Another fine stopping place may be right there just beforehand.

Second, look to the middle. Hopefully, when you went on a hunt for your opening, you found more than one strong sentence or story in the draft of your article, chapter, or blog. Pick one for the beginning and consider another for the end. To make it work, you may need to create some new paragraphs or rework some existing ones to lead into that last sentence.

Developing good endings can be hard work. Still it is worth the effort because they can linger like the smell of the beach at sunset long after the day has ended.

10

TITLES THAT WORK

O NCE I RECEIVED A PROPOSAL FOR A BOOK whose purpose
was to look at the passages in the Old Testament that seemed
to portray God as angry, sexist, violent, and racist. The author wanted
to help ordinary people see that things weren't exactly like that. So
instead of using an academic style, he wrote in a popular manner for
general readers with many cultural references to movies, music, books,
and the like.

The author's agent thought that something from popular culture
might be appropriate for the title. They picked a quote from a Jim
Carrey movie, *Bruce Almighty*, when Bruce was railing against God.
The title on the proposal, then, was *Smite Me, O Mighty Smiter*. Even
though I'd seen the movie, I didn't recall this quotation and thought it
sounded like it came out of the nineteenth century, so arcane as to be
nearly incomprehensible. But I knew the author personally so rather
than immediately toss the proposal, I read further. What I found was
a solid, engagingly written book.

I told my editorial colleagues, "The title will never work. But if we
call the book *God Behaving Badly*, maybe we could do it." That briefer,

catchier title was in fact an option the author had also considered independently. When we published the book a year later with that title, it was well received.

We all know titles are important for the success of a book. If we are self-publishing or titling a blog post, readers will decide to keep going or not based on those few words. Titles can even be important in getting a project a second look from an editor or agent. They are the first audience we may try to capture. So we shouldn't be satisfied with a placeholder title—the first thing that comes into our head—even when submitting a proposal. We need to work at it.

Books on writing regularly emphasize the importance of an opening sentence or paragraph, just as I do in this book. Few have much to say about titles, which are the very first chance you have to win your audience.

BAD TITLE STRATEGIES

If one of the most difficult writing tasks is coming up with a good concept for a book, surely a close second is coming up with a good title. Here are two opposite and equally bad directions we can travel in to title a book.

Bad strategy 1: Pour as much content as possible into the title and subtitle. As authors, we know everything there is to know about what we've written. And we are so in love with every fine distinction, every detail, every flourish of our pen that, naturally, we assume the best strategy is to reflect all this in our title. But doing so smothers the poor thing, giving it no air to breathe. A good title cannot possibly include everything a book or article says. It can't even include all the main things.

Perhaps surprisingly, the purpose of a title is not to completely summarize what we've written. We may resist when our editor tells us that a better title is one that doesn't include something we think is a main feature. What is the point of a title then? I'll get to that in a minute.

For now, just look at almost any fiction or nonfiction bestseller list. The vast majority will be populated with books whose titles have only two or three words. Occasionally you have successful six-word titles (*The Immortal Life of Henrietta Lacks*, *Astrophysics for People in a Hurry*), but they work for reasons that I discuss in a bit.

Bad strategy 2: Use an image or metaphor that, out of context, is completely devoid of content. Fiction titles often benefit from evocative images that we only understand after reading the book. *To Kill a Mockingbird*, *The Grapes of Wrath*, and *The Sun also Rises* are classic examples. But notice that Steinbeck and Hemingway also successfully employed very descriptive titles—*The Red Pony*, *The Old Man and the Sea*.

While fiction writers have the luxury of going either way, nonfiction authors do not. We are tempted to pick an alluring image off the forbidden tree of title metaphors. We have found an image that wonderfully communicates our idea—a garden, a toolbox, a highway, a family, an art gallery. But if we use that for the title without content, the game is lost.

> *Bad*: *The Hopeful Garden* (unless we are talking about actual horticulture here)
> *Possible*: *The Garden of the Mind*

> *Bad*: *The Uncanny Cockroach* (even alliteration can't save this puppy)
> *Possible*: *Thriving Against the Odds*

Again, look at a typical nonfiction bestseller list. How many consist entirely of a metaphor with no context? Probably none. Instead the title tells us immediately the book is about diets or relationships or business strategy or a true story.

Are there exceptions? Absolutely. Authors who are extremely well-known or who have had a previous bestseller can pretty much call their books whatever they want. Why? Because the author's name is now far more important than the title itself. This is the exception that proves the rule.

Consider one of my least favorite titles adorning the cover of a favorite book—*Outliers*. What the heck does that mean? But with two bestsellers under his belt, Malcolm Gladwell could call his book *Blank Pages* and it would sell just fine.

The problem with an evocative title (whether metaphor or well-known phrase from the wider culture) is that it can evoke entirely different things for different people. Worse, it can evoke the entirely wrong thing and thus totally miss the target audience, which brings me to the purpose of the title.

WHAT IS THE PURPOSE OF A TITLE?

The aim of a title is to grab the attention of the right audience. Note the two parts: *grabbing attention* and *getting the right audience*.

Grabbing attention is just that—arousing curiosity, provoking interest, getting people to look twice at it, remember it, and to peruse a few pages.

But if you grab the attention of the wrong people, all is lost. That's why metaphors alone can be so dangerous. An intriguing title about families may attract readers who are mothers, yet that is a disaster if the piece is for business executives. The mothers who start reading will quickly realize it is not for them and set it aside. In the meantime business executives will pass right over it without a thought. As a result, few read it.

Authors often assume what they've written is for everyone or at least a very wide swath of the reading public. In fact, most books and articles are for a very specific audience—not sports fans but soccer fans, not mothers but middle-class mothers of toddlers, not everyone but those who enjoy American historical biography.

How does a title grab the attention of the right audience successfully? Here are three strategies.

CONTENT, CODE, AND CREATIVITY

The best nonfiction titles combine content, code, and creativity. But if they do nothing else, they must clearly communicate the topic—the content. The title doesn't have to tell you everything, just something—and of course, the more central or core to the content of the book, the better.

Many successful books have straight-on, content-laden titles that (1) don't tell you everything about the book, (2) don't even tell you the main thesis of the book, and (3) aren't creative (or very creative). But, by gum, they work. Some from an Amazon.com bestseller list affirm this.

- *Act Like a Lady, Think Like a Man*—gotta be about relationships, and it is!

- *Get Motivated!*—what do you know, this woman wants to pump you up!

- *The Love Dare*—I guess lots of relationships out there need help!

- *Eat This Not That!*—chow down on this diet book.

Counterintuitively, one of the benefits of communicating clear content is that you narrow down the audience. You make sure you draw the attention of your target readership.

Closely connected to content is code.[1] What is code? Every genre (science fiction, cookbooks, textbooks, romance) has a certain set of characteristics that readers instinctively expect to find in a title. These telegraph what kind of book it is without saying explicitly, "This is a young adult novel."

The titles of most murder mysteries have a certain flavor to them. Consider these variations:

- *Murder on the Orient Express* (following the father of the genre, Edgar Allan Poe, and his "The Murders in the Rue Morgue")

- *Jack Knifed* (offering a hint of or direct mention of violence regarding the main character—Jack, of course)

- *Presumed Innocent* (using a legal term)

- *The Last Juror* (suggesting the end of someone in a legal context)

- *Still Life* (using an apt pun for a murder involving a painter)

Stray too far from the code and you risk losing your target readers. But if a title sounds like hundreds or dozens of others, how do you get it to stand out and be remembered?

That's where the third element, creativity, comes in. An effectively creative title is not one that is completely innovative and unprecedented (like *Smite Me, O Mighty Smiter*, which is so unusual most readers won't have a clue what it is about). Rather it combines the familiar (content and code) with the unfamiliar (something unusual, fresh, dramatic, helpful, unexpected, or arresting that makes it stand out). *God Behaving Badly*, for example, does this by offering clarity of content in a fresh, unexpected way.

Here are some other book titles that take the familiar and give it a twist.

- *7 Deadly Scenarios: A Military Futurist Explores War in the Twenty-First Century*

- *The Lost City of Z: A Tale of Deadly Obsession in the Amazon*

- *Team of Rivals: The Political Genius of Abraham Lincoln*

- *The Day Wall Street Exploded: A Story of America in Its First Age of Terror*

- *Collapse: How Societies Choose to Fail or Succeed*

These titles aren't perfect in my mind. They tend to rely too much on the subtitle to convey the familiar (the content). Still the titles are arresting. Also, two of the titles that don't clearly convey content (*Team of Rivals* and *Collapse*) are written by superstar, previously best-selling authors who have much more latitude in titling than most commoners like us.

The two that best combine the familiar with the unfamiliar, that is, content and code with creativity, are *The Lost City of Z* and *The Day*

Wall Street Exploded. Both convey specific information and intrigue. The one looks to be a true-life Indiana Jones (which it is); the other says it is a dramatic slice of the economic history of the United States (which it is).

The code for academic books, interestingly, is content. A scholarly tome that sounds too clever can be dismissed as "popular" and "not serious." These may not sound interesting to you, but they nail the code and the audience:

- *The Complete Adult Psychotherapy Treatment Planner*
- *A People's History of the United States*
- *A Handbook of Critical Approaches to Literature*

We have more titling freedom in magazine articles, blog posts, chapter titles, and subheadings. Why? Because readers already have a context that communicates code. They already know the magazine or blog deals with sports or news or cooking or cars or music. As a result, we can lean a bit more to the creative side. Here, then, are a few titles drawn from one list of the top twenty-five articles published in the United States in the last few decades.[2] Notice how they all combine the familiar with the unfamiliar, content with creativity.

- Gay Talese, "Frank Sinatra Has a Cold," *Esquire*, April 1966.
- Neal Stephenson, "Mother Earth, Mother Board: Wiring the Planet," *Wired*, December 1996.
- David Foster Wallace, "Federer as Religious Experience," *New York Times*, August 20, 2006.
- Hunter S. Thompson, "Fear and Loathing in Las Vegas: A Savage Journey to the Heart of the American Dream," *Rolling Stone*, part 1: November 11, 1971; part 2: November 25, 1971.
- Susan Orlean, "The American Man at Age Ten," *Esquire*, December 1992.

- George Plimpton, "The Curious Case of Sidd Finch," *Sports Illustrated*, April 1, 1985.

- Michael Lewis, "Wall Street on the Tundra," *Vanity Fair*, April 2009.

We don't normally associate a tennis player with religion. Las Vegas is supposed to be about fun and glitz, not dread and disgust. And what's Wall Street doing in a northern wasteland? We know in general what the articles are about, but we also are arrested by the unexpected.

What if we just can't come up with something that combines all three elements? Then we defer to content and code, and let creativity go. As I said earlier, only famous authors can get away with pure creativity for nonfiction titles. Thus, if we (who have not sold millions of books along with the movie rights) have two titles, and one is purely evocative but contentless while the other is full of content but dull, choose the dull title.

The fact is, with about a million new traditionally published and self-published books each year in the United States alone, 99.44 percent will not be by well-known people or have huge marketing budgets to give it mass exposure.[3] So the title must do the heavy lifting. That most titles don't achieve both clarity and creativity shows just how difficult the whole process is.

TITLES THAT STICK

In chapter five I mentioned *Made to Stick*, in which Chip and Dan Heath lay out how teachers, leaders, managers, preachers, and salespeople can make ideas memorable.[4] These same principles offer a slightly expanded set of criteria for developing a great title.

Great ideas (and titles) are:

- Simple

- Unexpected

- Concrete

- Credible

- Emotional

- Stories

It's not likely that any given title can have all six elements going for it, but the more the better. Here are some great titles:

- *Diary of a Wimpy Kid* (simple, unexpected, concrete, emotional, story)

- *Freakonomics* (simple, unexpected, concrete)

- *What to Expect When You're Expecting* (simple, concrete, emotional, story)

- *Moneyball* (simple, unexpected, concrete)

All these titles clearly communicate their code (juvenile fiction, economics, how-to, sports) in simple ways. Two of the titles are just one word—in fact, a brand-new word (unexpected)—but a word that clearly communicates the thesis (economics is weird; sports is about dollars). Notice that *Moneyball* doesn't tell us everything—it doesn't even tell us it's about baseball rather than basketball or football in particular. If the author or editors had tried to add that nuance to the title, it could have failed.

Economics is an especially complex and abstract topic full of arcane principles, mathematical formulas, and mind-numbing statistics. The authors of *Freakonomics* set aside all of that, along with the dozens of different subjects in the book, and settled on just one idea. Does the title completely communicate everything in the book and every audience that might be interested in those topics? No. And yes. It finds the core that is common to most: we are all afraid we are handling our money wrong. It makes us freak out. So maybe I should add *emotional* to the traits the title exhibits.[5]

It is possible to fail with a simple title, however. I already mentioned *Outliers*. Another is *Unbroken*. It's simple, but that's it. Otherwise it is confusing. Is this about materials engineering? What's not broken? In what way? Why should I care? Is there a story here? The title didn't help this book reach bestseller status at all. What did was the credibility of the author and the megasuccess of her first book, *Seabiscuit* (which is not creative but it got content and code right). It didn't hurt that the book itself is fabulous.

SUBTITLES, DRAMA, AND THE RULE OF THREE

But what about subtitles? Can't a nonfiction title be creative and let the subtitle carry the content and code? In a word, no. Why? Because while subtitles matter, they are, by definition, sub. Sometimes subtitles don't appear clearly in online listings. Even if the cover is pictured online, the font size of the subtitle may be too small to read—so potential buyers breeze right past it.

We can't rely on our subtitle to do the work of our title. Nonetheless, subtitles are worth crafting carefully to reinforce content, code, and creativity.

One way (not the only way) to construct an effective subtitle is by using the Rule of Three. Offering a list of three items gives a rising sense of movement, climax, and direction. Consider these subtitles:

- *A World War II Story of Survival, Resilience, and Redemption (Unbroken)*

- *The UltraHealthy Program for Losing Weight, Preventing Disease, and Feeling Great Now! (The Blood Sugar Solution)*

- *Is the God of the Old Testament Angry, Sexist, and Racist? (God Behaving Badly)*

In *Unbroken*, the subtitle seeks to make up for the lack of content in the title and shows a clear progression from not just surviving to thriving. The subtitle for *The Blood Sugar Solution* doesn't move chronologically but rather develops in terms of emotional benefit. For *God Behaving Badly* the subtitle makes a cumulative impact.

Titles or subtitles with two items can be helpful for purposes of comparison and contrast. But they tend to be (though aren't always) less effective because the items balance each other. On the positive side this gives a sense of stability, but negatively it can be less interesting because there is no sense of change. Consider two titles with paired items:

- *Empire and Honor*
- *Kinsey and Me*

Those are fine, serviceable titles, but they lack drama.

When using the Rule of Three in a subtitle, the longest item should almost always go last. Why? As noted earlier, rhythm overrides significance. Try reading (especially aloud) any of the following subtitles with the last item in the first or second place. Those options are flat. They lose their punch.

- *Global Cooling, Patriotic Prostitutes, and Why Suicide Bombers Should Buy Life Insurance (SuperFreakonomics)*
- *Superstrings, Hidden Dimensions, and the Quest for the Ultimate Theory (The Elegant Universe)*
- *Love, Terror, and an American Family in Hitler's Berlin (In the Garden of Beasts)*
- *A Chef's Story of Chasing Greatness, Facing Death, and Redefining the Way We Eat (Life, on the Line)*

It's not impossible to have a title with three items in a list. *Guns, Germs, and Steel* was very successful. But as important as the Rule of Three can be, it can be trumped (especially for a title) by the Rule of Memorability. If people can't remember the title of your book, that's trouble. And a sequence of three can be elusive.

THEY JUST LOVE MY TITLE

One way to find out which of several possible titles might be best is to survey potential readers. Authors have often told me something like, "I asked five friends, and they all told me they loved the title" or "I've been speaking on this topic lately, and when I mention my working title for the book, I get a very positive response."

They think this settles the question. It doesn't. Why? Because the results are not blind.

Blinding is a common tool used in research to take bias out of the results. Authors almost always have a definite bias about which titles they do and don't like, especially for their own work. If the presenter of the options is the author, respondents will pick up that bias (whether they are aware of it or not), even if they don't know the presenter is the author. Often respondents have a subterranean tendency to please the presenter. And if the responders are friends or family, the tendency can be magnified.

A far more objective approach is to give the task to someone else, to have that third party present several possible titles to people who don't know the author or anything about the book. Be sure the people surveyed represent the target audience for the book. Often Uncle Elmer, you see, is not in the bull's-eye. In addition, don't give any indication to your surveyor what your preference is.

When doing this, the survey taker should not tell participants what the book is about until after they have selected a title. You want first impressions to mimic as closely as possible the experience of someone browsing online or in a bookstore. In those situations the title must do all the work by itself. If respondents change their minds after hearing more about the book, note that also, but do keep the results of first and second impressions separate.

Another way to take the bias out of the process is to have an independent team of experts to advise you. If you are fortunate to have your book or article accepted for publication, the editors and marketers can be that team. You may have published dozens of articles or books. They have published hundreds or thousands and have a large base of experience to draw from. Listen to them. You can disagree with them, but always listen.

Is it a lot of work coming up with a great title? Definitely. With so many forms of entertainment flooding our world, with so much information coming at us, with so many demands on our attention from advertisers, a strong title is our best chance to break through and grab the attention of our target audience. Make it count.

PART 2

THE ART OF
WRITING

11

CREATIVITY, THE MYSTERIOUS MUSE

C REATIVITY IS THE X FACTOR.

How do we come up with new ideas? How do we develop or present something in new and beautiful ways so that it touches heart and mind, perhaps changing people in important ways? How can we keep from being stuck in a rut?

Not just authors and artists, but business leaders, cooks, sales people, parents, church leaders, computer geeks, athletes, and many others want to know the same thing. If we want to do something fresh, if we want to stand out, if we want to get ahead in a crowded field, creativity is the magic juice we want to drink. But where can we find it?

Some people seem to have an overabundance of creativity: Comedians who spontaneously crack one impromptu joke after another to the delight of their audiences. Chefs who spin out amazing new dishes every week to the delight of their customers.

Over two hundred years ago Mozart had such an overflow of inspiration he could "waste" it. He once wrote a divertimento for two horns and string quartet, calling it "Some Musical Fun" though we know it better by the name "A Musical Joke." The composition intentionally includes an abundance of "wrong" notes before it completely collapses in disarray at the end. Mozart was likely poking a little fun at the inept musicians he often had to endure who played his works.

Yet the composition contains themes that any composer of the day might have died for. Mozart, however, apparently had enough excess creativity that he could throw these away in a bit of satire.

With such geniuses around, should those of us without superpowers launch ourselves into the Slough of Despond? Can there be any hope for us? Seemingly, you either have the gift of creativity or you don't.

I disagree. While some people appear to be superabundantly creative, plenty of imagination remains for the rest of us if we are willing to work at it. In fact, we can use several nonmagical strategies to increase our originality. And yes, I offer some here. But first, what makes something creative? Let me try to take a bit of the mystery out of the magic.

COMBINE TWO THINGS NOT USUALLY CONNECTED

Way back in the twentieth century, two researchers wanted to find a means to measure creativity in people. So Sarnoff and Martha Mednick developed the unfortunately named RAT test (Remote Associates Test).[1]

The test consisted of giving subjects thirty sets of three words. In forty minutes the respondents were to come up with the one word that linked each set. So, for example, they might be given the words *cottage*, *Swiss*, and *cake*. The word linking all three, and the correct answer, was *cheese*.

Most helpfully the Mednicks defined the creativity they were trying to measure: "The forming of associative elements into new combinations which either meet specified requirements or are in some way useful. The more mutually remote the elements of the new combination, the more creative the process or solution."[2]

Essentially, creativity isn't concocting something entirely unprecedented. Rather it is bringing together two things that have been around for a while but previously hadn't been combined. Innovation almost always involves building on the past.

Clarence Birdseye went to Labrador in the early 1900s where he was taught how to ice fish by the Inuit. He noticed that at -40°C the fish they caught froze very quickly and tasted very fresh when cooked later. Birdseye was a naturalist, but fast freezing was the innovation that revolutionized the food industry and launched him into an entirely different career. He inaugurated a whole new sector of commerce based on combining two preexisting elements—food and freezing temperatures.

Then there was the Oxford philologist who invented a language. How did he do that? By combining several preexisting elements—his knowledge of languages and their histories, his Catholicism, his love of nature and suspicions of the industrial world, and his interest in Norse mythology—to create not just Elvish but what we know as Middle-earth. This didn't come to J. R. R. Tolkien instantly. He worked on it for decades, and only part of the outcome was *The Lord of the Rings*.

Here's another example to chew on. In 1928 Harry Burnett (H. B.) Reese started combining chocolate and peanut butter. Today it sells more than any other candy in the United States.

Or for book lovers, consider the printing press. Five hundred years ago Gutenberg created the printing press when he made a delightful combination of books and a wine press. Many people still think that's a good combo.[3]

When *Wired* magazine is trying to spot future trends (that is, creative ideas or products that will be important in the next few years), they do exactly what the Mednicks did fifty years before. They look for people who combine things in new ways. *Wired* calls them cross-pollinators.[4]

The novel intersection of two disciplines, two enterprises, two hobbies has been the source of new sciences, new marketing methods, new music.

> When the mathematician John von Neumann applied mathematics to human strategy, he created game theory—and when he crossed physics and engineering, he helped hatch both the Manhattan Project and computer science. His contemporary Buckminster Fuller drew freely from engineering, economics, and biology to tackle problems in transportation, architecture, and urban design.[5]

Such thinking about creativity is not new. In fact, the idea is hidden away in the Latin word *cogito*, translated "I think." Its literal meaning is a combination (appropriately) of *con* (with) and *agito* (to drive or put in motion). So even the ancients thought of thinking as driving or putting two things in motion together.

In just a moment I will look at practical, straightforward strategies we can use to increase the chances for coming up with new combinations, but first let me mention one other way of thinking about creativity.

While convergent thinking seeks to identify what unifies a set of different objects or ideas, divergent thinking goes the opposite direction. In this form of creativity, instead of starting with a diverse group, we start with a single entity and then try to go in as many directions as possible.

For example, to test one's ability to think divergently, start with a common object, like a piece of paper, and see how many uses for it you can come up with in sixty seconds. My list looked like this:

1. Write a letter.

2. Make a paper airplane.

3. Use as a bookmark.

4. Pick your teeth.

5. Cut a cake.

6. Make confetti.

7. Make a funnel.

8. Make a party hat.

9. Make a snowflake.

10. Put a footprint or fingerprint on it.

What both convergent and divergent thinking have in common is the potential for making unusual combinations, bringing two (or more) things together that aren't usually joined. That is the essence of creativity.

INCREASING YOUR RANGE

We come then to practical ways to train our creativity. To begin, if we are not catching any fish, maybe we need to restock the lake. That is, if new ideas seem to be hard to come by, maybe we need to replenish our minds. How? Learn more and experience more.

With a fuller life and mind, we have more options for things to connect in fresh and innovative ways. Some people might call it trivia, but I like to think of it as enriching life experiences. To start, we can get out of our routines.

We all have our favorite activities. They may be sports or cooking or reading or auto repair or crafts of some sort. Because we enjoy them, we do them over and over again. But if our goal is to become creative, we need to branch out.

That may not sound like much fun. If I really enjoy softball, learning to crochet may not seem all that exciting. Therefore I suggest we begin by branching out into another sport—say karate—instead of something entirely different like painting. Likewise, if I enjoy cooking Italian food, I could learn about Japanese cuisine.

What about for writers? If I write mostly romance novels, I might start reading true crime books or narrative history. Maybe I blog about parenting and families. Then reading classic literature like *Pride and Prejudice* or *Oliver Twist* or *Anna Karenina* could be fruitful. If I mostly read writers of one gender, I can read the other. If authors of one ethnicity are what I turn to most regularly, I will try some different ones. If I only read living authors, I read those of the past (or vice versa).

We can keep expanding our reading horizons into other unexplored fields like psychology, economics, science fiction, young adult fiction, memoir, or business books. While economics may seem like an arcane academic subject, I can still find books for a general audience that are quite stimulating, like *Freakonomics*, *Fast Food Nation*, or *The World Is Flat*. I try a variety of genres, and when I find a different one I like, I read more in that area.

Of all people, writers need to be lifelong learners with a curiosity about everything and anything. Who thought immunology could be interesting, but *The Immortal Life of Henrietta Lacks* is fascinating! Psychology may seem like a snoozer, but read Oliver Sacks's *The Man Who Mistook His Wife for a Hat*, and the world will seem wilder and more multifaceted than you ever thought possible.

Besides learning more in a wider variety of areas, we can up our creative game by expanding the range of our experiences. Don't go on vacation to the beach every year, try the mountains. Don't just watch musicals on TV, go to the theater and see a live production. And you won't have to sell your second car for tickets to a show at your community theater.

Maybe I have never volunteered at a food pantry or tutored at a nearby high school. Never been outside the country? Travel can be a terrific eye-opening experience, especially if we can get away from the top tourist sights and see how ordinary people work and live.

All these opportunities to learn and experience new things increase our treasure house of memories, knowledge, emotions, and abilities. The more we have in our bank, the more we can draw from, the more we have to combine and recombine in potentially new ways—in short, the more potential we have to be creative.

A LITTLE HELP FROM MY FRIENDS

Another key source of ideas is other people. Creativity need not be a solo; it can be done in chorus.

When my wife and I were working on our Bible study guide *Grandparenting*, we deliberately asked grandparents we knew what they thought we should include. What were the most important things other grandparents should know? What are the problems and difficulties that arise? How do they interact with their grandchildren? Their answers were a great resource that had a major impact on what we wrote.

Brainstorming with others helps us get out of our ruts. Get a group of people together, tell them everyone's contribution is welcome, that no idea is too crazy, and that in the initial phase no evaluation (positive or negative) is permitted. Write down every idea, preferably on a board where everyone can see.

When new ideas start coming more slowly, begin evaluating. Give everyone a chance to pick a couple ideas from the total list that they think have potential, and mark those with a star. That way you don't have to take time on the myriad of bad or mundane ideas that emerged. That's pretty much what advertising executive Alex Osborn had in mind when he first suggested brainstorming in the 1940s.

True, there can be problems with this approach. Some people don't think well on their feet. They may be intimidated by the group process. Another difficulty is that groups tend to converge, and the range of their ideas can narrow down quickly.[6]

To overcome this, Art Markman says to start by letting people brainstorm on their own first. Then compare lists. Studies show this results in a wider variety of ideas and possibilities.

One way to do this is called the 6-3-5 method. First, get six or so people together. Second, have them each write down three ideas on a piece of paper. Third, have everyone pass their paper to the person next to them, and each person writes down three more ideas. You end up passing the paper five times until everyone has seen each of the six pieces of paper, which now each have eighteen ideas on them.[7]

After that you can share the ideas together and start talking and evaluating, letting participants pick one or two they like best. The advantages are that people aren't limited by groupthink and those who are internal processors can participate in way that is more comfortable for them, thinking and writing on their own.

GET SOME EXERCISE

Bobby Fischer was a World Chess Champion in the 1970s who stood out as an eccentric genius in a field full of eccentric geniuses. As portrayed in the movie *Pawn Sacrifice*, he walked out of a chess match complaining about the lighting, ransacked his own hotel rooms looking for bugging devices, thought the Russians were watching him through his TV, and believed the US government was listening to him through (wait for it) his dental fillings. Though his mother was Jewish, he was vocally anti-Semitic, holding to many conspiracy theories about Jews.

He was also an astounding chess innovator in a traditional realm. He learned Russian so he could read the best Russian chess books and journals. He studied games and strategies of the previous century when others had discarded them as hopelessly antiquated. He devised a new kind of chess clock and a variation to the game called Fischer Random Chess.

His chess play itself was also innovative and risky. He played all out to win when the strategy of many grand masters was to settle for draws. His forceful end-game tactics often won him games that many considered to be inevitable ties.

One reason for this success was due to yet another Fischer innovation. His end games were so effective because he could push forward relentlessly and creatively even at the end of an exhausting four- or five-hour match when his opponent tired and lost concentration. How did he manage this? He played tennis.

During his famous World Chess Championship match with Boris Spassky in 1972, he would play tennis on free days. Throughout his career he would swim, lift weights, or engage in other exercise while his opponents didn't. He knew that to be in shape mentally he had to be in shape physically. To do his best in chess, his whole body had to be fit. Forty years later science has caught up and proven him right.

Not so many years ago, the brightest minds in neuroscience thought that our brains got a set amount of neurons, and that by adulthood, no new neurons would be birthed. But this turned out not to be true. Studies in animal models have shown that new neurons are produced in the brain throughout the lifespan, and, so far, only one activity is known to trigger the birth of those new neurons: vigorous aerobic exercise, said Karen Postal, president of the American Academy of Clinical Neuropsychology. "That's it," she said. "That's the only trigger that we know about."[8]

Writers, editors, programmers, students, and others who sit and use their brains in concentrated work for four or five hours at a time should take a tip from the grand master if they want to stay at the top of their game. For over thirty years I have run regularly, three to five miles several times a week. I am convinced it is something that not only kept me healthy but enhanced my creativity and kept my thinking sharp.

If the first way to enhance your creativity is to fill your mind and life with a wide range of information and experiences, and the second is to bring other people into your process, then the third is to regularly get good exercise. Fischer was an eccentric (okay, paranoid) chess master. But he was also right about tennis.

TAKE A VACATION

Several years ago I enjoyed reading *The Making of the Atomic Bomb* by Richard Rhodes. For my taste it was the perfect combination of science, history, politics, and World War II.

One thing that struck me, though, was how time and again during the late nineteenth and early twentieth centuries brilliant physicists like Niels Bohr would get stuck on a physics problem for months or even years. After working tirelessly they finally took a vacation and—boom (metaphorically)—the solution would come. Even though Rhodes recounted several such episodes, he never pointed out the pattern.

Wired magazine once ran a photo essay that chronicled the genesis of eight innovations. Again, the author of the piece failed to point out that only one (maybe) occurred at work. The idea for television came while plowing a field. Netflix was cooked up at home. Post-it Notes emerged in a church choir loft. The idea for Harry Potter came while J. K. Rowling was stuck on a train.[9] They could have also mentioned that the idea for bar codes came at the beach.[10]

Away from the pressures of the office, classroom, home, or laboratory, where the left brain (focusing on reason, logic, and problem solving) is working on overdrive, the right brain (where ideas often come from) can't get a word in edgewise. On vacation, on break, in the shower, in a new environment, the right brain has a chance to rise to the surface and contribute. The result can be a beautiful thing.

The point is clear: if you want to solve a stubborn problem or need some new, innovative ideas—leave work, go on a trip, get out of your usual environment.

FOUR STAGES OF CREATIVITY

What I have proposed here about creativity lines up well with the pioneering work of Graham Wallas.* Wallas based his work on the historical experiences of great minds like the German physicist Hermann von Helmholtz and the French mathematician Henri Poincaré, who followed much the same pattern as the nuclear physicists mentioned in *The Making of the Atomic Bomb*. Wallas suggested four stages.

Stage 1: Preparation. We investigate a particular problem from "all directions," involving wide-ranging research, study, and reflection. We talk to, interview, and work with others to give us new perspectives and data. We practice quickly coming up with new ideas such as through improv or writing exercises.

Stage 2: Incubation. We step away from the problem, think about other things, do other things. We go on vacation or take a sustained break to allow the background processes of our mind to work on the issue. Regular physical exercise can also stimulate our thinking capacity.

Stage 3: Illumination. Often suddenly, as if out of nowhere but grounded in the first two stages, a solution comes to mind.

Stage 4: Verification. We take the "happy idea" or burst of inspiration and work it out more fully in the laboratory, the office, the home, the classroom, the workshop, or the marketplace.

*See Graham Wallas, "Stages in the Creative Process," in *The Creativity Question*, ed. Albert Rothenberg and Carl. R. Hausman (Durham, NC: Duke University Press, 1976), 69-73. This was excerpted from Graham Wallas, *The Art of Thought* (New York: Harcourt Brace Jovanovich, 1926), 79-83, 85-87, 93-95.

IT TAKES PRACTICE

Learn as much as you can about everything. Brainstorm with others. Get some exercise. Take a vacation. Here's another very down-to-earth, very unmagical way to become more creative—practice.

A friend at work once offered improv training at lunch break for anyone who was interested. Improv (short for improvisational theater) has become a popular form of comedy in which most of what is performed is unscripted, unplanned, and unrehearsed. Audience members are often invited to shout out, for example, a place name, the names of some famous people, perhaps a fruit, and a type of crime. Instantly the players enact a scene based on these suggestions.

I, for one, am as spontaneous as a frozen lake, so this was a bit of a stretch. But I was fascinated that by regular practice of certain techniques and exercises, I could learn to think and react quickly (and sometimes humorously) to the cues, prods, and comments of others in the sketch.

One key improv guideline is to always accept what the other person says and build on it rather than contradict it.

PARTNER: What's that kangaroo doing in the office?

ME: That's not a kangaroo. How could it be? We don't live in Australia.

All my logic and curmudgeonliness bring the scene to a halt like the ground brings my gutter cleaning to a halt when my feet leave my ladder. Better to go with the premise of my partner than reject it.

PARTNER: What's that kangaroo doing in the office?

ME: I think he's interviewing for CEO.

Now my partner has something to work with. If I regularly practice with the "accept anything" rule in mind, I will rapidly improve my improv.

In one exercise, two players begin a scene with no instructions on the topic. They are also limited to just three lines. One starts with whatever comes to mind, then the other responds, after which the first player responds to the second. Then the scene is stopped. It is quick, with little risk if it turns out badly. But by doing this multiple times in the space of fifteen minutes (and then over a period of days or weeks), players will grow in their ability to quickly spit out dialogue. Dozens of other improv exercises can help us learn to quickly come up with ideas and invent dialogue.[11]

Blogging for over a dozen years has helped me do the same thing. Writing a blog is not the hard part, you see. Coming up with ideas for blog posts is. So over the years I have been training my mind to look for potential topics as I watch a movie, read a book, talk to friends, hear a lecture, or just people watch. Some ideas I immediately turn into blogs. Others I just keep in a list that I review regularly to see which may now be ripe for the picking.

Just like improv exercises, writing exercises can do the same thing.[12] I mentioned the game Balderdash in chapter seven on writer's block. You can find many other exercises online that often involve writing only a line or two. Just be sure you write quickly and don't get hung up evaluating. The purpose is not to come up with a perfect sentence but to train your mind to come up with something new quickly. There will be plenty of time to review and revise later.

Yes, the results of creativity can be magic, but it need not be mysterious. Stimulating creativity can be as ordinary as, first, branching out into new fields of learning and experience; second, getting ideas from other people; third, getting good physical exercise; fourth, taking a vacation; and last, practicing.

Now come up with three more ways.

12

BREAKING THE RULES

Forget everything you learned about English in grade school. None of it is true.

How many rules of grammar did you have to memorize growing up? Well, you only need to worry about two:

Rule 1: There are no rules of grammar.

Rule 2: When in doubt, refer to Rule 1.

Why are there no rules? Because there is no such thing as standard English. No authoritative body determines what is right and what is wrong. English is a free-for-all. It is constantly in flux—constantly being enlarged, reduced, modified, poked, pulled, distorted, bent, folded, and mutilated. Grammar changes almost as easily. Spoken English changes first; eventually written English catches up, at least partway. The good changes tend to stick, and the bad ones tend to fade away. It's all part of the genius of English.

Words are constantly being created and lost. Rather than decry this development, dictionary makers celebrate it. Each year Merriam-Webster, for example, makes a big splash with the new words they are adding. These are not words they created or approved of but which they determined had attained common enough usage that they merely recognized what was already a fact.

A couple years ago they added 250. What we used to call frozen yogurt we can now call *froyo*. I hope I never use business jargon like *onboarding*. Personnel departments around the country, however, are using the word to describe the process of training, orienting, and enculturating new employees into the organization. I need to know what it means and how to use it—so I can appropriately ridicule it![1]

What then is the purpose of grammar if everything is up for grabs? Certainly it is not to torture third-grade boys or even to give jobs to editors. Grammar has one—and only one—purpose: to facilitate clear, effective, powerful, artful communication.

Having certain conventions and regular patterns of words helps us do this. We don't have to laboriously unravel every single sentence we hear or read. We don't want readers stumbling and fumbling along as if they were trying to decode a foreign language. That would be counterproductive. It helps to follow the conventions—most of the time.

At other times, the conventions get in the way. And when they do, we shouldn't hesitate to throw them out. Ever.

Now look at that fragment: "Ever." It communicates much more effectively than it would as part of a complete sentence. It's like a verbal exclamation point. I admit, of course, that what makes it work is that the rest of my sentences are complete. If I only wrote in sentence fragments, "Ever," would lose its power. That's another reason to know the rules and follow them most of the time. When you unexpectedly break the rule, you can get added punch.

One quite successful author I worked with objected when I occasionally edited some of his prose into sentence fragments. "Good authors do it all the time," I explained. "It makes your writing more powerful." Still he insisted we change it back to the original. "Why?" I finally asked.

"Because if I don't," he said mournfully, "people will think I don't know how to write." This poor man was a victim of his third-grade education.

Consider the opening of one of the most beloved patriotic songs in the United States:

Oh, beautiful for spacious skies,
for amber waves of grain;
for purple mountain majesties
above the fruited plain.

The verb is . . . um, er, well, maybe it's above the fruited plain. In any case, its absence is proudly to be hailed in the land of the free and the home of the brave.

In chapter eleven we looked at ways to expand our creativity and art. Here we consider how rules can inhibit creativity. Breaking rules can be a step on the path toward art, toward touching our whole person rather than just one part.

Whether in grammar, structure, topic, or tone, when we say something freshly, readers can see things in new ways. The predictable will not do this quite as well. If Italian restaurants are popular, a Vietnamese restaurant stands out. If book covers are all dark, a white cover stands out. If pop music is loud, a quiet song stands out.

Stiffly following the conventions of grammar all the time can result in stiff writing, which creates boredom, which creates poor communication. If you want to communicate well, yes, learn the rules. But as soon as you do, figure out how to change them.

THAT'S UNHEARD OF!

Consider another supposed faux pas. Everybody does it. Besides that, it's not wrong. In fact, sometimes it can be a beautiful thing. No, I'm not talking about *that!* I'm talking about ending sentences with a preposition.

In the name of alleged grammatical correctness, how many ungainly sentences must we watch perambulate down a paragraph like a teenager with limbs too big for his body? If grammar gets in the way of clear communication, get rid of it. (Would it communicate better for the above subhead to read, "Something of Which We Have Not Heard"?)

As to everyone doing it, such well-known stylists as H. L. Mencken and Mark Twain joined in. Even a stickler like Lynne Truss did it in *Eats, Shoots & Leaves* when she asks, "So how should you use the colon, to begin with?"[2] Perhaps she was echoing Dickens. For goodness' sake, the very first line of *A Christmas Carol* is "Marley was dead: to begin with."

Sometimes we do need to get rid of prepositions when they are useless clutter.

Bad: When can we meet up?
Good: When can we meet?

Bad: That's where I'm going to.
Good: That's where I'm going.

Pointless prepositions deserve to be consigned to nether hell whether at the beginning, middle, or end of a sentence. But an absolute prohibition? Richard Nordquist quotes nine grammar authorities from over the last century who put the kibosh on this myth.[3] So where did it come from? *Garner's Modern American Usage* explains:

> The spurious rule about not ending sentences with prepositions is a remnant of Latin grammar, in which a preposition was the one word that a writer could not end a sentence with. But Latin grammar should never straitjacket English grammar. If the superstition is a "rule" at all, it is a rule of rhetoric and not of grammar, the idea being to end sentences with strong words that drive a point home. That principle is sound, of course, but not to the extent of meriting lockstep adherence or flouting established idiom.[4]

English, of course, is not Latin in its origins. It's Germanic. So get over it.

OTHER RULES WILLING TO BE BROKEN, WANTING TO BE BROKEN, WAITING TO BE BROKEN

When the television series *Star Trek* first aired in the 1960s, many objected to the famous split infinitive in the opening sequence: "To boldly go where no man has gone before." (Later series kept the split infinitive but made it gender inclusive: "To boldly go where no one has gone before.") The reason series creator Gene Roddenberry was right is that it sounds better to split the infinitive. Rhythmically it gives more emphasis to the word *go*. If it were "to go boldly," the phrase trails off awkwardly. In addition to rhythm and awkwardness, sense is a consideration:

The x-ray was ordered to adequately assess the extent of the break.

Other options just don't work as well:

The x-ray was ordered to assess adequately the extent of the break. *(Awkward)*

The x-ray was ordered adequately to assess the extent of the break. *(Was the order adequate or the assessment?)*

Sometimes, though, infinitives shouldn't be split. Consider:

I am going to morally, ethically, spiritually, physically, positively, absolutely, undeniably, and reliably annihilate my opponent.

This can work in a song, but the split is probably just a little too wide in prose to maintain the sense of what's being discussed.[5] So use your ear and your common sense to determine what's right. That's what I tried to do in all the split infinitives you'll see in this book.

You'll also see sentences that start with a conjunction. And that's not bad! As before, it's best not to do this frequently. But it can be helpful if you have a long sentence, if you want to give emphasis to what follows the opening conjunction, if you want to indicate a pause in thought, or if you want to emphasize a comparison or contrast between two ideas.

John F. Kennedy frequently began sentences with conjunctions in perhaps the most famous presidential inaugural address of the last century:

> We shall not always expect to find [new nations] supporting our view. But we shall always hope to find them strongly supporting their own freedom.

> Let all our neighbors know that we shall join with them to oppose aggression or subversion anywhere in the Americas. And let every other power know that this Hemisphere intends to remain the master of its own house.

> Let us never negotiate out of fear. But let us never fear to negotiate.

> And so, my fellow Americans: ask not what your country can do for you—ask what you can do for your country.[6]

Read almost any celebrated writer of the last century (Virginia Wolf, W. E. B. Du Bois, William Faulkner, and others), and you will find them doing the same.[7]

Elsewhere I encourage us to not use passive voice, but it can occasionally be the right thing to do. First, it can give variety in sentence structure, which can be a nice break from the constant use of active voice. Second, as noted, if we don't know who committed the action, it can appropriately communicate uncertainty. Third, passive voice can put emphasis in a better or more dramatic place. Consider these two sentences:

> The puppy was murdered. *(passive)*

> Someone murdered the puppy. *(active)*

The first is stronger than the second for the last two reasons given above. We don't know who committed the murder and to begin with

"Someone" is weak. It distracts from the distress we feel at an innocent puppy being killed.

Know the rules. Know them so you can break them. Don't break the rules most of the time because you want to communicate clearly. But break them sometimes to communicate more powerfully and more artfully.

13

THE KEY TO POWERFUL PROSE— TONE

IT IS NIGHT. TWO SOLDIERS ON WATCH suddenly meet in the darkness and shout, each demanding to know the other's identity. After a moment of panic, the two recognize each other and breathe more easily. These comrades have both been on high alert.

Twice before they've seen a ghost walking the castle grounds, a ghost who looks uncannily like the late King, Prince Hamlet's father. This cannot be an omen of good news. If this weren't fourteenth-century Denmark, they would both be trigger happy.

Two of Hamlet's friends join the soldiers, and then the apparition appears a third time. Dread descends on them all. Nonetheless, in their fear they try to speak to it. Yet the specter walks away silent, shrouded in mystery.

From this opening scene of *Hamlet*, Shakespeare sets a tone that hovers over the entire drama like a heavy cloud. Something terrible has happened and, we sense, will happen. Hamlet's own depression at his father's death, his suspicions that he was murdered by his Uncle Claudius to gain the throne, his loathing at his own mother for so quickly marrying Claudius, and his self-condemnation for not acting to avenge his father's death, all reinforce the dark mood.

This sense of unease works powerfully on us as well while we watch the story unfold, and its tone, its mood, hangs over us for days or weeks afterward. We wonder, as does Hamlet, if life is worth living in such circumstances. How are we to face "the slings and arrows of outrageous fortune"?

The most powerful and memorable stories, the most powerful and memorable prose, are those in which the tone communicates emotionally the very substance of the writer's theme. Tone is perhaps the single most important element in the art of writing.

Consider a piece of writing with a very different tone, a piece most writers can probably identify with, from *Blue Like Jazz* by Donald Miller.

> Writers don't make any money at all. We make about a dollar. It is terrible. But then again we don't work either. We sit around in our underwear until noon then go downstairs and make coffee, fry some eggs, read the paper, read part of a book, smell the book, wonder if perhaps we ourselves should work on our book, smell the book again, throw the book across the room because we are quite jealous that any other person wrote a book, feel terribly guilty about throwing the schmuck's book across the room because we secretly wonder if God in heaven noticed our evil jealousy, or worse, our laziness. We then lie across the couch facedown and mumble to God to forgive us because we are secretly afraid He is going to dry up all our words because we envied another man's stupid words. And for this, as I said before, we are paid a dollar. We are worth so much more.[1]

What's the tone here? Miller offers an amusing perspective on grumpy self-pity—but in a self-conscious way. He lets us know that while he overtly criticizes God and others for his plight, he is actually criticizing himself for being so self-absorbed.

How does he create the tone? Tone is achieved through the details included as well as the particular stylistic choices authors make—word choice, syntax, point of view, literary devices, and so forth. Miller's first choice is to write in first person plural ("we writers"). On the surface he appears to distance himself from this bad behavior and bad attitudes. But the details he includes like sitting around in underwear, smelling a book, "throwing the schmuck's book," clearly indicate he is talking about himself—and makes us chuckle in the process.

What's the message? Don't engage in self-pity and criticize others when I can very well do something about my own problems. They aren't the schmucks. I am. Miller's humor and implied self-criticism also signal to us that we shouldn't rely on his characterization of God as being capriciously vindictive. Rather, the opposite. God is there to help us be anxious for nothing.

How does the tone contribute to and make the message more powerful? If Miller wrote a straightforward paragraph like mine summarizing his message, full of dos and don'ts, shoulds and oughts, we'd all forget it in two minutes, if we didn't fall asleep first. By helping us laugh at him, he helps us laugh at ourselves. Yes, in a double reverse, he is not just talking about himself, but he is actually talking about us, about "we writers."

WHAT IS TONE?

Tone is one of five key elements of writing—plot, character, setting, theme, and tone.[2] While most writing includes all five elements to some extent, usually one or two elements dominate the others. These five elements may sound like they mostly concern fiction, but they are elements of nonfiction as well. While it is true that theme would normally be most prominent in nonfiction, the other elements can and do make appearances—in stories we tell, biography, and memoir. Let's look at each of the five.

Plot. We expect plot in a story. Something must happen. In some books and films the action dominates. We even call them action movies— such as the superhero, science fiction, and cops and robbers genres.

Character. Sometimes not a lot happens in a story. Instead, we go deeply into a character, such as in biographies of famous or less known but interesting people—*Hidden Figures* by Margot Lee Shetterly, *The Devil in the White City* by Erik Larson, or *Into the Wild* by Jon Krakauer. Examples from fiction include *The Help* by Kathryn Stockett, *The Catcher in the Rye* by J. D. Salinger, *Go Set a Watchman* by Harper Lee, and *The Joy Luck Club* by Amy Tan. The focus of attention is not the plot line but who the main character is and becomes.

Setting. In a few books and movies the setting itself becomes a character around which everything else seems to orbit. Weather and time period can be part of setting as well as geographical location. Even the title can tell us that setting is key—*Dakota* by Kathleen Norris, *Pilgrim at Tinker Creek* by Annie Dillard, *The Old Man and the Sea* by Ernest Hemingway, *Out of Africa* by Karen Blixen.

Theme. Theme is primary in almost all nonfiction. It can be important in fiction too. After reading a story or watching a movie, people often ask, "What did it mean?" or "What is the message?" or "What in the world was that all about?" Theme is the focus of books like *The Shack* or *Pilgrim's Progress*; primarily they want to teach us something.

Tone. So we have plot, character, setting, and theme. That leaves tone. Formally, tone is defined as the author's attitude toward his or her subject. Tone can be sentimental, optimistic, cynical, bitter, objective, compassionate, irreverent, or almost any other attitude. A tone can also be a mixture, such as sweet sadness, hopeful realism, or understated gratitude.

Emotion words are often used to define tone, but attitude describes tone better. It is a combination of what an author thinks and feels about a topic. I see it as the atmosphere that surrounds and permeates a piece. In the best writing, tone infuses the plot, the characters, the setting, and the theme with depth and significance. Tone harnesses the power of something deeply human. Tone offers a window into life, into who we are (good and bad), and into who we may become.

Look at the opening essay in Robert Fulghum's *All I Really Need to Know I Learned in Kindergarten*. What would you say is the tone?

All I really need to know about how to live and what to do and how to be I learned in kindergarten. Wisdom was not at the top of the graduate-school mountain, but there in the sandpile at Sunday School. These are the things I learned:

Share everything.

Play fair.

Don't hit people.

Put things back where you found them.

Clean up your own mess.

Don't take things that aren't yours.

Say you're sorry when you hurt somebody.

Wash your hands before you eat.

Flush.

Warm cookies and cold milk are good for you.

Live a balanced life—learn some and think some and draw and paint and sing and dance and play and work every day some. . . .

Think what a better world it would be if we all—the whole world—had cookies and milk about three o'clock every afternoon and then lay down with our blankets for a nap. Or if all governments had a basic policy to always put things back where they found them and to clean up their own mess.

And it is still true, no matter how old you are—when you go out into the world, it is best to hold hands and stick together.[3]

Many words could be used to describe this essay—playful, childlike, simple, innocent, calm. How does Fulghum achieve that? By using writing techniques that are consistent with the tone. He employs many simple one-syllable words and many short sentences. Even a long sentence like, "Learn some and think some and draw and paint and sing and dance and play and work every day some" works effectively by repeated use of *and*, which imitates a childlike manner of speech. Topics from an innocent time of life populate the paragraphs—naps, play, cookies, holding hands. The best sentence of all combines all these ingredients: "Flush."

What then is the theme? Life is not that complicated. Really. We've lost sight of what we already knew. Hold hands and stick together. *Life is simple.*

Fulghum doesn't rely on vague generalities. His concrete details create the tone—the sandbox, cookies and milk, three o'clock every afternoon. Likewise the tone, the word choice, the syntax, and the theme all reinforce one another. Simple words, simple sentences, a simple theme, and a simple tone work in unison. The medium is the message, making this an extraordinary example of effective tone.

Here's the title page to a book that offers something different, and yet not so different. How would you describe the tone and the theme?

The Shepherd's Adventure

or

A Practical Guide to Princess Rescuing

Al Anderson

(a learned discourse concerning the ancient and oft-neglected art of Princess Rescuing, with a complete account of the foibles, follies, mistakes, and miscues which commonly result when the untutored layman attempts to prosecute such a scheme; told in the similitude of a story, complete with beautiful but unnecessary descriptions, remarkably strange characters, countless classical references, brilliant effusions of poetry, several sage observations, and finally, several long badly-written passages which appear to have nothing to do with the story, but which the sagacious reader will do his best with, realizing that Princess Rescuing is, like life itself, not a simple thing, nor an exact science, and that the lowliest and most obscure people, are sometimes far greater and much more important than one might think)[4]

What's the tone, the feeling, the attitude the author expresses? It is fun and playful like Fulghum's piece, but with a difference. While being humorously self-effacing ("several long badly-written passages"), Anderson makes a dramatic shift into the seriousness of life when he writes, "realizing that Princess Rescuing is, like life itself, not a simple thing, nor an exact science."

How does the author achieve that tone? Both his humor and the seriousness of his tone are achieved through complex, multisyllabic words, numerous adjectives, a complex structure, and sophisticated literary devices like hyperbole, foreshadowing, and alliteration ("foibles, follies, mistakes, and miscues").

What is the most unusual aspect of how he achieves his tone? Grammar. This parenthetical statement is not a sentence at all. Though long and complex, it lacks a verb to go with its subject. The very structure is incomplete—like life itself.

What's the theme? Life is at once multifaceted yet incomplete. It's fun and serious. In a reversal of Fulghum, Anderson suggests that *life is complicated*.

Like Fulghum's essay on kindergarten, however, Anderson's piece achieves its compelling, dramatic tone by making theme, structure, syntax, and word choice all work together in a cohesive effort. The words are complex, the syntax is complex, the literary devices are complex, the theme is complex, the tone is complex—all reinforcing one another and coming together in a powerful unity.

CHOOSE YOUR TONE CAREFULLY

While the tone of a piece can be almost anything, not every tone works. Even the most sophisticated writers can get carried away. Consider the opening to D. H. Lawrence's essay "Benjamin Franklin."

> The Perfectibility of Man! Ah heaven, what a dreary theme! The perfectibility of the Ford car! The perfectibility of which man? I am many men. Which of them are you going to perfect? I am not a mechanical contrivance.
>
> Education! Which of the various me's do you propose to educate, and which do you propose to suppress?
>
> Anyhow, I defy you. I defy you, oh society, to educate me or to suppress me, according to your dummy standards.
>
> The ideal man! And which is he, if you please? Benjamin Franklin or Abraham Lincoln? The ideal man! Roosevelt or Porfirio Díaz?
>
> There are other men in me, besides this patient ass who sits here in a tweed jacket. What am I doing, playing the patient ass in a tweed jacket? Who am I talking to? Who are you, at the other end of this patience?
>
> Who are you? How many selves have you? And which of these selves do you want to be?
>
> Is Yale College going to educate the self that is in the dark of you, or Harvard College?
>
> The ideal self! Oh, but I have a strange and fugitive self shut out and howling like a wolf or a coyote under the ideal windows. See his red eyes in the dark? This is the self who is coming into his own.

The perfectibility of man, dear God! When every man as long as he remains alive is in himself a multitude of conflicting men. Which of these do you choose to perfect, at the expense of every other?

Old Daddy Franklin will tell you. He'll rig him up for you, the pattern American. Oh, Franklin was the first downright American. He knew what he was about, the sharp little man. He set up the first dummy American.

At the beginning of his career this cunning little Benjamin drew up for himself a creed that should "satisfy the professors of every religion, but shock none."

Now wasn't that a real American thing to do?[5]

You probably thought I should have cut down the size of this excerpt to the first few paragraphs. It doesn't take long to get the idea or the tone. Yet Lawrence persists in this outraged, hysterical tone for four thousand words, to the very last word of the essay! I only gave you the first 335 words, but they seemed like four thousand all on their own, didn't they?

A strong, intense tone can get very old, very fast. It will never do for a two- or three-hundred-page book. Such a tone will tire and discourage readers. A subtle, less overt tone usually works better. Readers can take it in larger doses, and it influences them at a more intuitive level.

What about the earlier examples from Miller, Fulghum, and Anderson? Aren't they rather intense, even if not as supercharged as Lawrence? Yes, they are. I chose them for that very reason, as clear examples of what tone is and how it works. The lesson here is to have a strong enough tone that it works, but not so strong that it chases readers away.

While Miller, for example, does maintain a rather humorous, self-deprecating tone throughout his book, he largely backs off from the intensity found in the excerpt about self-pitying writers. In Fulghum's case, the kindergarten essay is very short, and he uses different though related tones in the other brief, somewhat disconnected, essays found in the rest of his book.

Tone is an author's best friend. Tone is the sum that is greater than the parts. An effective tone is hard to achieve. It takes practice, experimentation, and the willingness to throw away multiple drafts. But the results can be magical.

14

FOR THE
LOVE OF
METAPHOR

Louise Strong, my mother-in-law, was a blunt-spoken, hard-smokin' woman from southern Illinois who died several years ago at age ninety-one. If she had an opinion, which she often did, she was not afraid to share it.

She grew up with five siblings, including her sister Bertha. The two of them were regularly at odds. While Bertha helped Louise get a job at the local Air Force base, she was anything but pleased that Louise kept getting promoted while Bertha did not. In turn, Louise didn't look very kindly on Bertha wearing the same color dress as she did to the wedding of Louise's oldest daughter.

Then there was Bertha's ability to make sure those in the family knew the indiscretions of everyone else in the family. Even some time after Bertha died, Louise still held a distinctively acerbic perspective on her sister. "Why, Bertha," she told me, "had a tongue that could sit on the front porch and pick grapes in the back yard!"

That exceptionally vivid and creative image has stuck with me. As with any good metaphor, this comparison communicated far more effectively, comprehensively, and memorably what Louise had on her mind than if she had baldly said that Bertha was a gossip.

Metaphors, similes, and analogies sharpen the sword of our writing. They allow us to cut quickly through the fat to the meat of our purpose. Metaphors are one way nonfiction can compete on equal footing with fiction writers who are always painting pictures. Fiction could hardly be much more colorful than the way Louise portrayed her sister.

One delightful creator of such comparisons is Fredrik Backman. He frequently uses apt similes and metaphors to paint vivid, miniature portraits of the cantankerous and lovable main character in his book *A Man Called Ove*.

Throughout the book, Ove endures a love-hate relationship with a stray cat. During their first meeting, "Ove stomped forward. The cat stood up. Ove stopped. They stood there measuring up to each other for a few moments, like two potential troublemakers in a small-town bar."

On another occasion, Ove encountered a driver in a Mercedes who tailgated him. After the driver passed him, Ove had the pleasure of tailgating the Mercedes in return at the next stoplight. Glares and gestures were exchanged. When they unexpectedly ended up in the same parking lot, Ove took the opportunity to block his adversary so a third car could have the last parking spot instead. Ove then "stepped out of the Saab triumphantly, like a gladiator who had just slain his opponent."

When the taciturn Ove recalls meeting the father of Sonja, his fiancée, he encounters his match in reticence. In a supreme effort to make conversation, Ove offers to see about fixing the old man's car. "The two men looked at each other for a moment. Then Sonja's father nodded. And Ove nodded curtly back. And then they rose to their feet, objective and determined, in the way two men might behave if they had just agreed to go and kill a third man."[1]

METAPHORS AND THINGS LIKE THAT

Metaphors, similes, and analogies are all comparisons of slightly different types. Though in this chapter I use the word *metaphor* as a collective term for all of these, here are the differences.

Metaphors compare two things that are basically different without using words such as *like* or *as*. One thing is used to mean the other.

- The highway was a white ribbon wrapping the green landscape.
- I am a prisoner of my own mind.

Similes compare two thinks that are basically different by using words such as *like* or *as*. One thing is similar in certain ways to another.

- He acts like a clown.
- Her eyes searched the room as a wolf hunts for prey.

Analogies are often extended comparisons used to further a rational argument. If something is true in one case, then we use the analogy to reason that it is true in a different situation.

- Just as a good roof protects a house as well as everything in it, a good insurance policy protects your health and everything that matters to you.
- Math is like mental weight lifting. You don't lift weights so you can do a clean and jerk in the Olympics but to improve your performance in any other sport. "You do math exercises so you can improve your ability to think logically, so that you can be a better lawyer, doctor, architect, prison warden or parent."*

*Dean Sherman quoted in Chip Heath and Dan Heath, *Made to Stick* (New York: Random House, 2007), 194.

We delight in the surprising absurdity of the comparison, yet it is dead on target. Why? While two men fixing a car together may seem trivial compared to deciding to kill someone, that is precisely Backman's point. Given their supreme reserve, for Ove and the old man to engage in this minimally interpersonal activity is in fact a grave and desperate act.

Strong metaphors like these are hard to come by. They take time, effort, skill, and a sense of what works that comes with hours of practice. But metaphors are quite common. They are so much a part of our language that we don't even notice them most of the time.

WIRED FOR METAPHORS

Take the way we speak of the financial world. It is *awash* in metaphors. We want to have plenty of *liquid assets* so that several *revenue streams* benefit our *cash flow*. Banks get *bailed out* and the government *pumps* money into the economy. As James Geary writes in his book on metaphors,

> When you need money, you can *tap* a friend, *sponge off* relatives, *dip into* savings or—if you're prepared to be unscrupulous—*skim* a little something off the top. When growth is *buoyant*, a rising tide lifts all boats. . . . Stocks do the most amazing things. They soar, surge, climb, leap, and perform all kinds of other super-heroic statistical feats. Sadly, they also plummet, slide, plunge, drop, and fall.[2]

We can't help but think and speak in metaphors. A hot temperature is the "high" for the day and a cold temperature is the "low." The future is "ahead" and the past "behind."

Virtually the only way to understand something new is in reference to the old. When the theory of plate tectonics was first used to explain continental drift in the 1960s, the earth was compared to rice pudding—hard on the surface but pliable and liquid underneath.[3] And electromagnetic fields were compared to two absolutely still corks floating separately in a bowl of water. Push one and the other moves. Not a perfect analogy, but helpful.

Why do we speak and write this way? Because metaphors aren't just clever comparisons. Metaphors are the way we think.

To illustrate this, Geary introduces us to Rebecca. When she reads a headline that says, "Belt Tightening Lies Ahead," or if someone says, "I'll show you the ropes," she has no idea what either means. She doesn't wear a belt, and no one showed her any ropes. Rebecca is an extremely intelligent person and a high-functioning autistic. Her brain is virtually incapable of processing metaphors. She only understands what is literal (or metaphors whose meaning she has memorized).

Research shows that our brains are voracious pattern seekers. As noted in chapter three on structure, we look for similarities in life around us so we don't become paralyzed analyzing everything we come across. If we see an object resting on the floor that has four legs supporting a horizontal platform about eighteen inches high with a vertical panel attached to and rising from one side of the platform—we know it's a chair, even if we haven't seen this particular style of chair before. Without pattern recognition, we'd never make it out of our bedrooms in the morning (though some of us who do use pattern recognition still can't manage that).

When children play pretend, they are engaging in a very complex kind of pattern recognition. "From a cognitive point of view, saying 'My job is a jail' is a lot like pretending that a banana is a telephone."[4] Not surprisingly, then, people like Rebecca also have difficulty with playing pretend. Scientists have traced the ability to pretend and under-stand metaphors to a certain category of neurons in our brain. For such people, these neurons malfunction.

The patterns our brains form do not always follow strict logic or mathematical exactitude. (If they did, Rebecca's literal mind would be able to decode what others were saying.) Our brains seem to require more latitude and flexibility to deal with life in all its messiness and complexity, if not randomness. This, too, may be a survival mechanism. The more supple our minds, the better we can cope with the unexpected. For the brain, precision and specificity are important but apparently not the most important values. Rather creativity, breadth, connection, and order are more central.

A good metaphor gratifies the mind like a good detective story. Both are puzzles where the solution is not obvious but plausible.[5] Our minds tend to put things in categories and patterns, and are restless till they finish the task. That's why finishing a jigsaw puzzle or a crossword puzzle is so satisfying. And figuring out the murder mystery before the author unveils the answers is like children climbing a tree, delighted to spot their father a block away as he rounds the corner for home.

Metaphors and analogies start with something we do know so we can more quickly understand something we don't know. They aid in learning. As physicist J. Robert Oppenheimer said, "We cannot, coming into something new, deal with it except on the basis of the familiar and the old-fashioned."[6] Multiplication is a kind of fast addition. Division a kind of fast subtraction. We learn by building on something similar that we learned previously. Metaphors are one way of being creative, as noted in chapter eleven—combining two things in a fresh fashion.

So if you can use a good metaphor, do.

STORIES IN MINIATURE

Metaphors are like miniature stories. In a world in love with stories, nonfiction writers need to take advantage of this. How do metaphors tell a tale?

Think about Ove and the cat—those two troublemakers confronting each other in a small-town bar. That quick image evokes a whole scene in our minds—a crowded tavern on a Saturday night, men and women laughing and talking, loud music playing in the background, a bar-tender or bouncer keeping things under control. It's the stuff of so many Westerns and action movies. Two punks trying to prove how tough they are, trying to impress a girl or some friends, find an excuse to take of-fense with each other. Will a fight break out? Will one back down? Will shots be fired? All of this and more we pour into those few words.

In a flash we wonder—*What does Ove have to prove? And what about the cat? How tough are they?* And we smile because again, the contrast is delightfully unexpected. On the surface Ove clearly outsizes the cat. But maybe, the analogy hints, the cat will be Ove's match. We'll just have to see how the story ends.

Two small-town troublemakers in a bar is a cliché, yes. But when you compare that to an old man and a bedraggled feline facing each other, it becomes fresh and vivid.

Metaphors, then, can serve several purposes. First, as we've seen, they can aid in understanding. They can quickly fill in a picture by allowing readers to draw on their own background and experiences. What we have to say becomes richer and fuller without laboriously providing all the details.

Second, they entertain. We find good metaphors simply en-joyable. Our minds and hearts delight in well-crafted connections. They can be the honey that helps us swallow otherwise tasteless (but nutritious) information.

Third, they can make what we have to say more memorable. We all know how hard it was to memorize disembodied dates from history class. But a good story sticks in our minds. We might not remember what year Teddy Roosevelt rode up San Juan Hill with his Roughriders, but the picture is locked in place.

When readers remember the miniature stories we've created with our metaphors, the advantage is clear. They are more likely to be con-vinced of the information or perspective we offer. Jesus was a master of storytelling. He was also a master of metaphor whose images still infuse our language whether we are religiously inclined or not:

No one pours new wine into old wineskins. (Mark 2:22)

If a house is divided against itself, that house cannot stand. (Mark 3:25)

Whoever wants to be my disciple must deny themselves and take up their cross and follow me. (Mark 8:34)

Can the blind lead the blind? (Luke 6:39)

Why do you look at the speck of sawdust in your brother's eye and pay no attention to the plank in your own eye? (Luke 6:41)

You are the salt of the earth. (Matthew 5:13)

A city set on a hill cannot be hidden. (Matthew 5:14 ESV)

They [the teachers of the law and the Pharisees] tie up heavy, cumbersome loads and put them on other people's shoulders, but they themselves are not willing to lift a finger to move them. (Matthew 23:4)

I am the bread of life. (John 6:35)

We picture one blind person leading another, the first bumping into a post and then the second. Ultimately, they both get lost and fail to reach their destination. The futility is poignant. The aptness of all these images has given them long lives and reinforced the influence of Jesus throughout history.

Such vivid images embrace a larger world of emotional, mental, and cultural connections we associate with each picture. Shakespeare's works have woven their way into our world for such reasons. Consider these:

In my mind's eye.

All the world's a stage, and all the men and women merely players.

Now is the winter of our discontent.

Love is blind, and lovers cannot see.

Why, then the world's mine oyster.

But, for my own part, it was Greek to me.

A dish fit for the gods.

Yet do I fear thy nature; It is too full o' the milk of human kindness.

Out of the jaws of death.[7]

I'LL HAVE A CLICHÉ WITH A TWIST, PLEASE

I mention Shakespeare's world-class metaphors as examples to inspire our work, not as phrases to unthinkingly copy. After all, some of them have been so overused that they have turned into background music we don't even notice. We have heard some phrases so often that they have lost their power to provoke, startle, or inspire.

Clichés are tired, dying, or dead metaphors or similes. They are viruses that have infected our language, reproducing with such speed and volume that they threaten to render our prose comatose. You know these and dozens of others all too well: *Filled to the gills. Selling like hotcakes. Raining cats and dogs. Happy as a clam. At the speed of light.* Every writing teacher, every book on writing tells us to eradicate clichés. Such advice has even turned into a cliché itself: "Avoid clichés like the plague."

But we can salvage clichés and give them new life. Consider my wife, Phyllis. She murders clichés. (But because these are unpremeditated, we should probably reduce the charge to manslaughter.)

Once, after a meeting, Phyllis was upset that the real issues had not been addressed. "There's a pink elephant on the table," she told me emphatically.

"You mean, 'There's an elephant in the room,'" I offered helpfully.

"No," she insisted, "my elephant is pink and it is definitely on the table!"

On another occasion Phyllis could tell I was about to say something that could get me in trouble. So she warned me, "You are treading on thin ground, Le Peau!" Well, at least if I fell through I wouldn't be in danger of drowning.

Another time someone had moved so fast, she said, "He made a beehive for the door." That way, I suppose, we could all use the door for something besides entries and exits.

Writers and speakers can (and largely should) just cut clichés completely, but Phyllis's verbal malfeasance suggests three ways to use them effectively.

Give clichés a twist. Suppose you are writing a detective novel. Your main character might say, "This guy had been a problem to me for years. As I held the gun I thought about how good it would feel to put him out of my misery." By switching one word, *his* to *my*, we make the cliché fresh, hopefully bringing a smile to the reader.

To contrast something effective in a small way with something big that is unnecessary and counterproductive, try, "Better to light a candle than burn down the whole house."

J. R. R. Tolkien offers an example in recounting the night Sam and his four friends had at the house of Tom Bombadil in *The Fellowship of the Ring*: "As far as he could remember, Sam slept through the night in deep content, if logs are contented."[8]

Extend the metaphor that the cliché suggests. In two earlier sentences in this section I extended the metaphor of a cliché. "Murdering a cliché" is not quite a cliché, but it is a somewhat tired metaphor in need of a rest. By extending the metaphor to include manslaughter, we gave it a good shot of caffeine.

Perhaps you want to consider the advantages of being sure to get something now versus the slim chance of getting everything later. This might do the trick: "Maybe you shouldn't count your chickens before they hatch, but at least you can have some eggs for breakfast."

If you want to express your dislike for someone, here's an option: "I held her at arm's length, wishing my arm was longer."

Create your own. I was reading a recent fantasy novel about an imaginary world. At one point a character offers the advice "Don't look a gift horse in the mouth." Really? Is it possible that the exact same proverb was developed in this alternate world as in ours?

To combat this, Tolkien once again shows us how it's done. In *The Lord of the Rings* he created dozens of his own adages such as, "The wise speak only of what they know."[9] While he put these into the mouths of his characters, we sense they were first formed in the recesses of the history of Middle-earth, adding depth and texture to his tale.

I had a teacher who said, "Just because it's a cliché doesn't mean it's not true." Clichés begin as hard-won pearls of wisdom that have been encrusted in shells of overuse. But if we can give a cliché a twist, perhaps it can become the best of all possible pearls.

WHEN METAPHORS MISS THE BOAT

Good metaphors are key to good writing. We already use metaphors without realizing it, whether we are offering information about science, history, or culture, whether we are writing about our growing up years, a book we read, or a way to do something better in business, in church, or in relationships. The goal, then, is to use them intentionally, in fresh and apt ways, no matter what we are up to. Then our readers will be happier than gymnasts in zero gravity.

Not every metaphor will do, however. We need to be alert not only for clichés but also for mixed or failed metaphors.

Mixed metaphors combine two pictures or images that just don't go together. Here's a headline from the *Tulsa World:*

Step Up to the Plate and Fish or Cut Bait

It's hard to play baseball while you are in a boat trying to catch trout. It is also confusing to readers. Or consider this sentence from *Our Town, N.Y.:*

The moment that you walk into the bowels of the armpit of the cesspool of crime, you immediately cringe.[10]

Personally, I think I would do more than cringe if I found out my armpit had bowels. The writer of this sentence may have been trying to extend the metaphor. Unfortunately, he just ended up inappropriately combining two trite, though connected, phrases. The failure becomes complete when he adds unrelated body parts.

Failed metaphors, on the other hand, use an image that is not appropriate for what you are trying to explain. A regular source of entertainment is deliberately creating such grammatical monstrosities. The *Washington Post's* Style Invitational has for years asked readers to create bad to outrageous metaphors. They willingly oblige.

It was an American tradition, like fathers chasing kids around with power tools. (Brian Broadus, Charlottesville)

He was deeply in love. When she spoke, he thought he heard bells, as if she were a garbage truck backing up. (Susan Reese, Arlington)[11]

One last caution remains. Don't use too many metaphors. A little garlic or cumin can be great when cooking. Too much can make your dish inedible. Likewise, too many metaphors, even good metaphors, can overload your text and slow down your readers. If they have to process too many comparisons, your content will be hidden rather than enhanced. Using a single metaphor to unify an article, a chapter, or a book can be just fine. But don't reference it too often.

So be careful that your metaphors are not as common as one-liners at a comedy convention, as numerous as drunks at a tailgate party, or as bountiful as bribes in Chicago politics.

15

LESS IS MORE

I WAS SITTING IN AN AUDITORIUM at the Calvin Festival of Faith and Writing in Grand Rapids, Michigan, listening to a filmmaker talk about his craft. He showed us some clips from his movie, talked a bit about his process, and took questions from the audience. Somewhere in the middle of his presentation he said in passing, "I'm not sure I'm supposed to say this because we're on a Christian college campus, but I generally don't like faith-based movies. They don't trust their audiences."

I thought I knew what he meant, but I wanted to be sure. So I asked him to say more. "Often Christian films don't trust their audience to get their point," he said. "They feel they have to spell everything out. Ironically, faith-based films don't have enough faith that their viewers will understand what the movie is saying. I like movies that give enough without giving too much. They show respect for their audience by letting them figure things out for themselves without spoon-feeding them."[1]

One movie with religious themes, he said, that did trust its audience was *Tender Mercies* with Robert Duvall, who won the Oscar for Best

Actor for his role. The movie tells the story of Mac Sledge, a country music singer who seeks to recover from his alcoholism through his relationships with a widow, her son, and the church.

The film shows the development of these relationships in only a few scenes with very little dialogue. First, we see Sledge approach the widow asking for work on the farm. Shortly after that Sledge is eating silently at the dinner table with the widow and the son. Then we see Sledge ask the widow if she'd "consider marrying" him. Yes, she'd consider it. After that we see no wedding, just the two dealing with life as husband and wife.

Courageously the writer and the director trusted the audience to fill in what was not directly portrayed, that their relationship had developed over a period of months into a romance and a commitment. In the rest of the movie we see a powerful story of grace and the redemption of a frail and fallen human being.

Whether writing fiction or nonfiction, we are often too concerned about whether our audience "gets it." We don't want them to miss the point. Ironically, however, spelling everything (or too much) out creates flat writing, which lessens impact. Ambiguity (but yes, not too much) can be the writer's best friend. When we trust our readers, we engage them three dimensionally. If we leave room for them to fill in the blanks we have left, they internalize our story or message more deeply. As a result, what we write sticks better.

When we are too focused on readers getting our point, we can become didactic and perhaps preachy, engaging only one dimension— perhaps just the mind or just the will. Art engages the whole person— will, heart, soul, mind, and strength. Sentimental or manipulative writing has the same problem but from a different angle. Books like *Old Yeller* and *Heidi* (sorry, if these were some of your favorites growing up) may be worthwhile entertainments, but they tend to be a little too precious.

The principle of *less is more* makes room for art by making room for all of who we are.

Yet how can *less is more* be true when so often we are also told, "Tell 'em what you're going to say. Tell 'em what you have to say. Then tell 'em what you said"? How is that trusting your readers?

Summarizing is not the same as overdoing detail. I believe it is valuable to give signals to readers about where you are and where you are taking them. And the more practical or utilitarian the purpose, the more appropriate that is. Writing how-to manuals and cookbooks can be worthy endeavors. We need to use common sense as we write, applying guidelines such as *less is more* in ways that make sense for the genre.

Regardless of what we are writing, however, we must treat our readers with dignity. Don't announce that you are going to tell a funny joke or story. Give readers the dignity of deciding for themselves if it is humorous. Besides, doing so makes it less funny because you have given away the element of surprise. Don't say a story will be sad or happy or startling. That inoculates the reader against sadness or happiness or shock. Just tell the story.

LESS EXPLAINING, MORE DESCRIBING

Certainly, *less is more* has everything to do with narrative nonfiction—memoir, biography, autobiography, and the stories we tell in essays, blogs, or articles. Here we should especially resist the impulse to overtell, overexplain, overwrite. Describe what we see and what we have experienced rather than overinterpret.

Kathleen Norris's spiritual memoir, *Dakota*, offers one example of how less is more in the opening paragraph.

> The vast high plains, the beginning of the desert West, often act as a crucible for those sturdy folk who inhabit them. Like ancient Jacob's mysterious angel, the harsh region requires that you wrestle mightily with it before it bestows a reluctant blessing. This can

mean driving through a furious snowstorm on icy roads, wondering whether you'll have to pull over and spend the night in your tin box of a car, only to unexpectedly emerge under tag ends of clouds into a clear sky blazing with stars. Suddenly you know with certainty what you're seeing: the earth has turned to face the center of the galaxy, and many more welcoming stars are visible than the ones we usually see on our remote wing of the Milky Way's spiral.

Not bad. But how much better it is without the verbiage I added in the previous paragraph. Here is what she actually wrote:

The high plains, the beginning of the desert West, often act as a crucible for those who inhabit them. Like Jacob's angel, the region requires that you wrestle with it before it bestows a blessing. This can mean driving through a snowstorm on icy roads, wondering whether you'll have to pull over and spend the night in your car, only to emerge under tag ends of clouds into a clear sky blazing with stars. Suddenly you know what you're seeing: the earth has turned to face the center of the galaxy, and many more stars are visible than the ones we usually see on our wing of the spiral.[2]

Less has become more. Now the sparseness of the land is matched by the sparseness of the prose. By not saying too much, Norris allows us room to feel the weather ourselves, to see the sky in our own way. By not including every nuance of her thoughts and experiences, she doesn't crowd us out but invites us in.

We can use many effective ways to say less when writing nonfiction, and end up with more powerful prose. Cutting adjectives and adverbs is common advice, and it is good advice. Hemingway pioneered unadorned fiction a century ago. Orwell, Strunk & White, and Zinsser then took up the cause for nonfiction. And happily this approach still holds sway.

Art goes through phases, and I suppose there will come a time when spare prose will fall out of favor and something different will replace it. In music, hauntingly beautiful and mysterious-but-stark Gregorian Chant gave way to the polyphonic style of the Renaissance, which in turn was replaced by the ornamental baroque period (think Bach and Handel) which, after running its course, opened the way for the cleaner, more uncluttered classical era epitomized by Mozart and Haydn. In reaction to that and the overly rational influences of the Enlightenment, the Romantic style with its emotional emphasis emerged with champions such as Liszt, Brahms, and Tchaikovsky.

No doubt we are already seeing that shift in fiction with the rise of magical realism (*Like Water for Chocolate* by Laura Esquivel, *Life of Pi* by Yann Martel, *American Gods* by Neil Gaiman) as well as portrayals of multiple realities and parallel universes (*The Man in the High Castle* by Philip K. Dick, *Dark Matter* by Blake Crouch). Sometimes books in this genre have gone way beyond trusting audiences to intentionally seeking to confuse and disorient audiences. Which is the real story and which isn't? We have almost no way to know, which is part of the point. And I appreciate that. There can be value in shaking expectations and perspectives.

Such directions have influenced nonfiction as well, though in more subtle ways. Narrative nonfiction has traditionally taken a straightforward approach—telling the story from start to finish. In recent years we've had any number of excellent best sellers using this approach, such as *Unbroken* and *Seabiscuit* by Laura Hillenbrand and *The Glass Castle* by Jeannette Walls. Much narrative history, such as that of David McCullough and Candice Millard, also follows this path.

Alongside such time-honored patterns have come volumes influenced by the notion that there is no such thing as a purely objective observer. We all have our own perspective and prejudices, regardless of how expert, professional, educated, or well trained we are. (Remember the story in chapter one about the trombonist auditioning for the

Munich Philharmonic?) If this is so, what are nonfiction writers to do when their goal is to be accurate, honest, and faithful?

One approach gaining favor among some is to magnify their personal involvement with the subject rather than try to hide behind a curtain of impartiality. This can make their writing both faithful and more enjoyable to read. Rebecca Skloot's *The Immortal Life of Henrietta Lacks* and David Grann's *The Lost City of Z*, mentioned in chapter six on narrative, are just two examples.

Instead of trying to remove personal involvement or perspective, some authors thus glory in it. This can make the story more human and therefore more interesting. In ways it is a more complex and challenging task for writers, but the results can be worthwhile.

I am not ready to side with those who absolutely declare there is no absolute reality. Yet when writing nonfiction, even nonfiction that isn't substantially narrative in form, we still, I believe, have something to learn from recognizing our limits in objectivity. Yes, as writers we should have passion and conviction, but we should marry those with humility, a virtue far older and more venerable than any postmodern philosophy, any cutting-edge scientific discovery, or any fad of the day.

WRITE LIKE LINCOLN

What does spare, uncluttered writing look like when it is also filled with conviction, passion, and humility? We need search no further for a model of *less is more* than the mere seven hundred words of Abraham Lincoln's Second Inaugural Address, given on March 4, 1865. Here was a man who was so convinced of the importance of the Union and the injustice of slavery that he was willing to commit the wealth and lifeblood of a mighty nation to preserve the one and eradicate the other.

And yet, on the eve of Union victory, after the Union alone had spent over $3 billion and suffered more than six hundred thousand killed or wounded—see how he begins:

Fellow-Countrymen: At this second appearing to take the oath of the presidential office, there is less occasion for an extended address than there was at the first. Then a statement, somewhat in detail, of a course to be pursued, seemed fitting and proper. Now, at the expiration of four years, during which public declarations have been constantly called forth on every point and phase of the great contest which still absorbs the attention and engrosses the energies of the nation, little that is new could be presented. The progress of our arms, upon which all else chiefly depends, is as well known to the public as to myself; and it is, I trust, reasonably satisfactory and encouraging to all. With high hope for the future, no prediction in regard to it is ventured.[3]

Lincoln begins low key, in passive voice, avoiding any direct reference to himself as the one who was making a "second appearing to take the oath." Next he notes what won't be said—no details about the hostilities. After all, everyone knows them already! And when he does mention the recent military successes pointing to final victory, he calls them "reasonably satisfactory"—understatement in the extreme.

After four years of so much pain, loss, frustration, and delay, many in the nation were ready to celebrate loud and long. Thousands had come to the inauguration in Washington for just that purpose. But Lincoln avoids any triumphalistic chest thumping, any arrogant "I told you so." If any one person was responsible for the Union maintaining a steady course toward victory in the face of not only impassioned Southern resistance but also perpetual Northern vacillation, it was Lincoln. Yet he said nothing of this.

Neither did Lincoln give grand assurances of victory, which was imminent ("no prediction in regard to it is ventured"). Instead, he reflected back on the mood of everyone as they had stood on the precipice of war in 1861.

On the occasion corresponding to this four years ago, all thoughts were anxiously directed to an impending civil war. All dreaded it—all sought to avert it. While the inaugural address was being delivered from this place, devoted altogether to saving the Union without war, insurgent agents were in the city seeking to destroy it without war—seeking to dissolve the Union, and divide effects by negotiation. Both parties deprecated war; but one of them would make war rather than let the nation survive; and the other would accept war rather than let it perish. And the war came.

Lincoln emphasizes what the two sides had in common: "all thoughts," "all dreaded," "all sought," "both parties." Yes, he contrasts his devotion "to saving the Union without war" with "insurgent agents . . . seeking to destroy it without war." Yet even in this he holds back. He does not call them rebels or traitors, which would have ignited the approval of the crowd.

He makes his viewpoint clear that one party "would make war" while the other "would accept war." Nonetheless, he continues to curb his language. He doesn't conclude this paragraph with a rousing "So they began the war, but we will finish it!" Unexpectedly he returns to passive voice, "and the war came"—as if neither North nor South was responsible. But if not them, if not us, then who? Lincoln's remarkable reflection on that question begins in the next paragraph.

One-eighth of the whole population were colored slaves, not distributed generally over the Union, but localized in the Southern part of it. These slaves constituted a peculiar and powerful interest. All knew that this interest was, somehow, the cause of the war. To strengthen, perpetuate, and extend this interest was the object for which the insurgents would rend the Union, even by war; while the Government claimed no right to do more than to restrict the territorial enlargement of it. Neither party expected for the war the magnitude or the duration which it has already attained. Neither anticipated that the cause of the conflict might cease with, or even before, the conflict itself should cease. Each looked for an easier triumph, and a result less fundamental and astounding. Both read the same Bible, and pray to the same God; and each invokes His aid against the other. It may seem strange that any men should dare to ask a just God's assistance in wringing their bread from the sweat of other men's faces; but let us judge not, that we be not judged. The prayers of both could not be answered; that of neither has been answered fully.

Many in the world hold religious convictions dearly and passionately. So much of our identity and sense of worth can be tied to the God we worship and the community we worship in. Yet Lincoln holds these with an open hand. The prayers "of neither has been answered fully" because God is not a puppet under our control. He is not a celestial dispenser of favors under our command. He is not "a tribal God who would take the side of a section or party."[4]

Lincoln does not demonize the South or canonize the North. He clearly expresses his disapproval of many in the South who overtly held to the "strange" practice of daring "to ask a just God's assistance in wringing their bread from the sweat of other men's faces," (referencing Genesis 3:19). But the North does not get off the hook.

Up until the war began, the North benefited economically from slavery. Though slavery was banned in northern states, slave-grown and slave-harvested cotton largely flowed through New York City, employing and enriching bankers, insurance companies, traders, shipping firms, and more.[5] As Lincoln says in the next paragraph, the problem is not "Southern slavery" but "American slavery."

Even so, many in the North wanted to harshly punish the South after the war was won. They were ready for revenge. There was to be no compromise with rebels, no amnesty for traitors. Their punishment was to be swift, severe, and complete. Therefore, Lincoln directs the second half of the sentence and his second biblical reference (Matthew 7:1) to the North. We should be cautious in judging others since we ourselves are to be judged.

The question he hinted at earlier, however, still hangs in the air. Slavery, both sides knew, "was somehow the cause of the war." But for Lincoln, that does not completely answer the question of why "the war came." So he continued:

> The Almighty has His own purposes. "Woe unto the world because of offenses! for it must needs be that offenses come; but woe to that man by whom the offense cometh!" [Matthew 18:7 KJV]. If we shall suppose that American slavery is one of those offenses which, in the providence of God, must needs come, but which, having continued through His appointed time, He now wills to remove, and that He gives to both North and South this terrible war, as the woe due to those by whom the offense came, shall we discern therein any departure from those divine attributes which the believers in a living God always ascribe to Him? Fondly do we hope—fervently do we pray—that this mighty scourge of war may speedily pass away. Yet, if God wills that it continue until all the wealth piled by the bondsman's two hundred and fifty years of unrequited toil shall be sunk, and until every drop of blood drawn with the lash shall be paid by another drawn with the sword, as was said three thousand years ago, so still it must be said "the judgments of the Lord are true and righteous altogether."

Lincoln finally offers a tentative yet startling answer to the question, Who caused the war? Perhaps, he says, God in his sovereignty did. Perhaps the "offense" of slavery meant that "all the wealth piled by the bondsman's two hundred and fifty years of unrequited toil shall be sunk, and . . . every drop of blood drawn with the lash shall be paid by another drawn with the sword." The two sides spent $6 billion directly on the war.[6] Over six hundred thousand died and an additional four hundred thousand were wounded. Did this equal the treasure and blood extracted from two hundred and fifty years of slavery? Lincoln did not know. But if that was God's will, would it not be just? If judgment may rightly fall on us all, then we should all look for mercy, and we should all seek to be channels of mercy, even to our enemies.

Lincoln does not conclude with an obligatory "God Bless the United States of America," which "fails to come to terms with the evil and hypocrisy" woven into the fabric of the country along with whatever grace God had given us.[7] No matter how just we see our cause to be— and both sides saw it as just and worthy of God's assistance—Lincoln remembers that the Bible which both sides read portrays God as sovereign while we are not. Lincoln instead concludes:

> With malice toward none; with charity for all; with firmness in the right, as God gives us to see the right, let us strive on to finish the work we are in; to bind up the nation's wounds; to care for him who shall have borne the battle, and for his widow, and his orphan—to do all which may achieve and cherish a just and lasting peace among ourselves, and with all nations.

Lincoln once more balances conviction ("with firmness in the right") with a humble recognition that we are finite human beings who dare not claim too much either for God or for ourselves ("as God gives us to see the right"). The action, therefore, that he calls the nation to is not final victory but to binding wounds, caring for widows, seeking peace.

In the Second Inaugural we have *less is more* and nonfiction at its best. Yes, at a century and a half old, some of the sentences seem a bit convoluted for our twenty-first-century taste. The King James Bible and some vocabulary (*charity* meaning "love") seem archaic to us. But this was not the case for his audience for whom it was entirely contemporary. Also note that five of every seven words are single syllables, a proportion we can all well imitate. We don't need an overblown vocabulary to achieve depth and substance.

His skill and artistry are seen in other ways. He includes an abundance of striking parallels ("All dreaded it, all sought to avert it," "Both read the same Bible and pray to the same God"), contrasts ("devoted . . . to saving the Union . . . seeking to dissolve the Union," "malice . . . charity"), and alliteration ("directed . . . dreaded . . . delivered . . . devoted . . . destroy . . . destroy . . . divide . . . deprecated," "Fondly do we hope, fervently do we pray," "borne the battle").

He also deftly organizes the whole speech with a simple and forward-looking structure—from the past ("four years ago all thoughts were anxiously directed to an impending civil war") to the present ("if God wills that [the war] continue") to the future ("let us strive on to finish the work we are in").[8]

His use of *less is more* is just as impressive—indirect references, muted emotions, simple vocabulary, understated appeals.

Many have questioned the genuineness or depth of Lincoln's faith given his lack of church membership and sometimes spotty record of church attendance. But certainly no US politician has ever publicly embodied the best of Christian theology and ethics more fully than Lincoln. Here strength of conviction is matched by strength of humility.

As I've written this book, at times I've sensed how the lines blur between the craft of writing and the art of writing. Sometimes it's hard to clearly identify where one stops and the other begins. When it comes to the precept *less is more*, the same can be said of the line between the art of writing and the spirituality of writing. As we consider how humility can be one embodiment of *less is more*, perhaps that precept embraces all three.

The craft of writing with less decoration leaves room for more art. The art of writing with less certainty in ourselves leaves more room for faith, hope, and love; that is, for more spirituality. And so, in part three, it is to spirituality that we go.

PART 3

THE SPIRITUALITY OF WRITING

16

CALLED TO WRITE

"D AD, WHAT'S YOUR CALLING?" Several years ago, my then college-age daughter, Susan, was standing in the kitchen with me when she casually popped this rather colossal question.

"Well," I said, collecting my thoughts, "I think it is to glorify God with words, whether written or spoken."

"Hmm," she said, "That's what I thought."

Whew! Passed that test! I then turned the question to her. "What do you think is your calling?"

Without much hesitation she responded, "I think it is to help children somewhere in the world in an urban context. I don't know exactly how, where, or in what capacity, but that's what I think."

Not bad, I thought. Not bad. That's a pretty clear sense of vocation in the service of others.

When Susan asked me that question in the kitchen, I had been an editor for over twenty-five years. I had written books and articles and had done a good deal of teaching, speaking, and preaching in various contexts. However, I had not thought much about my calling or vocation during my adult life, and I had never articulated it in that way before. Yet after decades of following the abilities and interests God gave me as well as the paths he had opened to me, my response to Susan came to mind in the moment. I seemed to know my calling in retrospect rather than beforehand.

Christians are often concerned about their call—to the mission field, to a vocation, to a cause, to a group of people. The impulse is good. If Jesus is Lord of all of life, then I should follow him where he leads. And if he wants to send me someplace or use my gifts in some way—well, I don't want to miss that for lack of attention.

FIVE RUBRICS

So how do we find out? Here are five rubrics that have guided me.

First, keep your eyes open to what God is already doing. We can get caught in a trap of thinking we should do something entirely new, that we need to have a major influence in some dimension of life or ministry that has never been done before. Such are the visions of our youth, which are not to be disparaged because they can get us moving in positive directions. Yet we can also benefit from a sense of context.

This is the context: God is active everywhere and not just through us and not just through our churches. In sports arenas, in banks, in schools, in state capitals, in retail shops, in neighborhoods, in courtrooms, in factories, in countries with Buddhist or Hindu majorities, everywhere. All we have to do is open our eyes, open our hearts, and pay attention. Our aim, then, is to join God's work already in progress.

Andrew Purves reminds us, "We don't bid Christ into the hospital room; he is already there. Rather let your prayers be oriented toward thanksgiving for blessings given and expected."[1] Christ is already present with those who suffer, who grieve, who are anxious, who rejoice in a good outcome. How can we join him as he offers grace to them?

The question is not, What can we do for God or his kingdom? Rather it is, What is God already doing around us? What themes, people, events, ideas keep coming up in your life? Maybe it's people who need prayer or homes repaired or job leads or nonjudgmental friendship amid life's hardships. Maybe it's a particular country or those in a certain stage of life. Whatever it is, ask what God is already doing and then consider joining in his work.

Writing might be part of our response. If we are asking ourselves, *What should I write about?* Likely it will be on a subject we are already a bit familiar with. We need to ask ourselves, *What do I already know? What have I already done or been involved with? What has God already taught me, or where has he already taken me?*

Common advice given writers is this: Write what you know. That's been the case for everything I've written. I was involved in leadership in various settings, and then I wrote a book on leadership. I taught the Gospel of Mark for fifteen years and then wrote *Mark Through Old Testament Eyes.* I have written and edited for decades, and the book you now read is the result. Every blog or article started with something I knew. In every case it meant I needed to know more and grow more. So I did more research or got more experience. But that's where it started.

Second, pay attention to what gives you joy and energy. What do we find ourselves doing even when we don't have to or when no one asks us? Organizing files? Working on bikes? Reading fiction? Making meals? Visiting friends? Helping friends with tech problems? Making and editing videos? Maybe we find ourselves writing letters, blogs, or a daily journal.

When I was in grade school, I found myself making my term papers into "books." I created chapters, a cover, a table of contents, and bound the pages together with yarn—all things that weren't required by my teacher. I wasn't thinking about being a book editor at the time, but looking back, this seems somewhat telling.

Then in high school I self-published a humor book with a friend. We went to a local printer, had five hundred copies printed, and sold them by hand to friends and family for a dollar apiece. No one made us do this. We did it for fun. I also joined the staff of the high school newspaper and became its editor my senior year.

Despite all this, in college I was a typical student, clueless about the future. But once when I was standing around with a group of friends, almost in passing one of them said, "You know, you should go into publishing." That had never occurred to me. I hadn't been paying attention. Making books for fun, editing newspapers and newsletters, doing unassigned writing for my school projects—I had just not put it all together. My friend understood me better than I did myself.

Another way to ask this question about joy and energy is: What makes me feel great afterward? What gives me a sense of satisfaction and accomplishment? That might be a calling.

Then we consider how we can turn that activity to the benefit of others if we are not doing so already. Do we make delicious meals that we or a few others enjoy? Is there a way to expand or redirect that? Do we spend extra time tinkering with our car? Are there others we could help in a regular way with their cars? Does writing for the sake of others make us excited? Or does that leave us a bit flat?

Just because we are good at something doesn't mean it's a calling. We may be great at music or at accounting, but simply don't enjoy it much. Then it's probably not a calling. And it is probably not something we would want to write about.

Third, listen to others. Do others affirm what I am doing and encourage me to keep at it? Do I get compliments and words of thanks for my efforts in a particular area? Do those who have expertise in that sphere tell me they see real possibilities for me?

One friend believes he has the gift of encouragement. But no one else does since sadly his comments usually come off as criticism. No one affirms his "gift." Alas, he isn't listening, and he keeps offering his "gift."

My wife, Phyllis, and I have tried over the years to nurture relationships with longtime friends, colleagues, and mentors so we can come to them for counsel about issues we are facing. If we are dealing with a crisis or a decision point in life, we are quick to get their advice. We have gone to them when considering job changes, parenting challenges, or opportunities that could fall into our area of calling. Because they know us well and because we trust the wisdom they have gained over the years, we listen carefully to what they say.

Much of what I've written is because wise people who know me said, "You ought to write about that." I almost always start with doubts, questions, and objections, but I usually conclude they are right. Al Fisher has been a good friend in the publishing industry for many years. Once he told me, "The history of every publishing house is important. We've got to get the stories of the ups and downs, of the lessons learned from the previous generation before they disappear. You need to do that for the publisher you work for." I was startled by his directness, but his comment led to a multiyear effort that resulted in a book: *Heart. Soul. Mind. Strength.: An Anecdotal History of InterVarsity Press.*

Fourth, don't ignore dreams. One way key figures in the Bible received guidance was from dreams, including Abraham, Jacob, Joseph (Jacob's son), Pharaoh, Gideon, Solomon, Nebuchadnezzar, Daniel, Joseph (Mary's husband), the Magi, and Pilate's wife. But we cannot rely on dreams apart from other forms of guidance such as Scripture and the counsel of others. After all, dreams may come from an evil source, or those who say they had dreams may lie (1 Kings 22:22-23; Jeremiah 23:25-32).

Joseph had a dream about his brothers' sheaves of wheat bowing down to his sheaf, and another dream about the sun, moon, and eleven stars bowing down to him. While the dreams accurately symbolized that he would be second in command in Egypt when his brothers came for help during a famine, Joseph failed to listen to or show respect for his family.

As a result, Joseph became prideful, which was followed by resentment, violence, and deceit in the family, certainly not what God wanted.[2]

Once I had a dream just before dawn about a writing project. In the dream were both the words and melody for a song I'd never heard. When I awoke, even though I could remember only some of the words and half the tune, I thought I should write them down. In the days that followed I completed the music and filled out the verses. Afterward I saw, as I looked over the text, that it largely drew from images in the book of Revelation.

I then sent it to several friends, who were trained musicians, to critique it and help me revise it. After that, without mentioning where the song came from, I showed it to the music director at church and told her she was welcome to use it but that she should feel no obligation to do so. Rather, I said, she should exercise her judgment as the person primarily responsible for music. She responded, "Yes, I think this would work well as a Communion song." And our church has used it ever since.

I paid attention to the dream, but I did not assume that the song's origin gave it any special quality or priority. I never presumed I knew what was supposed to happen as a result. I relied on my community for that.

Fifth, follow Jesus. We already know most of God's will and don't have to look far to find it. As others have said, the vast majority of what God wants from us is already found in the Bible and is summarized in both the Ten Commandments and the Two Great Commandments. After all, loving God and loving others summarizes the whole of the law (Matthew 22:37-40). If we can do that, we can confidently say we have fulfilled our call.

PAYING ATTENTION

What all five of these rubrics boil down to is cultivating the spiritual discipline of paying attention—to what God is already doing, to what gives us joy, to what trusted friends say, to dreams, and to what God has already said. Doing that can require times of quiet and silence. Often when we pray we are busy telling God what we think and what we want. We don't stop long enough to give him time to get a word in.

Steve, a longtime friend, told me he makes a regular practice of stopping during his time of prayer to ask, "Lord, what do you want to say to me today?" Then he pauses and waits. A minute, two minutes, ten minutes, or maybe more. He doesn't empty his mind. Instead he allows God to fill it. Sometimes a word comes to his mind from God. Sometimes not. If not, it doesn't bother him. He simply takes the time to enjoy being in God's presence.

When a word does come, it may be as simple as "I love you." It may be a general word of encouragement or challenge. At other times it is very specific.

How does he make sure this isn't his unconscious talking or "an undigested bit of beef," as Scrooge thought Marley's ghost might be? Steve tests it against the Scriptures, the tradition of the church, reason, and the counsel of friends. If it is consistent with those, he moves forward. If not, he waits and doesn't make a decision. He continues his process of discernment, prayer, and listening.

Some other thoughts on calling.

First, don't expect your job to fulfill your calling. It's especially hard to make a living by writing. Out of hundreds of thousands of people publishing books and writing articles each year, maybe a few thousand are making a living by writing what they love. Many more are writing for organizational websites, magazines, or newsletters while they write fiction on weekends. Most have a job that has very little to do with words. Even T. S. Eliot, one of the best-known and successful poets of the twentieth century, was a banker. Poetry simply did not pay the bills.

Second, some people ask themselves, "Am I a writer?" I don't think this is a very helpful question because it implies we must have some degree of innate talent to earn the title—and if we don't have that inborn ability, we should just do something else. If you write, you're a writer. If you work hard to improve your craft and to communicate clearly to others, you're a writer. And if others read what you write, let them decide what they think about it and you.

Third, sometimes we just need to relax, give ourselves a break, and not overanalyze what God has in mind for us. Sometimes writing is just what needs to be done in a given moment to serve a particular purpose. It's not essential to have a call to write for us to do some writing for the sake of the kingdom. The church needs a nursery manual, so we write it. It's not a calling, and that's just fine. Writing is simply an extension of what God has called us to do otherwise in the arts or church or family or business or society. We simply need to write what needs to be written and move on.

Fourth, we may have several calls in our lives—some major and some minor, some temporary and some longer term. As we grow and change, as our circumstances alter, God may have new challenges awaiting us. A calling does not have to be a once-for-all, lifetime commitment. So relax.

How do you find out if writing is your call? Write. Then write some more. Then write a lot more. Try fiction. Try nonfiction. Experiment with different styles. Get suggestions for improvement from qualified people. Revise. See how you like it. See how others like it. And if those things check out, keep going. That might be a call. And if not, no problem. Just keep listening, and maybe keep writing anyway.

What about Susan? After college she worked with children in Peru for two years in a *pueblo joven* or "young town" of dirt streets and half-finished dwellings. When she came back, she went to law school and then worked for several years as an attorney for a legal aid nonprofit, doing advocacy work on behalf of children in the city. She and her husband, John, are also raising three bright, active children in Chicago.

While being a parent is a lifelong commitment, working on behalf of children in an urban setting may not be her calling forever. If not, she'll know because she pays attention.

17

THE QUEST FOR VOICE

I N WRITING CIRCLES, FINDING YOUR VOICE is a common topic
of conversation. Much anxiety and distress are often generated
about this, especially for young, up-and-coming writers. We want to
be great or at least good, fear we aren't, and so obsess over our style,
our tone. For many it is the holy grail of writing.

A writer's voice is generally considered to be something personal,
authentic, and unique. Mark Twain, James Thurber, Dave Barry, Bill
Bryson, David Sedaris, Tina Fey, and Joel Stein, for example, are all
humorists. They all employ exaggeration, irony, absurdity, confusion, and
surprise in their craft—but with very different voices, unique to each.

While they all frequently use a narrative form, Twain is particularly
known for his witticisms—aphorisms at once cynical and wise.

Always do right. This will gratify some people and astonish the rest.

Nothing so needs reforming as other people's habits.

Always obey your parents, when they are present.

True patriotism, the only rational patriotism, is loyalty to the Nation
ALL the time, loyalty to the Government when it deserves it.[1]

Dave Barry tends to emphasize exaggeration and absurdity to carry his humor. He once observed that skiing "combines the element of outdoor fun with the element of potentially knocking down a tree with your face."[2]

Or in describing the laxative he was given to prepare for his colonoscopy, he writes:

> The instructions for MoviPrep, clearly written by somebody with a great sense of humor, state that after you drink it, "a loose watery bowel movement may result." This is kind of like saying that after you jump off your roof, you may experience contact with the ground.
>
> MoviPrep is a nuclear laxative. I don't want to be too graphic, here, but: Have you ever seen a space shuttle launch? This is pretty much the MoviPrep experience, with you as the shuttle.[3]

And consider this analysis that Barry offers about writing:

> If you look at any list of great modern writers such as Ernest Hemingway, William Faulkner and F. Scott Fitzgerald, you'll notice two things about them:
>
> 1. They all had editors.
>
> 2. They are all dead.
>
> Thus we can draw the scientific conclusion that editors are fatal.[4]

Voice, like tone, is characterized by and created via word choice or sentence structure, but it can also express how writers see the world. Voice can be more personality based. Tone on the other hand is the atmosphere or mood that penetrates the substance of a piece and may differ from work to work.

One reason voice becomes such an important topic for writers is that they often find themselves imitating authors they admire—and doing a second-rate job of it. This can paralyze writers, sensing they are just not good enough.

The solution, it is said, is to find your own distinct way of writing. I love Anne Lamott, but I can't write like her. So I don't try. I write the way that works for me instead. Better the unknown me than a poor imitation of someone who is famous. This gives me the freedom I need to move forward positively without worrying about being compared to someone else.

Voice is also important in the sense of having a right to speak because not everyone has always had one. The sad reality is that often certain groups of people in society have been silenced or muffled. What they have to say has been sidelined because they came from a certain place, looked a certain way, grew up in a certain culture, did a certain kind of work, or didn't have enough money.

God, however, created all of us in his image. We all have a role to play as his stewards on earth in proclaiming his rule and righteousness. He gave us all voices to praise him as well as to speak words of comfort, justice, correction, and encouragement.

Those who have found themselves excluded in the past need to know with certainty that what God has taught them, shown them, given them is important. We all need insights and perspectives from every part of the body so that we can all be whole. All have a voice, a voice shaped by our specific culture, language, ethnicity, gender, history, and circumstances. That fact, and that diversity, is something to celebrate because it is how God made and shaped us.

UNIQUE VOICE

So far so good. Yet I have a lingering question—not about the right to speak from and with one's unique background but about what can become a driven quest for an individual voice. Let me begin with a practical point. Sometimes our unique voice isn't critical. If I am a writer trying to get paid for the words I put on paper, I am subject to someone else's standards or style—that of the magazine, website, corporation, or educational press I am writing for.[5] Certain types of voice may be inappropriate for certain situations. Twain's cynicism would be wrong for most funerals or obituaries. A chatty voice may be wrong for a news article. And there can be honor in using our craft well to serve the honorable purposes of others.

A second concern is that if authors find a voice and use it consistently, everything they write can begin to sound the same. Eventually, they could lose their creative edge.

To be sure, we need a balance here. A writer with a recognizable voice becomes something of a brand. Readers know what to expect and keep coming back for more. That can be good. But if the voice is overused or too intense, readers can become tired of it, feeling like they've read this book or article before. Part of the art for a writer is being able to write differently for different occasions, purposes, genres, and topics.

IS VOICE THE HOLY GRAIL?

Another question I have is that the search for authenticity can become the ultimate goal. Such discussions are often filled with the angst of the passionate artist seeking deep, genuine self-expression. Writers are told they must dig down to find the dirty demons inside, let them out, and experience the freedom of their own voice. Even my hero Anne Lamott says this about the dark places in our lives that we keep shut behind closed doors:

> We write to expose the unexposed. . . . Truth seems to want expression. Unacknowledged truth saps your energy and keeps you and your characters wired and delusional. But when you open the closet door and let what was inside out, you can get a rush of liberation. . . . The truth of your experience can *only* come through in your own voice.[6]

And I think, yes . . . but. Yes, I understand that we should not present ourselves artificially cleaned up and shiny. I understand the desire for authenticity in an image-obsessed world full of false fronts and con artists making big bucks by constantly selling us clothes, cars, and techno-gadgets we don't need so we can seem cool when we know we aren't. I understand that cloyingly sentimental stories can be manipulative as well, having no power to change the world.

But the individualism of it all, the intense self-centeredness of such a search can't be right, can it? What about community? What about the world outside my head? Isn't it just a bit narcissistic to think ultimate truth must be found inside my little soul?

Yes, because deeper truth is found elsewhere. It is found via a very scary concept T. S. Eliot commends to us—*tradition*. I remember first coming upon Eliot's "Tradition and the Individual Talent" and thinking it was completely nuts. I was in high school at the time.

Though this is one of the most important and influential essays of the twentieth century, I thought Eliot was crazy to say artists should seek to extinguish their personalities. Wasn't individual expression at the heart of what art was all about, as Lamott suggests? And wasn't Eliot a quintessential modern artist standing for freedom against the chains of the past? Yet here he was upholding the importance of tradition (by which he largely meant Western literary tradition). What could he possibly have been thinking?

Eliot contends that we don't move forward by breaking from the past but by building on the past. Without knowledge of our past, our accumulated wisdom of the human condition with all its failings and successes, we are in a quagmire. Unless we recognize that our very present is shot through with the past, we will misunderstand ourselves and the world. We will fail to contribute anything new. Yet when we do listen to the past, our new work becomes part of the tradition and alters all previous works as introducing a new planet into a solar system would alter the orbits of all the other planets.

Eliot writes, "Some one said: 'The dead writers are remote from us because we know so much more than they did.' Precisely, and they are that which we know."[7]

The goal of writers is not complete originality but to take the past and give it a shake, a fresh look that helps us see reality differently and better. Our task is not to destroy the past but to build upon the past.

And what does our tradition tell me? That I am not at the center of the universe. I am not the goal of the ultimate quest; goodness, truth, and beauty are. We aspire to these for the sake of others as well as for ourselves. Whatever encourages people to be their better selves, to be more closely connected to reality, to delight in creation—this is our noble aim in writing.[8]

Sometimes we have to go through the bad, false, and ugly to get there, and sometimes that rotten stuff is in me. This can be a fruitful source of creative material. Sometimes we have to bring the evil of the world to light in order to defeat it. But inner darkness is not our final aspiration, even if it is authentic.

Writing is not merely an inward, self-referential exercise. It is, or should be, outward. Writing can help our therapy, but we shouldn't expect to publish it.

Set your sights higher than finding your voice. Set them on making the world a better, truer, more beautiful place.

18

THE SPIRITUALITY
OF WRITING
ABOUT YOURSELF

ALL WRITING IS AUTOBIOGRAPHY.
We write what we know, what we learn, what we experience. If we write about business or biology or barbecuing, it is because those are things we've studied and experienced. If I write a book on structural engineering that never uses first-person singular or tells a personal anecdote, it is still autobiographical. It chronicles what I learned and thought about the topic. It means I think what I have learned in my life is worth being studied by other people.

Since we inevitably write about ourselves, a spiritual question immediately arises. How can we spend so much time and effort focused on ourselves if our own self is not the final aim of our writing? If, as I suggested in chapter seventeen, we write not just for ourselves but so others can flourish, how do we not fall victim to pride or self-absorption? Or to put it another way, How can we keep ourselves in perspective, keep others in perspective, and keep God in perspective?

EXAMINING OURSELVES

Just asking such a question, even if we aren't sure about the answer, can be the most helpful thing we do to keep life in balance. Self-examination has been a common spiritual discipline for centuries. It may seem counterintuitive to try to solve the problem of thinking too much about ourselves by taking time to regularly think about ourselves, but bear with me for a moment.

Part of maintaining physical health involves paying attention to our bodies. Does my heart beat funny sometimes? Am I suddenly having digestive problems on a regular basis? Why am I tired all the time? Answers to those questions can lead us to change our diet or our exercise routine, or take us to a doctor. Of course, how often we ask such questions should also be part of our balance in life. Too much of this kind of thinking can lead to hypochondria. In moderation, noticing and questioning ourselves in this way is beneficial.

Likewise, engaging in regular spiritual self-examinations can help us stay healthy. Often around the dinner table, for example, we will ask each other, "What was a high and a low of your day?" In doing this we take time to notice our emotions—what has made us sad or happy or excited or feel down. God does not just speak to us through words or thoughts. Sometimes he is trying to get our attention through what we experience.

If something is weighing on me or energizing me emotionally, the Spirit may be trying to help me notice something. Maybe I should try to find ways to put more of those energizing activities in my life. As for what's weighing me down, maybe I just need to recognize this is something temporary. Winter may be cloudy, but it is only a couple months. If winter has a major debilitating effect on me, perhaps a more significant response is needed.

One of the best ways to carry out this reflection is by writing. Spiritual journaling has been practiced and encouraged for centuries.

Writing in this way is valuable because sometimes we don't know what we think until we write it down. We get to know ourselves, our thoughts, our feelings, our values, our goals, our circumstances, our ups and downs, by writing about ourselves.[1]

Asking about something we liked and didn't like in our day also helps us remember what to thank God for and what to ask him about. This is key. The purpose of the exercise is to turn our attention away from ourselves. What is *he* doing in my life or around me? If it's good, then I can express gratitude. If it's a problem, I can focus on his grace and strength.

Just as writing is autobiographical, likewise we can't help but think about ourselves and see life through our own eyes. We need to intentionally look at our day differently. Ultimately, spiritual self-examination turns our attention back to God and his way of seeing.

Here are some other similar pairs of questions we can ask ourselves and each other:

- For what moment today am I grateful? For what moment am I not grateful?

- What was a life-giving part of my day? What was a life-thwarting part of my day?

- When today did I have a deep sense of connection with God, others, and myself? When today did I not have a sense of connection?

- Where was I aware of living out the fruit of the Spirit? Where was there an absence of the fruit of the Spirit?[2]

You might find one of these pairs more to your liking. Or you could use different questions from time to time for variety.

Spiritual self-examination (called *examen* or *examination of conscience* as originally developed in the Ignatian tradition) has another dimension, that of confession. Each Sunday at our church in prayer and song we begin by remembering the love, greatness, and holiness of God. He is cause for celebration, praise, and thanksgiving.

And in focusing on who he is, we can't help but see a contrast with ourselves—our weaknesses and failings. So we then take a few moments, in God's presence, to confess our sins. We are asked to look back on our week and ask ourselves, *Where did I miss the mark? When did I fall short of God's will? How do I need forgiveness?* After this we have pronounced over us wonderful words of Christ's love, announcing that by him we are reconciled to God.

Participating in confession in the context of Christian community offers a dimension I don't experience on my own. When I see lawyers and truck drivers and teachers and nurses and writers and parents and students and executives and handymen all confessing together, I cannot pretend this isn't for me as well. I am reminded of the reality of God's forgiveness, a gift held out for us all.

I go to church to remember and give thanks for the good I have experienced during the week—the breath of life, my daily bread, love and companionship of others, small miracles and large. I also go to remember my sin. That may seem morbid and depressing, but it is a healthy reminder that I am a creature, one who is created, one who is dependent on my Creator. In remembering my weakness and my foolishness, I am pushed into the arms of One who is the essence of strength and wisdom.

In this way, self-examination turns my heart and mind away from myself and toward God. This weekly rhythm can become a habit in the best sense. By practicing a habit enough, it becomes part of my character. In finding reasons to thank God and in identifying my need for God, though it is by looking at myself regularly, I actually end up thinking about God more.

GETTING PERSPECTIVE

Granted, to say everything we write is autobiographical does stretch how we normally understand the genre. I say it to underline the point that anything we write is intimately personal. Obviously, writing explicitly about ourselves is very different from my hypothetical book on structural engineering. If I write a memoir, tell a story about myself in an article, or reflect on the events of my day in a blog, I am the main character, the main subject—not a bridge or a skyscraper. So, yes, such writing can present unique spiritual challenges.

Writing is a tightrope because on the one hand we are told as Christians not to think more highly of ourselves than we ought, and on the other we are told that as writers we should talk about ourselves so audiences can identify with us. By being vulnerable we can draw readers in and so help them benefit from our life and work.

John Stott, the well-known London pastor, writer, and speaker who died in 2011, was famously reluctant to say anything about himself. Though his books sold millions and he spoke to thousands all over the world, he almost never said anything about his own life. Stott navigated the tightrope by simply getting off it. He remained staunchly Bible focused.

That is clearly one valid way to resolve the issue. As noted earlier, however, we can benefit greatly from writing directly about ourselves, telling stories about ourselves, writing in first-person singular. Doing so can be an exercise in remembering. And when we remember, we have an opportunity for confession and for thanksgiving to God.

If we do decide to write directly about ourselves, how can we be sure we don't fall into self-absorption? Perhaps we can gain some clues from one of the most famous instances of a Christian writing about himself. In fact, his book essentially created the entire genre of spiritual memoir over fifteen hundred years ago.[3] I'm talking, of course, about Augustine and his *Confessions*.[4]

Augustine, the great African theologian and churchman, lived from AD 354 to 430. He was perhaps the preeminent theologian of the first thousand years of the church—and maybe of the second thousand as well. Even the towering intellectual figure of the Middle Ages, Thomas

Aquinas, was thoroughly indebted to him. Augustine's just war theory is even widely taught today, including at US military academies.

He was born in North Africa and then migrated to Italy, where he converted to Christianity. He then returned to Africa and became bishop of Hippo (in present-day Algeria). He was a prolific writer, producing many commentaries on Genesis, Psalms, and Romans, works countering the heresies of the day, as well as doctrinal works on topics such as the Trinity and free will. Other than the *Confessions*, his book *The City of God* is probably his best-known volume.

Confessions chronicles his life from his earliest days (even offering reflections on what was possibly going on in him while still in his mother's womb!) into early adulthood. He does not systematically tell us everything about himself but instead focuses on his moral and intellectual development as they relate to and culminate in his conversion to Christianity at age thirty-one. He notes his propensity for stealing, gluttony, and cheating as a child and teen along with his strong sexual urges. Augustine also portrays his intellectual development, first being enamored with the Manichaeans and then the Neoplatonists. In doing so he recounts different ways he tried to puzzle out such questions as the problems of evil and free will.

Since Augustine is the father of the spiritual memoir, it is worth taking some time to consider how he went about it. For me, several aspects stand out regarding how he exercised the spiritual discipline of gaining perspective even while focusing on himself.

First, the book is called *Confessions* for good reason. Augustine confesses to God in two ways. One, obviously, is by confessing his sin. Besides the offenses already noted, he confesses disobeying parents and teachers, as well as his thirst for the praise of others. He also confesses his narrow, inadequate intellectual efforts. He evaluated some of his previous thinking this way: "I didn't yet see that the pivot of such an important matter is in your artistry, All-Powerful One, since on your own you make wonders."[5] He couldn't really understand the fullness of beauty or reality if God was not in the picture—especially if he didn't see that God was the artist who painted the picture.

In addition he doesn't just mention sins he's already conquered but is honest enough to discuss those he still struggles with. "Actual drunkenness is a far cry from my life; you will be merciful and keep it from coming anywhere near me," he tells his Master. "But sometimes too much drinking creeps up on your slave; you'll be merciful in putting that, too, at a great distance from me."[6] Yes, this is *Saint* Augustine. I don't think he's being overly prudish here since he doesn't claim all alcohol is wrong. But he knows what too much is (as do the rest of us) and acknowledges his dependence on God for the fruit of the Spirit of self-control when it comes to the fruit of the vine. Augustine's honesty calls me to ask, *Am I being completely honest about myself as I write?*

Augustine doesn't just confess his faults, however. He makes a confession of faith. He confesses God's mercy, grace, generosity, wisdom, and more. Thus he balances his weaknesses with God's greatness. He is asking himself, *Where do I see God's hand in this episode, this story? What do I learn about God and his world as a result? What can I praise him for?* The answers to these questions may or may not work their way into our writing, but asking and answering them should work their way into our lives.

Second, Augustine puts himself in perspective by using self-deprecating humor. Famously he says that before his conversion he had prayed to God, "Give me chastity and self-restraint, but don't do it just yet."[7] Learning to laugh at ourselves is one of the healthiest spiritual exercises we can engage in. When we take ourselves too seriously, we are more prone to be offended by others, to let ourselves get in the way of what God is up to.

Making myself the butt of my own jokes is good for my spiritual and psychological health. It also has the advantage of reducing the distance between me and my readers. I'm not an authority seated high above them but one of them, on a journey as they are, trying to make some sense out of life. We are alike.

Third, Augustine makes sure he is not always the hero of his own story. His mother Monica stands out. She is tenacious in prayer and even follows him from Africa to Milan after he left town on a ship, keeping his plans hidden from her. Ambrose, the bishop of Milan, is another major influence who helped him begin to see there was some sense in Christianity after all.

We don't have to be perpetually revealing our thoughts. But when we learn something from others, we should be quick to give credit. Once when writing on hospitality, I used this example:

> On the plains of Illinois on our way to visit relatives, we ended up in a fifty-car pile up on the highway in the middle of a blizzard. Our car was eventually able to limp to a nearby exit for a small town where we sheltered in a restaurant with four young children, all of us dazed and uncertain what to do. As we were standing there among many other stranded motorists, we heard rumors that the town was going to open up the local high school gym so people would have a place to sleep for the night. But a local family saw us and our four small children and said, "You're not staying in the high school gym."
>
> "We're not?" we responded somewhat confused.
>
> "No," they replied, "you're staying with us tonight." So they welcomed a houseful of strangers into their home, interrupting their own plans, feeding us, finding places for us to sleep and inviting us to join in their family activities. We were reminded vividly how God welcomes us into the hospitality of his love through the gift of his own Son to the people of earth. This was especially so because that night was Christmas Eve.[8]

I couldn't have been more passive in this episode. We were bewildered, stuck in a blizzard with a wrecked car, and had no place to stay. The heroes were people who didn't know us, who didn't have to help us, but who offered us not just hospitality but an example to follow.

Fourth, Augustine puts himself in perspective by putting himself under the authority of Scripture. Though Augustine occasionally references passages explicitly, he regularly alludes to the Bible without directly quoting, usually once, twice, or three times a paragraph. Footnotes in modern translations show this clearly. His mind was saturated with the language, the stories, and the teaching of the Bible.

He also overtly submits himself to Scripture. When talking about the authority God has given humans to judge, he offers this exception:

> It doesn't apply to your book [the Bible] itself, even if something's unclear, since we subordinate our understanding to the book, being sure that even whatever in it is shut off from our view has been rightly and truly stated. Thus, a person, though he's already of the Spirit and renewed by the recognition of God according to the image of the one who created him, ought to be a doer of the law, and not a judge of it.[9]

To achieve perspective in this way we need to read the Bible regularly and widely, but we also need to study it in a way that shows respect for the Scripture. Too often we atomize the text, pulling out isolated verses here and there and smashing them together as seems right to us. The Bible, however, is not a book of timeless truths or the "Sayings of Chairman God."[10] Instead of putting ourselves in charge of how Scripture is organized, we let the Bible itself guide our study. We do this by emphasizing the study of whole books of the Bible, trying to discern what the author was aiming to get across in the entire book, not just in pieces.

Matthew didn't think we could understand his Gospel only by comparing it to various texts from Luke and Romans. Doing so not only distracts us from what Matthew had to say but can make us mis-understand him. No, Matthew expected we could understand it by reading Matthew.[11] Likewise, for each book of the Bible, we start by focusing long and hard on the book as a whole.

At the end of his *Confessions*, Augustine spends the last three of his thirteen chapters not by talking about himself but by offering a thorough and deep reflection on an extended passage—the first chapter of Genesis. He analyzes it as a whole. Yes, he is a man of his times and often resorts to an allegorical reading that I wouldn't generally en-courage. Nonetheless, he shows his intent to have his mind and heart fully shaped by God's Word taken as a whole.

This shift from his own story to Genesis can seem odd, however. Why, after spending three hundred pages on himself, does he switch in the last hundred pages to the beginning of Genesis? It seems like he has started an entirely different book.

In doing this, however, Augustine puts himself in perspective in a fifth way—by setting his story in the context of a larger story. His story is not the main event. It is one piece of a majestic cosmic narrative of God and his works. This gives Augustine's story and mine a sense both of proportion and of significance. My story is only part of a larger whole, so I do not take too much credit. But, oh, how magnificent is that story—from creation to consummation, from promise to ful-fillment, from death to life—and I am a part of it!

Confessing our faults and our faith. Using self-deprecating humor. Making sure we are not always the hero. Submitting to Scripture. Seeing ourselves as part of a much grander story. The sixth and final way Augustine helps us is by his example of offering his writing to God.

Remarkably, Augustine addresses the entire book to God. He writes to an audience of one. Primarily he is not speaking to parents or pastors or people struggling to get through life whole and holy. In every section he keeps his focus on God. The book is about Augustine, about himself. But in addressing it to God, it also becomes entirely about his Lord.

Doing this makes sure he continually redirects his focus away from himself toward God. It gives him perspective on his life, reminding him that he is not the primary character in the story of his life. Rather God is. He credits God, for example, with giving him the ideas that expose the errors of the Manichaeans, saying, "It's you, truthful God, who repudiate these people, proving them wrong, and find them at fault."[12] Augustine then proceeds to lay out an argument on why they are wrong. Obviously, these are Augustine's arguments, but he acknowledged God as their source.

All the while, Augustine is clearly aware other people will be reading the book. He asks, "To whom am I telling the story? It isn't of course to you, my God, but in your presence I'm telling it to my race, the human race, however minute a snippet of that might stumble on my writing, such as it is. And what's the story's purpose? Obviously, it's so that I and whoever reads this can contemplate from what depths we must cry out to you."[13]

Augustine wrote the *Confessions* about a dozen years after becoming a Christian and just a few years after becoming a bishop. As a result, a significant part of his purpose seems to be pastoral. He wants to offer a model, one way in which someone might become a Christian, whether the struggle was moral, intellectual, or both. He wants to show a way that seekers in Hippo and elsewhere might come to know and love the Lord he has come to know and love. What God has given him, he offers back to God.

> What is the benefit they [my readers] want from this [my testimony]? . . . It's no small benefit, God my Master, that many give thanks to you on our behalf, and that on our behalf many plead with you. Let a brother's mind love in me whatever, according to your instruction, should instill love, and let it grieve for whatever in me, according to your instruction, should instill grief.[14]

We don't have to write a whole book addressed to God to practice the spiritual discipline of perspective. But we can still ask, *Where did my ideas come from? Who gave me this facility with words? Who was the main actor in my life as I experienced success or failure? What am I learning about God even as I tell my own story?* Such a focus takes the pressure off me. I can worry less about how many readers I will get or if they will be pleased with my work. I can instead concentrate on whether it pleases God.

The spiritual discipline of perspective. That is the gift Augustine offers those of us who write about ourselves. It is a gift we can give thanks for.

19

SPIRITUAL AUTHORITY AND WRITING

WHEN WE WRITE AND PUBLISH about spiritual matters, we stand in a pulpit.

We may think we are just journaling in public, writing about our day, and how we interacted with God. Readers may find our experiences and reflections helpful or not. We don't require or even expect them to agree with us or follow our example. It all feels very low-key, just a way to express ourselves. But inevitably it is more.

Even when we just post on social media or blog, we expect and look for others to read and interact. Otherwise we'd just privately put it in a notebook or computer file and leave it there, unseen by the world. Something just between me and God. Occasionally we may share some of what we write with close friends, a church leader, or family members. However, publishing such thoughts to a wide circle of friends or acquaintances or the public generally is a qualitatively different matter. Why? Because doing so raises issues of spiritual authority.

Authority is the power to act granted to us by others. Authority can be positional—like being hired on a church staff. But authority can also be ascribed—granted to us in unofficial ways by others. Another way to say this is that authority can come from above (like a president appointing a cabinet member) or from below (like the Dalai Lama who, while living in exile from Tibet with no official office or power, has tremendous worldwide authority). In a previous generation, Martin Luther King Jr. and Billy Graham held relatively minor positions of organizational authority compared to the much larger ascribed moral authority they wielded.

Regardless of which kind or how much authority we have, it is derived. We do not give it to ourselves. It is bestowed on us by others (Matthew 8:5-13; John 5:19-23). We may not be famous, but even if only a small group follows us as we "express ourselves," we bear a responsibility.

We write. People choose to listen to us, follow us, maybe even pay money to support us, to hear us speak, or to buy our books. They give us the gift of some measure of authority in their lives. That is a trust we need to handle with care.

CREDIT WHERE CREDIT IS DUE

That care begins with nurturing integrity in our writing. In chapter four I consider character, especially as it relates to persuasion. This means we avoid manipulation. We seek to be honest by checking our facts and respecting viewpoints that differ from ours. We give proper credit for quotations, information, and ideas. We are vigilant against plagiarizing. We don't make up things about ourselves or present ourselves as better or more knowledgeable than we are. We show humility, recognizing our own limitations and celebrating the good things others do and say.

Taking seriously the trust others place in us goes further. More than once as an editor I've worked with writers who are about to publish their first book. They have great stories, great content, and a compelling speaking style. So I ask, "Are you ready to be famous? You might not become well-known or a bestselling author. But if you do, it can really cause trouble for your spiritual well-being. You need to think ahead of time how you will deal with fame because afterward it may be too late."

We've all seen the negative effects that success, notoriety, and admiration can have. People begin abusing their power, thinking that rules about money, truth, and relationships don't apply to them. When news of their moral failings becomes public, their authority to write can collapse along with much else that was once valuable.

When we are successful, we can tend to take too much credit, believing it is just our own smarts, effort, or talent at work. We forget we are beneficiaries of accidents of birth that gave us a family, a culture, and a moment in time that nurtured us in so many ways.

I know I am such a beneficiary. I owe my DNA to others—my parents, their parents, and so forth. I also had nothing to do with my grandparents and great-great-grandparents emigrating from Europe to America. Both sets came to avoid violence and conflict that could have ended their lives. If they hadn't, I might not be here. If my parents hadn't been raised in a culture with a certain history and values, hadn't been educated and made a good living, I might not have either. If I hadn't graduated at a time when publishing was flourishing, that might not have been my career. Yes, I have often been able to make the most of my opportunities by hard work, but I didn't create many opportunities. They were there waiting for me.

When my decisions (among many good possibilities) keep turning out well, it is easy to take credit I didn't earn. I may then start listening less to the advice of others. This pattern is true in business, in churches, in families, in life—not just in writing.

Whether we become wildly successful or just mildly successful, we always need to watch the state of our own souls. Humility is where we start.

One way to nurture a sober view of ourselves is to listen to others. Do we have a friend, a spouse, a pastor, a relative in our lives who can and is completely honest with us about who we are and what we do? Politicians and others in authority have advisers they listen to—but too often they are all yes men and yes women. Those with differing points of view are deliberately excluded or inadvertently pushed aside. The result, then, is a damaging downward spiral into groupthink.

Some people at church, at work, in the neighborhood, or in the family bother me with their contrarian views. Why do they insist on saying things so outrageous and so clearly mistaken? But in my best moments I stop and realize they are good for me. I need to hear viewpoints I disagree with. I don't have the corner on truth or wisdom. I am limited and fallible. After considering their thoughts, I may still disagree. Usually, though, if I have truly considered what they've said, I have a better, more nuanced perspective.

I have the gift of a wife who loves me so completely that she tells me when I am wrong. I write that without any sense of irony. If I say something that might have hurt someone, she tells me. If I decide something too fast or slow, she tells me. If I need to ask someone for forgiveness or forgive someone, she tells me. She doesn't berate or belittle. She simply tells me. This is a gift because I know her love for me is total. She wants all that is best for me. At first I may not like what she says, but I am incredibly blessed to have her in my life.

UNDER AUTHORITY

If we are to exercise spiritual authority, we must have people who exercise true authority in our own lives. This is a foreign concept to many from conservative or independent church backgrounds. Much of the history of Protestantism is shot through with reactions against abuses of hierarchy. Sadly, unaccountable pastors are not immune to abusing power themselves. Pastors who are under the authority of superintendents or bishops are in a better spiritual position for themselves and for their congregations.

Yes, authority structures can be abusive too. Still, a structure that can be self-correcting, however haltingly, is better than no structure at all.

The independent blogger who writes on spiritual themes can be one example of the viewpoint that all I need is me, God, and the Bible. But I need more because my heart is so prone to self-deceit. If something like that is my situation, how can I put myself under authority? Several options are available.

One is to find people who will read what I write before I make it public, people I will actually pay attention to, not those who work under me. I need readers I already look up to who have expertise or spiritual maturity—a pastor, an older Christian, someone who has mentored me, or a longtime friend I have such a strong relationship with that disagreements or corrections won't threaten the relationship.

When I worked at InterVarsity Press, I often blogged on its website. I always had someone review my blog before I posted it. I wanted to make sure not only that it was written well but that I wasn't saying something inadvertently that could be taken the wrong way or harm the organization. Even though I worked hard on those pieces, my reviewer would often spot awkward sentences and sometimes more problematic issues. That was a gift.

I have also had editors review all my books. They made multiple suggestions for change. Many were simply stylistic, but a number were much more substantive. I always took them seriously.

Once I submitted a draft of a book manuscript and was greeted in return with a ten-page single-spaced report of comments and suggestions. As a lifelong editor and writer, I could have been offended and irritated. Wasn't I a well-trained, longtime professional with a proven track record?

The truth is that I, just like any writer, was too close to the material and couldn't see what was needed. So I read the report openly, and it was amazingly on target. Even when I disagreed, I often made the change anyway. After all, maybe I was wrong. After revising the book, I resubmitted the text.

Following my revision I received a second ten-page report. And again, the editor was right. I reworked it once more and ended up with a far superior manuscript than I could have completed on my own.

Part of the advantage I had in this was working with a traditional publisher rather than self-publishing. By working with an existing organization that had its own procedures, culture, and trained staff as well as a doctrinal statement, I was automatically submitting myself to an authority.

Many of us, however, are suspicious of institutions. As those immersed in the Western mind, we highly value individualism, freedom, and independence. These are near godlike ideals not to be tampered with. To be responsible to others (both above and below us) is a countercultural concept, if not heresy. Anything that limits us can feel like a virtual assault on our very humanity. We have forgotten that the whole point of institutions was not to increase power but to limit power.

Over centuries, millennia really, philosophers and political theorists wrestled with how to tame the arbitrariness of distant power. At a glacial pace—taking different courses if you compare China after Confucius with the West after Plato and Cicero—societies gradually hedged in those at the pinnacle of power with what we conventionally call institutions, systems bigger than the powerful themselves that held the powerful in certain ways to account. None was anywhere near perfect, and the institutions themselves could be bent to terrible ends. But nonetheless, over a long

period of time and with countless fits and starts, we learned
something about how to tame the worst of power.[1]

Yes, finding someone we can hold ourselves accountable to is good.
So is finding an existing organization to work with. Submitting to
others is a spiritual discipline that reminds us that we are not God and
that he is.

Patrick was an associate pastor in a West Coast church that was part
of a denomination with European roots. While performing his duties
well, he also wrote a personal blog on his own time that took up issues
regarding the Bible, theology, the church, history, and more. Over time
his blog began offering ideas on the Trinity and in particular the deity of
Christ that were at odds with the denomination's confession of faith and
most of church history. After carefully following the church's procedures
in such cases, the denomination removed Patrick from his position.

Of course, Patrick found this all very painful and difficult. How
would he support his family now? And what right did the church have
to take this action based on his personal writing that was done on his
own time, not as part of his employment? Wasn't he being persecuted
by a backward, fossilized institution? These are important questions.

One thing Patrick had failed to recognize, however, was that he was
also part of a community. He could not separate himself (or part of
himself) as an isolated entity, responsible only to himself. He was be-
holden to the Western idol of idealized freedom. As a result, he had
not consulted with church authorities before publishing what he knew
would be contested viewpoints. He had an ill-formed appreciation for
the biblical nature of the church of which he was a part.

Marie walked down a different path. She worked in the research
department of a Christian nonprofit and began writing a book she
knew might not sit well with the history and values of her employer.
So she went to the organization's president and said this. "I have
written a manuscript that wasn't part of my job which I hope to publish.

But I know it could be viewed as problematic by the organization. I'd like you to read it first, if you would. I'm not asking you to approve it or reject it, to tell me what to say or what not to say. What I'm asking is that you point out places to me where I could reword things so they would cause you less trouble. I will be happy to take those suggestions under consideration as I proceed."

Here Marie showed respect for the organization's culture, beliefs, and leaders. She showed wisdom by getting advice at a preliminary stage from those above her, making sure they were not caught by surprise. But she also retained the right to make the final decision, maintaining her integrity as a scholar. She didn't want to leave the organization, but she was savvy enough to know that publication could potentially lead to this. As it turned out, she got her input, incorporated the president's suggestions as she could, published the book, and has remained an employee in good standing.

Social reality, biblical norms, and church practice all affirm that we inevitably belong to a larger whole. All our actions reflect on our community, and our community is the source of whatever authority we have. Most of the cultures in the rest of the world understand this implicitly. That is the way the cultures in the Bible also operated. We do not have the unfettered freedom to do, say, or write whatever we please.

WHEN LEADERSHIP IS RESTRICTED

While aligning ourselves with existing organizations may sound good in theory, one legitimate concern comes from women and people of color. Many institutions, including those in some conservative Christian traditions, are largely led by white males. As a result, the ability of marginal people to lead and be heard has been limited. The digital revolution has given voice to many who were once voiceless. Wouldn't putting ourselves under authority potentially mean returning to obscurity? This is a legitimate issue.

One solution is for such organizations to begin deliberately (yes, institutionally) making diverse leadership a core value, giving visibility and responsibility to groups that have only been incidentally represented before. Even organizations that might have theological or philosophical reasons for limiting some positions to certain categories of people can creatively find ways to give others more influence.

I was fortunate to work for over forty years for an organization that had this core value, making progress (three steps forward, two steps back) over decades. For several years my boss was a woman. And when I had the opportunity to groom my successor as editorial director when I retired, I had the freedom to do that with the person I thought was the best for the job. Nobody offered the slightest objection that I was mentoring a woman. The only response I got was, Yes, of course, she's the obvious choice.

Many denominations, service organizations, and parachurch ministries have very open policies regarding leaders and speakers. It may take some investigation, but I believe most of us could find a group that would embrace us and whose other core values and beliefs we could also embrace. A home may already be prepared for us if we will only look and be willing to step away from the idol of individualism.

Still there may be times when aligning with an existing group is not an option. Then we should try to build up a structure around ourselves that gives advice (if not actual direction) and keeps us accountable. This may start with one or two people; more can be added as appropriate. A board or council of advisers should consist of strong, independent-minded people who will not be afraid to tell us what they think is right.

Such counselors offer another advantage—defense and protection when unfair criticism comes. They are there to come to our aid when challenges arise from the outside. By placing ourselves under authority, we can be assured that we won't stand alone.

And what should guide our guides? Certainly we need to produce key documents like a statement of faith, a mission statement, core values, and so forth, which we might model after those from likeminded organizations we admire. These can be used by us and our board or support team to discern, as time goes on, if we are staying true to our purpose and goals.

One helpful touchstone for developing and evaluating such key documents is the Wesleyan Quadrilateral. While John Wesley never explicitly articulated these four resources for his work, he clearly used them all. They are Scripture, tradition, reason, and experience.

The first is Scripture. We begin with God's Word. We want to know what it says, what it means, and what it means for our life and work. It is the measure of truth. It evaluates us. Not the other way around.

Second is tradition. With so many apparently different interpretations of Scripture, how do we know if ours is correct? One approach is to weigh it against the consensus of the church throughout its history. That is, by tradition. If we are coming up with a view that is at odds with the creeds or the historical views on the Trinity, the full divinity and full humanity of Jesus, his bodily resurrection, or other core tenets or practices of the faith, we should be suspicious of ourselves. We may be right, but probably we are not.

One argument against tradition as a guide and guard is the history of the church's views on slavery. Did it really take us one thousand eight hundred years to figure out that Scripture is against slavery? Wasn't the tradition massively and tragically wrong on that point?

What is ignored is that as Christendom took hold in the Roman Empire, slavery began to wane and eventually disappeared. In the early years of the church, slaves were accepted as full members. Also "the clergy began to argue that no true Christian (or Jew) should be enslaved" and urged owners to free their slaves. Almost a millennium before the Civil War, the church (convinced by Scripture) ended the last remnants of the institution.[2]

The problem in the West was not that the traditional interpretation of Scripture supported slavery (it didn't) but that the traditional interpretation against slavery was ignored.

The third leg of the quadrilateral is reason. We should not be afraid to use the brains God gave us to think through issues. As I wrote elsewhere, "The ability to think, to think logically and carefully is not a merely human exercise. It is a God-given ability. And if we don't use it, we disparage not only the gift but the Giver. Education, learning, logic should all come into play as we seek to hear Jesus's voice."[3] Reading widely and learning from experienced, educated authorities can be invaluable as we shape our goals and make our plans. Research can also be key. What other organizations are doing similar work? What can we learn from them or how could we partner with them?

Last is experience. What has life taught us? Do we find certain types of events repeating in our life that we should pay attention to (successes, failures, joys, problems)? What are we good at? What motivates us?

Frederick Buechner famously said, "The place God calls you to is the place where your deep gladness and the world's deep hunger meet."[4] That nicely puts all this into one bundle. With some thought, prayer, research, and discussion with others, we can discern our answer. Buechner's axiom can also be used by an organization (or your newly forming group) to set direction and parameters. Combining that with the other sides of the quadrilateral (Scripture, tradition, reason) we can have assurance we are starting on solid footing.

We have no perfect solution for assuring that our writing is under adequate spiritual authority. But lacking perfect solutions is true in all of life. That should never stop us, however, from taking a step forward and seeking to do what is right for us, for others, and for the kingdom.

20

THE COURAGE
TO CREATE
AND LET GO

RECENTLY I WAS TALKING WITH ROB, a friend who had been an editor for decades with several prominent publishers. Rob told me he was working informally with Harvey, a longtime friend in the sciences.

Harvey had been asked to write a history of a well-known science foundation that he had worked with for many years. The foundation wanted something they could use with supporters and the general public to help them grow in appreciation for science. Harvey knew many of the famous scientists of the era and had a first-row seat at the development of many key scientific breakthroughs. The foundation thought he was the perfect choice.

Yet the project stalled.

"He can't seem to get started," Rob told me. "He thinks he needs to write a history of the whole of Western thought and is mired in research."

"Has he written a book before?" I asked.

"No," said Rob.

Immediately I knew the problem. First-Book Syndrome.

What is first-book syndrome? It's a common malady that can afflict ordinary people as well as those who have worked with words all their lives. It is a special form of writer's block deserving attention. What can be the symptoms?

One of the most common is what we see in Harvey. He thinks the book must be about everything. It doesn't and shouldn't. A book about everything is really a book about nothing. Readers don't want to know everything about everything. They want to know how to barbecue vegetables (not cook everything) or make better use of social media (not all technology) or get their young children to bed at night (not learn about all parenting at all stages) or learn about how people lived in medieval France (not in the entire history of the planet). But Harvey can't see that the book will be better if it is more limited, if a slice of his vision becomes the whole project.

Related to first-book syndrome is not knowing where to start. Since the topic of our first book seems vast (it must be since it needs to be about everything), we could start in a dozen different ways. Too many options can create paralysis.

Another symptom can be never-ending research. We can always find more books to read, more people to interview, more places to visit. The possibilities are limitless. How do we draw the line? In this case paralysis is not the problem but the opposite—perpetual motion. We never stop preparing to actually write.

The last symptom can be the inability to let go of our image of the ideal book. We have a vision of what we want to accomplish and what the book can be—it is good to read, delightful to the eye, and desirable for gaining wisdom. Nothing else will do. Our hands are tightly gripped around this ideal, and we just can't let go.

In Harvey's case, I suggested that Rob try to get him to start small. I said, "Ask Harvey to pick one anecdote from one scientist he knew that was funny, surprising, or revealing of a larger truth. Just write that one story. After that, Harvey could pick another anecdote from another scientist and write that."

Another strategy would be for Rob to suggest changing the mandate. Put the book on hold. Change the goal to something less intimidating, like writing a series of blog posts or articles made up of these anecdotes that could be serialized over a period of months.

If that goes well, after a year or so, Rob and Harvey could sit down, look over the pieces, and revisit the idea of a book. Maybe a new vision for the project will emerge. If it does, it will likely have a much narrower focus and be a much better book.

BEHIND THE SYNDROMES

If you manage to overcome first-book syndrome, you can always look forward to second-book syndrome. James W. Sire almost never wrote another book because his first book, *Papers on Literature, Models and Methods* bombed, selling less than a thousand copies. Fortunately, he overcame second-book syndrome, listened to the encouragement of others, and eventually wrote *The Universe Next Door*, which to date has sold over three hundred thousand copies.

If failure doesn't produce second-book syndrome, success just might. Alan Fadling's first book, *An Unhurried Life*, won a book award, sold well, and enjoyed great reviews. Now he thought, *How in the world do I top my first effort? How can my second book be anything but a disappointment to readers of the first?*[1] Eventually, he too managed to overcome this barrier and wrote *An Unhurried Leader*.

How did these authors rise above these syndromes and similar writing afflictions? In chapter seven I offered some practical ideas for dealing with writer's block. In this chapter I want to take a closer look at some of the emotional and spiritual dynamics that can be at play.

Ironically, paralysis and perpetual motion can both result from the same source—fear. We fear we won't measure up, either to our own standards or to those of others. We fear the criticism we imagine could or will come our way. It's too long. It's too short. It's too loose. It's too rigid. There's too much humor. It's too sober. There's not an original thought. It's too idiosyncratic.

The solution? Don't ever finish. Keep working and fussing and revising. Never say you are done and never send it off into the wide world, alone, and unprotected.

An even better solution is to never start. If we never begin, we will never finish. Problem solved! Write a paragraph and delete it. Write a few sentences and scratch them out. Sit and look at the wall or at the ceiling. Play with the cat. Straighten the desk. Get another cup of coffee. Certainly we can't go wrong with caffeine.

With all these dynamics at work, even starting small may not be enough to get someone like Harvey unstuck. Something more may be needed.

That something can be courage. It takes courage to write, to create. And it takes courage to finish. I remember hearing pastor and author Calvin Miller give a talk about the first chapter of Genesis—the most cosmic creative effort in the history of, well, the cosmos. And how did God go about it?

First, he created light. Then he did something very interesting. He stepped back for a moment to consider what he had just done. Yes, he thought, it was good. Maybe we need a little more though.

So next he separated the waters above from the waters below. After that he separated dry land from the seas. And once again he took a moment to review his effort. Once more he thought it was good. But again he decided something else was needed.

Through six cycles God proceeded in this same way—creating, evaluating, doing more. Then he does a remarkable thing. He stops. He stops creating and he stops evaluating. He stops adding, reworking, tinkering. He rests. He sends his world out for others to look at, enjoy, use, contemplate, watch over, and, yes, to criticize and abuse.

Whether you are making a meal, painting a landscape, devising a curriculum, or cultivating a garden, there comes a time when you need to serve the food, hang the picture, let others study the material, or harvest the fruit of your labors—all the while knowing it won't be perfect. It takes courage to create and courage to stop creating.

Where does the courage come from? From trust. First, we trust in ourselves, in our experience, our hours of training, our instincts honed over months or years of learning our craft. Courage comes from trusting in what we enjoy and delight in, not worrying overmuch about what others might find funny or entertaining or enlightening or moving. Then we are at rest in ourselves, even with our weaknesses and limitations.

In *The Screwtape Letters* C. S. Lewis offers this famous description. Someone with humility "could design the best cathedral in the world, and know it to be the best, and rejoice in the fact, without being any more (or less) or otherwise glad at having done it than he would be if it had been done by another." The idea, Lewis continues, is for someone "to be so free from any bias in his own favour that he can rejoice in his own talents as frankly and gratefully as in his neighbour's talents—or in a sunrise, an elephant, or a waterfall."[2]

No morbidity here. No sourness. No being glum and gray. Humility instead allows us to see all the light in the world.

THE COURAGE TO LOVE AND LET GO

Courage also comes from trusting others, from entrusting our work with others. We trust our readers enough to enjoy it, benefit from it, or to disagree with and even dislike it. We allow them to give their honest opinions and trust that they are not making a personal attack or superficially saying it's wonderful because they are your mother.

If we are wise, we will trust our work with people to get their input before it is offered publicly. If we have a writing assignment as a student, employee, or volunteer, the one who gave us the task is our reviewer. If the piece is to be published, we trust the comments and suggestions of editors who have professional expertise. They can save us from embarrassing errors and make our work better. One writer I worked with always said, "Blessed are the wounds of a friend—prior to publication." How much better to get criticism from one in private than from a thousand in public! After all, criticism is not just something to be endured. It is something to help us grow and improve.

Yet not taking criticism personally is one of the hardest parts of writing. What we create reflects who we are or who we think we are or who we want to be. When our writing is criticized, do we not hurt? When it is cut, do we not bleed? So we tend to protect, guard, defend what we've written or maybe just keep it under wraps indefinitely. At some point, however, we must separate ourselves from what we have created.

The mindset that helps me gain some emotional distance is to think of writing as my job. I am working for others, not for me. I'm trying to serve them and meet their needs, not mine. Jobs have sales and production goals. Likewise, I cold-bloodedly set a target to produce a certain number of words each day or to finish a project by a certain date. Criticism from "customers" is not about me but about the product. I use that to help me do better and produce more.

When God rested from all his work, he faced criticism too. Adam complained about "the woman you put here with me." Eve complained about the snake. The people of Israel complained about not having enough food or drink in the desert (Genesis 3:12-13; Numbers 20:4-5). We complain about the problems in our lives and our world. Yet God sent his creation out, knowing these disappointments would come. He sent it out because of love.

Courage also comes from trusting God. I've studied and taught the Gospel of Mark for years. One of the first things I learned was that early in the Gospel, running from about the end of chapter 4 all the way through the end of chapter 6, fear becomes a prominent theme.

The disciples are in a boat afraid of a storm, and then, ironically, they are suddenly afraid of Jesus when he calms the storm. Next some demons, calling themselves Legion and who possess a man, are afraid Jesus will torture them, though he doesn't. Then the townspeople are ironically afraid when Jesus stills the demonic storm in the man by sending the evil spirits into a herd of pigs. A sick woman fears exposure after touching Jesus to be cured of her twelve-year malady. A prominent man named Jairus fears his twelve-year-old daughter will die.

Intertwined with this theme of fear in Mark is that of faith. Often we think of faith as having a resolute state of mind. Faith, we think, is not letting any doubts seep into the foundation of our thoughts and undermine our positive attitude. If we can just screw up our conviction tightly enough, we can banish all uncertainty.

Frankly, I am just not very good at that. Problems, worries, and difficulties are frequent visitors who overstay their welcome all too often. Money, illness, conflict all play a part. So do the larger issues of hatred, violence, inequality, the environment, wars, and rumors of wars that plague society.

Despite such flaws, I am encouraged that the Bible rarely portrays faith as mental toughness and mere positive thinking. Nor is it as simple as an absence of fear. Rather, faith is much more closely aligned with something we *do* than with something we *think* or *feel*. Faith is more about obedience than inner certainty.

By faith, we are told, Abraham went to a country he knew almost nothing about. By faith Moses went to Pharaoh even after arguing with God about his deficiencies. By faith the people crossed the Red Sea. By faith the sick woman touched Jesus' garment. By faith Jairus let Jesus see his daughter even when everyone else thought it was pointless. By faith the disciples kept following Jesus despite their fears, misunderstandings, and failures.

By faith, then, I go to resolve a conflict even when I fear rejection. By faith I give a tenth of my income to kingdom work even when resources seem meager. By faith I volunteer at a food pantry even though that seems futile in the face of the immensity of the world's needs. By faith I stop writing and revising, call my work finished, and send it out for people to read and perhaps benefit from, even though I could be criticized.

Courage is not the absence of fear or doubt. Courage is doing the right thing in the presence of fear or doubt. In that I take comfort.

21

STEWARDS WITH
A MESSAGE

Lauren DeStefano tells us, "Give someone a book, they'll read for a day. Teach someone how to write a book, they'll experience a lifetime of paralyzing self doubt."[1]

The psychological, spiritual, social, and emotional pitfalls of writing are so numerous and varied that writing anything seems nothing short of a miracle. Throughout this book I've sought to provide the tools and skills needed to write better and to give you more confidence as you do so. It is time to face a few last challenges.

MAKING OUR MESSAGE KNOWN

Many questions crowd into the seats next to us as uninvited traveling companions on our writing journey. The first is a topic we considered near the beginning—our audience. This time, however, the question is not, Who is my audience? but, How do I attract an audience? We want others to enjoy and benefit from our work. While writing is one thing, however, advocating for what we have written feels like something entirely different.

Some of us are naturally gregarious and have no trouble connecting with people, chatting about ourselves, our work, our ideas—all the while making those we talk to feel like the most important people in the world. Many of us, however, are quiet souls who love nothing better than working alone in an office or in the splendid solitude of a crowded coffee shop, tapping away at our laptop with earbuds firmly implanted to block any last distractions. For us, speaking to five or ten or a hundred is as appetizing as eating charcoal.

The reality is, however, that more and more publishers depend on authors to build a following to help ensure success in the marketplace. One author told me, "After I finished writing my book, I thought my job was done. I then discovered that my job was only half done."

The traditional model is, of course, that authors write books and publishers sell books. But, as explained in appendix A, that has changed. Publishers rely on authors to make a book visible—in fact, to make themselves visible so they can make the book known.

Authors, they say, need a platform, a place to stand where they can be seen above the crowd. In practical terms this means obtaining endorsements from well-known people the authors have personal contact with, networking with interested organizations who can publicize or sell the book, writing blogs and articles, being active in social media, speaking regularly to groups where their books can be sold, and much more.

All this can seem unnatural to many or unpleasantly self-promotional. Whether it comes easily or not, however, we need a framework for understanding these efforts that centers not on ourselves but on our message.

The psalmists, the prophets, and the apostles were not shy about proclaiming or (to use the language of the King James Bible) "publishing" their message. Their goal was not to have their name in lights, to sell out Madison Square Garden, or to live in a celebrity mansion. Their goal was to proclaim their message, a message of the greatness of God and his wondrous works as well as his judgment. The apostles proclaimed the cross; the resurrection; the One who triumphed over death, sin, and hell; and the new era that had dawned. If they drew attention to themselves, that was to serve the larger purpose of giving voice and credibility to their message.

We, likewise, don't seek to build a platform for ourselves but for our message—so it can be heard. Do we want people to flourish in some particular way socially, culturally, mentally, physically, emotionally, or spiritually? Do we believe we have something to say to nurture that? Then seeking to build a platform is as proper as seeking to write.

What if we do not succeed in building a platform? What if our writing does not get published or find a wider readership? What if our message doesn't get a broad hearing? This can be the second uninvited traveling companion on our writing journey. The best way to deal with such fears is to be clear about our goals. If our goal is to have a popular blog, be a sought-after columnist, or sell tens of thousands of copies, we may succeed, but we may not.

As writers we need different goals. The first is to be faithful. Are we following as God has guided us through prayer, Scripture, experience, using the reason he gave us, and the counsel of others? If we are, we have not failed. The second goal is to grow and flourish as God desires. We aim to improve in our craft as writers, to learn something as we research and write, and put out a strong effort. We always have room for success in these things.

AWKWARD PRAISE

If we are fortunate enough to gain a readership, the third uninvited traveling companion still may await to question us. When people find out we are an author or make a point of meeting us because we have published, we may suddenly feel like a rare mammal being gawked at in a zoo. The attention we sought to put on our message, despite our best efforts, can become focused on us.

When excessive flattery or even honest praise comes our way, we may not be sure how to respond. What do we say? Should we deflect the compliment and say other writers are better? Is some profound or witty comment expected? Or is a simple "Thanks" or "I appreciate that" right?

If we've been fawned over and heard too many admiring comments, it may drive us away from our admiring public. Even though we know as an author that success can involve building some name recognition and a following, the last thing we may want is to stand in a crowd with everyone's attention focused on us. A desire to resist flattery could seem noble, but it may also be a desire to escape.

After all, God gave you a gift—of communicating, maybe clearly, perhaps compellingly, possibly artfully. He's given you particular experiences and insights. Yes, we can exercise that gift by writing in our study with little or no human contact. But our writing may not be the only way to give to people.

Leonard Nimoy, best known for playing Spock in *Star Trek*, went to many public events he was invited to, even dressed as his TV and movie character. Some might consider that demeaning, but he considered it his job. He also knew fame is fleeting. There was no guarantee how long he could support his family in this way. To him, connecting with the public was just part of what it meant to be an actor.[2]

In contrast, one Olympic skating medalist in a Disney parade with Mickey Mouse was overheard to say, "This is so corny. This is so dumb. I hate it."[3] I can understand that. Mickey can be pretty commercial. Yet here might have been an opportunity to reframe such an event. Certainly many children and parents were excited to see a world-famous athlete in person. Perhaps we could see the occasion as a way to say thank you and give a bit of happiness to others.

We might have another reaction to such attention and praise, however. We may quietly, secretly begin to hope for it, to look forward to it, to expect it, and then to need it—like an addiction.

If some of us shy away from an adoring public, others of us are energized by people. They give us a buzz that makes us feel alive. We can't get enough.

We need to be careful that people who admire us become neither victims of our scorn nor objects for gratifying our own egos. The balance point, I think, is to treat all our readers (whether they are positive or negative about our work) with respect, gratitude, and generosity. We do this by turning our focus away from ourselves and toward others, to see life through their eyes, to take time to understand what they need instead of what we need.

They are the ones who read what we write. We might be happy to create amazing prose that no one reads, but most of us want our work to give joy or insight or make a difference in the lives of others. Being willing to interact with our readers prepares us for the upsides and downsides of praise and criticism.

STEWARDS OF A KING

By exercising the spiritual disciplines of generosity and gratitude we also turn our attention to the One who is the source of our gifts and abilities. We don't have ourselves to congratulate for our talents. We are stewards. We have been given certain resources we are responsible to handle wisely, increasing and expanding God's presence in the world.

The idea of stewardship is deeply rooted in what Genesis has in mind when it says humans were created in the image of God (Genesis 1:27-28). When God gave the first man and woman in the garden a calling to be fruitful, to multiply, and to subdue the earth, this was not a command to dominate nature. Stewards are given something that belongs to another and are made responsible to not just protect it but to use it as the owner intended (see Matthew 25:14-30). God's intention was to expand his loving presence throughout his creation. As stewards we join in that work.

Genesis 1 describes the formation of the cosmos the way the building of ancient temples was often described in ancient literature.[4] Temples were places where the deity resided. The implication is that the whole cosmos is like a temple where God resides.

From descriptions in the Old Testament of the tabernacle and temple, we see that various parts were intended to represent the whole earth and the whole cosmos, symbolizing God's presence throughout creation. A large brass bowl filled with water was called the sea (1 Kings 7:23-26). The altar was to be made of earth and uncut stones (Exodus 20:24-25). Representations of vegetation were to adorn the temple (1 Kings 7:18-26, 42, 49-50). The seven candles represented the five visible planets, sun, and moon (Exodus 25:31-35). The colors of the curtain and the priests' robes were of the sky (Exodus 26:31, 28:5).[5]

The first chapters of Genesis also present the sanctuary in the garden as a kind of cosmic temple in miniature where God was also to dwell. Why does God do this? Because his plan is for his ruling presence to expand from the garden (representing the cosmos) to eventually fill the whole earth.

That is the context in which the man and the woman are said to be in God's image. They are appointed vice regents to participate in filling the earth with God's presence. When we parent or develop software or make a meal or do plumbing, truck driving, table waiting, emailing, or nursing—we are living out the image of God in us. When we make something orderly or beautiful, when we bring joy or comfort, when we live out and tell others of God's grace, we are being stewards of what God has given us, bearing witness to his kingdom that will fill the earth.

This is the stewardship God has called us to when we write and when we connect with our readers. Setting limits on our interaction with others is sensible and appropriate. We need to preserve time for our other responsibilities. But when we do get reactions to our work, we can respond with grace—with the grace he has given us.

PEACE TO SERVE

Being annoyed by or attracted by the attention of others may be the least of our troubles. We may have an even harder time with the fourth and last uninvited traveling companion. What do we do when people are critical, especially in the anonymity of social media? Even those we know personally may react negatively, perhaps out of jealousy, perhaps especially if they are writers themselves who have been less successful. Because how people respond to our writing can feel so personal, the effects of praise or criticism can send us into levels of Paradise or the Inferno that Dante never imagined.

How do we deal with all this? Here are a few final words for your encouragement.

Remember, it's just about me. Why did I write? Probably, first and foremost, I wrote it for myself. And that's not a bad thing. I wanted something inside me to get out. So I did it. Was the process enjoyable? Did I improve my skills? Was I pleased with the result? Did I learn something along the way? Well, then, that's worthwhile. It's enough. If people are critical or dismissive, I still got something out of it. Did people like it? That's a bonus.

Remember, it's not about me. A pastor told me that sometimes he preached and felt dry, but the Spirit took what he said and moved people in amazing ways. At other times he preached with joy and energy, only to see no response. These reactions helped him learn that preaching is not about him or about how well he does. It is about whether or not the Spirit shows up, and that is the Spirit's decision, not his. His job is to preach faithfully. So he does.

Say thank you. Gratitude keeps life in perspective. We didn't write alone. We owe a debt to those who taught us, encouraged us, guided us, to those whose writings influenced us, whose words we've heard, who gave time and supported us in our writing, who gave us advice along the way, who bought and read our work, who recommended it to others. We need to say thanks to them. This is not just to deflect praise but to keep us grounded.

Expect criticism. It happens. Just being aware of that ahead of time can help you deal with it when it comes. Publishing publicly means we open ourselves to public criticism. This should neither surprise nor dismay us. In the case of reviews on websites or in magazines, we should almost never respond. Our job was to write. Their job is to review. This is simply part of being in the public square.

Social media is generally not a good place to try to resolve criticism. Again, people are going to say what they are going to say. You had your say; let them have theirs. If you have a personal relationship with someone who has said something especially problematic, handle it personally if possible, away from the often-distorting glare of the internet.

Dan Reid, the illustrious (now retired) academic editor of Inter-Varsity Press, once said, "If you are starting out as a biblical scholar and the notion of having your dearly held 'contribution' summarily overturned in twenty to thirty years unnerves you, may I suggest a career in accounting?" Which is to say, grow a thick skin and realize that others shall dish it out to you as you have dished it out to others. That's part of how scholarship works. I critique those who came before me, and those who follow me critique me. Hopefully, we all learn and move forward because of these discussions, even if not in a straight line.

Get a support team. The equally illustrious editorial director of InterVarsity Press, Cindy Bunch, notes that some authors develop a launch team to help them promote a book when it is published. Maybe we also need a spiritual launch team. They can help us sort through the spiritual and emotional implications of praise and criticism. In addition, the book may or may not sell well or few may read our blogs. Or something in between. It's always a guessing game in publishing. Any possible result can have spiritual implications. Our team can help us there too.

Remember, my identity is in Christ. I am not defined by what I write. I am not defined by the praise or criticism or sales of my book or the number of hits on my blog. My identity is in Christ, who loves me with an everlasting love, who made me, who put that urge to write in me, and who helped me get it out. I look at him and find myself.

Now go in peace, to write and serve the Lord.

Appendix A

GET THEE TO
A PLATFORM

W HY DO PUBLISHERS OFTEN EXPECT AUTHORS to help promote and sell books? Publishers still send out books for review; set up media interviews for authors; get the books into the wholesale and retail distribution systems; publicize them through direct mail, in catalogs, and on websites; and much more. But all of these efforts have in recent years been less effective in selling books. Why?

Primarily because the number of bookstores has declined, to perhaps half of what there was twenty-five years ago.[1] And why is that?

First, in the late 1980s a wave of megabookstores began (Borders, Barnes & Noble, etc.) that sucked away a lot of business from smaller bookstores. Then came the wave of the big-box stores (Walmart, Target, Costco, etc.) taking business from the megabookstores and the remaining independents with massive discounting on a few bestsellers. By the late 1990s Amazon.com and other online booksellers hit the scene, giving bookstores another blow.

The rise of self-publishing has not made it easier for publishers either. From 2010 to 2016 the number of new, self-published books *per year* rose from one hundred fifty three thousand to seven hundred eighty seven thousand.[2] This increased competition makes it harder for any book to stand out and get noticed.

Publishers have learned to survive by increasingly going direct to consumers, since retail outlets collectively aren't there to do the job they used to do (though there has recently been a slight rise in the number of independent stores). Sometimes a publisher will send out catalogs or other mailings to consumers. And they also rely on authors to be directly in touch with potential readers and make the book available.

The lesson for authors, of course, is you can't just pitch your ability to write a good book to a prospective publisher or agent. You also have to pitch your ability to promote and to directly reach people who will buy your book.

While this can at times seem commercial, Al Hsu offers this perspective:

In Nehemiah 8:4-5, we see a Biblical example of several key components to a good platform. "Ezra the teacher of the Law stood on a high wooden platform built for the occasion." It goes on to say that a small group of 13 people stood on his left and right. "Ezra opened the book. All the people could see him because he was standing above them." This passage highlights three crucial pieces in developing platform.

Visibility. Ezra stood on a high platform. The people could see him and he could be found amidst the crowd. For an effective platform, you have to be seen somehow, somewhere—through social media, writing, conference speaking or other ways. This will look different to different authors and genres of books.

Credibility. The passage highlights that Ezra was a known teacher of the Law. He had the knowledge, the authority, the wisdom to teach. For an effective platform, you need some degree of expertise in the topic, research, positional authority, or in other ways be someone that people will listen to.

Community. The wooden platform was built by others, and Ezra was accompanied by 5 people on his right and 7 people on his left. He wasn't alone. For an effective platform, you need friends, networks, organizations, communities, launch teams, etc. that magnify your voice and take your message further than you could go yourself.

Our platforms are a mix of visibility, credibility, and community. We need all three. As you think about your own platform, it might be helpful to consider where you are stronger and where you are weaker and focus your initial efforts in the weaker areas.[3]

BUILDING A PLATFORM

Here are some thoughts on how you could develop more in these areas:

Expertise. Your credibility on a topic comes from the education and experiences you've had in that area. This can be due to a job you've had in a certain field or in years of significant volunteer work. If you lack formal training or education in that field, it can be beneficial to get it. Credibility may also come from important personal experiences you've had with hardships or successes. If you publish online or speak regularly to groups, this can give you recognized authority as well.

Connecting. Network with those who are interested in and care about the same things you do. Find and join the organizations that focus on your areas of interest. These can be professional organizations or volunteer groups. In this way, you can find out who are key figures. But don't look at it just as an opportunity to get support from them. Find ways to support others in their work.

Influencers. As you network with like-minded people online or in person, start making a list of those you encounter who are themselves networked to your target audience. These are people who could be endorsers, who might be able to promote your book within their organizations, who could invite you to speak in certain venues, or who would simply be happy to have a copy of your book and talk to others in their circles about it. This list will come in handy when your book releases.

Support team. Pulling together a support team can be worthwhile. This could be six to sixty people you ask to join you in making your book known by talking about it in their circles, reviewing it on Goodreads and Amazon, getting copies into the hands of well-known people, mentioning it on social media, and so forth. This can be the most important single thing you do, especially if you are in a culture that does not encourage putting yourself forward. But there may be no problem with others doing that for you.

Writing. One way to build a platform toward book publication is by writing for magazines, newspapers, or journals. To build credibility for periodical publication, write for websites. To build credibility for that, write on your own blog or website.

Social media. Facebook, Twitter, and Instagram are some of the key social media outlets today. Take time to add friends and followers to your lists. Follow and engage with others as well. Social media needs to be a two-way street, so interact with what others post rather than merely focus on what you post. And when you post items, use the 80/20 rule. Most of what you post should be general, everyday items about your life that don't particularly tie in to what you are writing. The other 20 percent can be about your books, blogs, articles, speaking, and so forth. You might want to aim to post daily or several times a week.

The book community. Create an author profile on Goodreads and Amazon. Especially notice those people who regularly post reviews of books in the areas you are writing in. Make note of them and when your book comes out, ask them (along with a couple dozen other friends) if they'd be willing to read your book and post an honest review. (Offer to send a free copy.) If your publisher agrees, you may want to send a prepublication electronic copy to some so they can have their review ready to post right when your book releases.

Distill. One of the most helpful tools you can have is a thirty-second summary of your key idea and motivation for your book. This is the proverbial elevator pitch—the best, briefest way to explain what you are writing and why it matters. My publisher asked me to do this in fifty words for this book. Here's what I wrote:

Writing is hard work. Writing well is even harder. But there are ways not only to make it easier but better. Having spent my whole career as a writer and editor, I offer a book on craft and character for nonfiction writers.

Websites and blogs. Having any kind of internet presence is extremely helpful. Even a simple web page can be valuable. A blog can be a good way to get your thoughts out so people know your areas of expertise. One caution: don't give too much of your book away in a blog or web page.

Podcasts. A podcast can be helpful. While equipment can be inexpensive, the sound quality can also seem cheap. Good editing can be costly as well. Consider whether you are good verbally or not. Have a regular dialogue partner to pitch you questions and offer some entertaining repartee. In any case, don't decide on this in isolation. See if it fits into your overall strategy, abilities, and platform.

Speaking. Look for opportunities to speak. These can come your way because of the networking you do. At first, don't be concerned if some of these are small and informal. Any practice you get in front of groups will be valuable. You'll begin to see what works for you and for your audiences. As you get more speaking opportunities, you may need to be selective based on how closely they fit your target audience or other criteria. Keep a list of your annual speaking events so in a book proposal publishers can see where you are speaking, what sizes the audiences are, and what groups/constituencies you are networking with.

Much more could be said about all this. Many books are available with dozens or hundreds of ideas. Check them out, but don't be overwhelmed. Pick just a few ideas that fit you and work with your audience. Some of the authors who regularly blog and publish books on platform and marketing include Michael Hyatt, Seth Godin, Jeff Goins, Chad R. Allen, and Terry Whalin. Check out these and others to find what's most helpful for you.

What if you work hard at all this and it just doesn't seem to be coming together? In that case, Al Hsu writes, "authors may need to readjust their expectations and discern whether they are truly called to a particular writing ministry. Counsel and discernment from a trusted Christian community will help authors sense whether a particular book project or ministry involvement lines up with their vocation and calling."[4]

In any case, seeking to build a platform may present challenges to what I've said elsewhere in this book about pride, humility, and the need to keep yourself in perspective. But balance is possible. If God has given you a light, you shouldn't hide it under a bushel basket. As noted in chapter nineteen, however, we need to make ourselves accountable to others when it comes to removing the basket. If we have something of value, we should be willing to share it. We just shouldn't think that we are the light!

EDITORS AND AGENTS DO MAKE COWARDS OF US ALL

F OR THOSE ON THE OUTSIDE, the publishing world can be strange and mysterious. It can seem half art and half business—or none of either. It can also feel clubby and ingrown. Allow me, then, to try to demystify what goes on inside the minds of agents and editors.

WHAT EDITORS AND AGENTS WANT IN AN AUTHOR
Perhaps surprisingly, when it comes to getting published, the most important thing may not be your idea but you. Agents and editors are looking not just for books that will sell but for authors they can work with over the long haul. When you meet or query an agent or editor, here are some dos and don'ts.

Do your homework. Show familiarity with what the publisher has produced or with the authors the agent has represented. Don't send your children's book proposals to agents or publishers who don't do children's books. Sending only to the right ones will increase your odds of success. Follow editors and agents on LinkedIn and Twitter to see what they are thinking and doing (but don't stalk them). Often they mention new projects they think are great and pet peeves they have. If a publisher's or agent's website says not to submit unsolicited proposals, don't. Find another way to connect. (See "The Biggest Mystery" at the end of this appendix.)

Be courteous and professional. Be gracious in your tone and confident in your presentation. Don't downplay your proposal ("I know it needs work"), but don't overplay it ("Sure to be a bestseller and blockbuster movie!").

Take advice. Be ready and willing to follow suggestions about the shape of the book, the nature of your platform, or anything else. When an agent or editor doesn't give an outright no, be cooperative. This is your chance to get in, remember. So don't aggressively push back or contradict. They probably know more about the business than you do—certainly more about *their* business. But they aren't perfect. So if you have questions, ask them straightforwardly, without an edge. On the other hand, don't act desperate or gush either. Be receptive to appropriate feedback.

Build your platform. Before you ever send in a proposal, it is best if you have already spent two to five years in building a platform (see appendix A).

Don't bad-mouth other agents, editors, or publishers. Don't say things like, "This other publisher I worked with didn't understand the project and let it die." If they hear you say bad things about others in the business, they will anticipate that you will spread bad opinions about them if things go a bit sour.

Don't send an angry response to a rejection. After all, you may want to work with this person down the road on something else. Don't burn your bridge. Rejection happens. Take it as an adult. It's not personal, really. Editors and agents manage huge workloads. They are also under financial pressure to produce for their organizations, which they must take seriously when evaluating book ideas. (See the following section on what they look for in a proposal and why.) If you want to respond, do so by saying thanks. Agents want polite, professional authors who will reflect well on them and enhance their relationships with publishers when the book finds a home.

WHAT EDITORS AND AGENTS
LOOK FOR IN A PROPOSAL

Agents and editors usually have a formal or informal grid they use to evaluate new proposals. Even with just a few years in the business they become adept at spotting good and bad ideas quickly. When I was a new editor, my boss, James Sire, told me, "You don't have to eat the whole pudding to tell if it's bad." Here are some of the questions editors or agents ask themselves to come to a quick decision.

Does this fit us? Agents immediately wonder, "Are there publishers I can send this to, those I've worked with before, who know me, who have a track record in this genre or topic?" Editors ask, "Is this a genre, topic, or format we've done before?" If not, it could be rejected before they finish the first sentence. To avoid this, do your homework (see above).

How is this new? While editors and agents look for perennial subjects in their sweet spots, they also look for fresh explorations or angles that haven't been addressed. Don't propose a book that covers the waterfront of parenting, which has been done many times. Pick something specific like helping middle schoolers with homework or helping toddlers eat well without battles or guilt. (Books on these topics probably already exist, but you get the idea.)

Did it grab me right away? An idea can't just be new. It should come early in the proposal (don't bury the lede) and present itself in an arresting way. Agents and editors are busy people. They may get hundreds of proposals a month. They have dozens or hundreds of existing authors they are working with. The proposal, the title, and any sample of the manuscript you send must pull them in immediately. Don't exaggerate the significance or sales potential of the project. Do present it as compellingly as possible. (See chapter one on opening lines and chapter ten on titling.)

Is this a new or published author? Although agents and editors tend to pursue previously published authors, many want to find a strong debut author with whom they can nurture a successful long-term relationship. In fact, counterintuitively, new writers can have an advantage over published authors. How? It can be hard to repeat one bestseller with another. And if the first book was a flop, well, that does not bode well for a second book. A new author is not encumbered by either kind of track record. Anything is possible.

Small- and medium-sized publishers are especially interested in new authors. Writers who succeed are often lured away by the large advances big publishers can offer. So smaller publishers always need new writers to fill the void.

Can I clearly see how the book needs to be revised to get it into publishing shape? Agents and editors want to see a proposal's potential and have a clear vision of how to get there. If it will take a lot of work, they may not have the time needed. So, as stated earlier, if they have suggestions to make, usually it is because they see possibilities. Be ready to respond positively.

Is the proposal sloppy? Proofread your proposal—many times. Typos look unprofessional. And if you can't even bother to get a proposal right, why should they trust you to take the time needed to get your ideas and research right?

Use a clean, simple format. Don't get fancy with layout or font choice. It can look like you're trying too hard—and unless you have design training, it may look amateurish.

THE BIGGEST MYSTERY

Often the biggest question writers have is, How do I find an agent or editor? It all seems so mysterious and frustrating. Some ideas include:

Go to writers' conferences where you can find an opportunity to sign up for a fifteen-minute conversation with an agent or editor.

Get an introduction from an established author you know or meet one at a conference and ask for help. Yes, it is about networking and who you know.

Check the agency or publisher website to see if unsolicited proposals will be reviewed or not. If they say no, they mean no.

While I can only give these few ideas here to find editors and agents, you can find more help in *Writer's Digest* or other online resources such as www.pw.org/literary_agents.

THE COAUTHOR DOTH PROTEST TOO MUCH, METHINKS

CONTRARY TO COMMON EXPECTATIONS, coauthoring is not easier than authoring a book on your own. Every editor knows this, but the myth persists. Why?

Primarily because it seems self-evident. Two authors bring twice as much experience and knowledge to a manuscript as one. So far so good. Their different areas of expertise can complement one another.

Maybe one author is a practicing marriage counselor while the other does marriage research. Maybe one is an entrepreneur and the other teaches business in college. Maybe one has lots of ideas and stories (about education, science, helping the jobless, raising teens, or doing youth work) and the other knows how to write. The two perspectives make for a stronger, more balanced book, right?

The different perspectives or areas of expertise, however, can also be a source of conflict. Practitioners and theoreticians see the world differently. Idea people have their thoughts and experiences organized in a certain way—which a writer will tell them just won't work in an article or book. One couple told me they almost didn't make it through coauthoring a book on marriage.

Another reason the myth persists is that we think coauthoring should cut the time of writing in half. If it takes twenty hours to write an article, then we assume each coauthor only spends ten hours each on it. But what often happens is that both authors end up spending about as much time on it as if each had written the whole thing (and still they get only half the fee). Why?

First, planning the research, the outline, and the stories must be discussed and agreed upon. Sure, when working alone you have to think it through, but ultimately you can just decide and start.

Second, remember those disagreements that arise when coauthors have different viewpoints? They take time to negotiate.

Third, often coauthors will divide up the writing responsibilities, then they rewrite or edit each other's portions. That is needed to give the piece a consistent voice so readers don't feel jerked back and forth between two very different styles from one section or chapter to the next. Again, this part of the process can take more time and negotiation than just revising your own draft of the whole.

Another challenge related to voice is, Who is speaking? Who is the "I" in the text? Is it author A or author B or both? I have not seen any perfect solution, but here are a few alternatives.

Option A. The voice is that of one author, in which case the other author is referred to in the third person (or not at all). The advantage is that this is less jarring for readers than the other options. The disadvantage is that one author may feel relegated to the position of junior partner.

Option B. The author's voice is always "we" unless a personal story is being told. In that case, the "I" is identified in parenthesis. For example, "I (Andy) got stuck on an airplane once when . . ." The advantage: each author is treated equally. The disadvantage: it is a bit jarring for the reader to swing back and forth between authors.

Option C. The author's voice is always "we," and when a personal story is being told, it is done in the third person for both authors.

("Once when Andy was stuck on an airplane . . .") The advantage is consistency of voice, but the disadvantage is that the book feels more impersonal when there is no "I."

Option D. Each chapter or subsection leads off with the name of the author of that portion of the book, which is then written in first-person singular. This may not work, however, when the stories from both authors are mixed in the same sections.

One more issue needs attention. Tom Woll in *Publishing for Profit* thinks certain understandings should be documented in the contract of multiauthor books to make sure things go smoothly. The reason: he has seen way too many projects break down entirely over such issues.

One author tells the publisher one thing, and the other author says the opposite. If the authors have an agent for the project, the agent can (and should) negotiate the differences for the publisher. Ultimately, the publisher needs to "know precisely who has the final contractual authority [and] . . . can provide definitive, *legally binding* solutions."[1] Contractual terms may be overkill, but he is right to point out the need to clearly (and in writing) settle these things beforehand.

Multicontributor books organized by a single person are usually easier and more straightforward in this regard. This person is the volume editor whose name appears on the title page. The volume editor is usually the one contractually responsible to the publisher for the book as a whole. (The volume editor is not the same as the house editor, an employee of the publisher who shepherds the book through the in-house publishing process.)

I may seem unnecessarily negative about coauthoring. After all, co-authors who work well together and complement each other can make for a stronger book produced in less time for each. In addition, I've enjoyed coauthoring many books and articles. My wife and I have had our differing views at various points in projects we've worked on, but for the most part we've divided the labor in ways that lean to each of our strengths. Thus we have tended to defer to each other in those areas, minimizing conflict and maximizing benefit.

Many authors are surprised at the difficulties that they may encounter. A wise editor will spell out for authors ahead of time what to anticipate and help them make key decisions (like voice or who has the last say) before work on the manuscript begins. That can facilitate a positive experience.

Appendix D

TO SELF-PUBLISH
OR NOT TO
SELF-PUBLISH

I SPENT DECADES AS THE EDITORIAL DIRECTOR for a traditional publisher. Do I encourage and support self-publishing—even self-ebook publishing? You bet.

Self-publishing used to be the crazy uncle in the attic of the publishing industry—awkward, embarrassing, and something you wanted to keep out of public view. Even its name, *vanity publishing*, sounded a bit sleazy. Paying a "publisher" to print and distribute your work had negative connotations. If a legitimate firm won't produce your book and pay you royalties, there must be something wrong with it. Right? Either it is commercially unviable or editorially substandard. It means someone is putting it in print just to satisfy their own vanity.

So why my change of heart?

First, just as I encourage people to read most anything (magazines, blogs, newspapers, websites, books, journals, and more), I think it is good for people to write (articles, fiction, nonfiction, poetry, letters, memoirs). Reading stimulates the mind and writing clarifies thought. Writing and reading are foundational to a good society—not only for entertainment but to transfer information and wisdom from one generation to another. So self-publishing? Of course.

Second, people want to write far more books than traditional publishers can absorb. The explosion of self-publishing in the last couple decades has put an exclamation point on that.

Third, self-publishing is easier than ever with more options than ever. Some services allow you to do most everything (and you pay them only as each book sells), others will handle all the headaches for you (in exchange for a large check from you), and still others offer an intermediate option between these extremes. Rather than try to provide more detail on this rapidly changing landscape, I suggest you research it online and talk to some who have already self-published.

I have several friends who have self-published memoirs or family histories. I think they are doing the right thing—for now. They produced them largely for themselves and their relatives, and they offer them for sale when they speak publicly. There may come a time, though, when they need the help of a traditional publisher.

TRANSITIONING TO TRADITIONAL PUBLISHING

Self-publishing can lead to successful traditional publishing. Andy Weir initially self-published *The Martian* with great success before he accepted Crown Publishing's offer. The same thing happened to Amanda Hocking. Fifty literary agents turned down her paranormal romance manuscripts, so she self-published an ebook. She writes fast (finishing a book in about a month) and her ebooks caught on, and now she is $2 million richer. As a result, not surprisingly, a traditional print publisher released her Trylle series.

Why go to a traditional print publisher when she was doing so fantastically well on her own? Amanda said she did it for a couple reasons: "E-books are taking up more of the market, but it's still somewhere between, like, 10 and 30 percent of the market. But also, I was kind of overwhelmed with the amount of work that I had to do that wasn't writing a book. I was writing more when I worked a day job than when I was writing full time because of how much time I devote to the whole publishing part."[1]

Even though an author gets more money than just a royalty from self-publishing, being responsible for preparing ebook files for multiple platforms, and printing, warehousing, shipping, marketing, and billing for print books can be a hassle. Self-published authors may also have trouble getting into many traditional outlets such as bookstores. In addition, even with lots of design software out there, the final product may just not look as professional as what an established publisher can do.

Instead of self-publishing being the Island of Misfit Books, it is now a place traditional publishers look to as a good potential source for their own programs. In appendix A I talk about the need for authors to establish a platform, that is, create a place from which they can be seen by the reading public. This means speaking, getting endorsements, blogging, and networking with organizations who might promote the book. And even when an author does all that, sometimes a publisher still will not believe that an author has enough platform to economically justify publication. So the book is turned down.

When books are successfully self-published, however, authors have absolute proof that they have a platform. Of course, successful self-publishing does not automatically turn into successful traditional publishing. Sometimes instead of creating a market, self-publishing can exhaust a market, so some caution is in order. But the days of editors automatically consigning self-published books to the reject pile are over.

REACHING THE WORLD (OR NOT)

With all the expectations for authors to do so much promotion, are there any other reasons to go with a traditional publisher over self-publishing? One consideration is selling rights.

A book is not just a physical object or a digital file. It is intellectual property that can be developed and disseminated in a variety of forms. All or part of a book can appear in audio form, in magazines and newspapers, on websites, and in blogs. Book clubs may be interested in licensing their own edition, or college professors may want to use a chapter in a custom textbook. Sometimes a book can inspire movies or ancillary products like greeting cards and T-shirts.

Most authors don't have the experience, time, or networks to maximize intellectual property rights. Many publishers, on the other hand, have full-time staff devoted to just this sort of activity.

One of the most common adaptations of a book is a translation. What can a publisher offer? Most have lists of hundreds of publishers around the world, to whom they regularly send promotion via mail or email. Rights managers may annually attend book conventions around the world, where they meet with international publishers to show them new books and make recommendations tailored to each publisher.

Based on years of corporate and personal experience, rights personnel will know which publishers will do well with certain types of books and authors. They will also know which international publishers to shy away from.

While a publisher can't guarantee rights sales, it can guarantee widely promoting subsidiary rights that the self-published are unlikely to undertake. In addition a publisher will manage all of the administrative details involved, including sending complimentary reading copies, negotiating contracts, collecting royalties, dealing with currency exchange, and following up when books are not published or royalties are not paid on time.

Here are a few stats to consider:

- Approximately 80 percent of the world's population lies outside the West.[2]
- Over half of all Christians now live outside the West.[3]

- Over 70 percent of books published in the world are in languages other than English.[4]

So if, as an author, your focus is on reaching your friends, family, those you speak to, and those connected to your organization, self-publishing may be for you. If you have wider desires and ambitions, a traditional publisher may be your choice.

A decision to self-publish is as individual as the author and the book. There is no one right answer. But if you are aiming for traditional publication and are having trouble getting a publisher to accept your book, self-publishing might be your next best bet.

Appendix E

THE COPYRIGHT'S
THE THING

C OPYRIGHT IS ONE OF THE MORE DIFFICULT and complicated concepts to wrap our minds around. That's largely because it has to do with an intangible object—the rights for intellectual property. Copyright is not the physical object of a book or a magazine. That is all the more obvious regarding blogs and other internet content. And to make it more complicated, you can't copyright an idea—only a fixed, tangible expression of an idea such as in a painting, recorded song, software program, or essay. So what is copyright? Simply put, copyright is the right to copy.

The law begins by assuming that the author owns the right to copy (works made for hire being the major exception). Copyright begins the moment of creation. It does not have to be registered with a government office, though that can help ensure legal protection.

Once a work is created, the author can permit others to copy the work. Authors can do this piecemeal or they can authorize one party to exclusively administrate rights to the work. That's where many publishing contracts come in.

In such agreements authors grant the right for a publisher to copy and sell the work. They can also allow the publisher to authorize others to copy the work—such as permission to quote, to include extracts in an anthology, to adapt the work to another medium like TV, to publish translated and other special editions, and so on. The publisher in that case functions like an agent for the author. In exchange, the publisher retains a percentage of the income the publisher receives through negotiation and sends the rest to the author.

If there is no publishing contract, then the author is responsible to sell rights and negotiate all these other uses. This can be time-consuming and challenging without experience, but the author will retain all the income paid for the right to copy.

While international copyright law has made things somewhat uniform around the world, variations exist from country to country. A great deal of helpful general and specific information on copyright and practices is available through national government websites like the following:

- United States: www.copyright.gov
- Canada: www.canada.ca/en/services/business/ip/copyright.html
- United Kingdom: www.gov.uk/copyright
- Australia: www.copyright.org.au

SELL OR RENT?

Over the years I've tried a variety of ways to explain how copyright and contracts work in practice. Here's one.

Copyright is like real estate. If you own a piece of property, you can do two things with it to get some money. First, you can sell the property. Second, you can rent it.

If you sell the property, you are relinquishing all rights to the property in exchange for payment. The new owner may build a sky-scraper on the land and make a gazillion dollars or lose a bunch of money because she paid you way too much. In either case, it has nothing to do with you. You are not helped or harmed, because after the sale you have no legal interest in the land anymore.

That is like a work for hire (selling some writing outright to another party). You simply don't own it. You are paid a one-time fee for the copyright, and after that you have no say whatsoever as to what happens to the work. Work-for-hire agreements are often used with employees (who get their salary in exchange for the intellectual property they create on the job). Freelancers often sign a work-for-hire agreement to do some writing that is part of a larger project or collection.

Now, instead of selling, what if you decide to rent your property? In doing so, you agree to allow someone to use the land and structures for a certain amount of time for certain purposes in exchange for an agreed upon periodic payment. But since you have transferred certain (not all) rights to the renter, you can't just do anything with the property you choose. You can't rent it out to a second renter while your original renters still live there. You can't tear down the building on the property. You can't hold a fiftieth anniversary party there for your parents.

At the same time you still have certain obligations. You probably have to keep the building in good repair. While you are restricted in many ways, you are nonetheless still the owner.

Likewise, you can also "rent" your copyright. You transfer certain rights for your creation for a certain period of time. But again, after having signed such a "rental" agreement, you can't do just anything you like with it. In many book contracts, all rights are transferred from the creator to the "renter" (or publisher), though usually not permanently. Now the publisher can exploit the work in a variety of ways and is obligated to compensate you, the creator, as agreed.

The benefits of such an arrangement are that you as an author don't have to deal with all kinds of details, problems, and questions you don't have the time or the desire to handle. In a sense, the publisher acts as both your rental agent and property manager.[1] That way you don't have to deal with renters—who don't pay or who annoy neighbors with loud music—or with finding new renters to keep the income flowing.

At the same time you are limited in what you can do with your own work by the terms of the publishing agreement you have signed. You are no longer allowed to give others permission to copy the work in an article, in a translation, in a collection, or otherwise. You have granted all those rights and responsibilities to the publisher for as long as the publishing agreement is in force. If someone comes to you with such a request, you must refer them to the publisher to handle things.

In such a case you may always own the copyright, and the work itself may still be copyrighted in your name (indicating that you are the owner). Because of your (rental) publishing agreement, however, what happens to your work is now in the hands of another until the agreement comes to an end. That could happen when the work goes out of print or when some other event happens as defined in the agreement, such as you or the publisher failing to fulfill certain terms of the agreement.

So if you have questions about how your copyright works, you can answer a lot of questions by remembering if you have sold your work or are renting it to others.

A VISIT TO OUR LAWYER

I am neither a lawyer nor the son of a lawyer (though I am the father of a lawyer), so I am legally unqualified to give you any advice about anything. (Enough for the disclaimer.) But I get asked questions.

Once an author wanted to make sure that royalties would be handled properly after her death and wondered what would be the best way to do that.

I told her that most book contracts include a standard provision for the publisher to pay out royalties according to the author's will. All that most publishers may need, then, is a copy of the final will or a letter to that effect from the heir or executor. Then further payments would be made accordingly. She thought that was very helpful and cleared things up for her. If the will was clear about who would get such income, she would be in good shape.

Then it was my turn to ask a question, "Who will hold the copyright after you die?"

"What do you mean?" she asked.

"Well," I said, "what if your books go out of print after you die? Maybe another publisher will want to pick up the rights and republish. Who would the new publisher write the contract with? Who would own the material? You need to answer two different questions. The first is, Who will get the income (royalties) from my intellectual property after I die? The second is, Who will own my intellectual property after I die and be authorized to make decisions about it? You as the owner of the intellectual property may want those questions answered the same or differently."

"Oh," she said, "I see. That's how all those books that Google wants to put online get caught in publishing limbo."

Exactly. Having a will is always a good thing. Just as we'd want to make sure it is clear who owns our other property after we are gone, authors may want to make sure that a will provides clearly for who will own the copyrights to their works.

Recently my wife and I were revising our wills. (Don't worry, kids. You're still in.) You see, we figure every ten years or so we ought to consider how things have changed or not. Being a writer and editor, I took my own advice and asked our lawyer about our copyrights, which was not in his standard will. I wanted a clause in our wills that designates who will inherit not only our royalties but who will own and be able to make decisions about our intellectual property (meager as it may be) after we are gone. So he did.

You should consider putting ownership of intellectual property in the hands of one person, even if you choose to distribute the income to several. One reason for this is that shared ownership can make decision making complicated if the new owners disagree with each other. And if you have an even number of owners, who breaks a tie?

In addition, when one of the new owners dies, what if that person hasn't designated an owner—or has named multiple owners? You see the difficulties.

With a clear will, we can rest easy at night knowing that all our brilliant prose, heartbreaking poetry, and highly imaginative, realistic, magical, narrative, postmodern, antirealist, traditional fiction (not to mention our patents, inventions, software, and all manner of artistic works) will have a secure future. We will not have left them destitute, homeless, or orphaned, but will have provided a happy home that will serve them through their full term of copyright.

ONLINE RESOURCES FROM ANDREW T. LE PEAU

MORE ON WRITING AND PUBLISHING

You can find a link to the following resources related to *Write Better* at www.ivpress.com/write-better.

Appendix F. Brevity Is the Soul of Blogging

Appendix G. The Dictionary and Google Hits Are Dead

Appendix H. Though This Be Academic Publishing, Yet There Is Method in It

Appendix I. What a Piece of Work Is Academic Writing

Appendix J. Questions and Exercises for Students and Others

ANDY UNEDITED

Andy Unedited (andyunedited.com) is my blog that explores the world of books, publishing, ideas, writing, history, editing, leadership, scholarship, and life. You can sign up to get email alerts whenever I post something new, and you can search more than ten years' worth of ideas, suggestions, information, and perspective. If you have a topic you'd like me to address, just leave a comment on any recent post, and I'll do my best.

RECOMMENDED READING

ON WRITING

Dreyer, Benjamin. *Dreyer's English*. New York: Random House, 2019.

Lamott, Anne. *Bird by Bird*. New York: Anchor Books, 1994.

McKee, Robert. *Story*. New York: HarperCollins, 1997.

Orwell, George. *All Art Is Propaganda*. Compiled by George Packer. New York: Harcourt, 2008.

Strunk, William Jr., and E. B. White. *The Elements of Style*. 4th ed. New York: Longman, 2000.

Sword, Helen. *Stylish Academic Writing*. Boston: Harvard University Press, 2012.

Truss, Lynn. *Eats, Shoots & Leaves*. New York: Penguin, 2003.

Zinsser, William. *On Writing Well*. New York: Harper Perennial, 2006.

ON PERSUASION

Guinness, Os. *Fool's Talk*. Downers Grove, IL: InterVarsity Press, 2015.

Heath, Chip, and Dan Heath, *Made to Stick*. New York: Random House, 2007.

Heinrichs, Jay. *Thank You for Arguing*. 3rd ed. New York: Three Rivers Press, 2017.

Kahneman, Daniel. *Thinking, Fast and Slow*. New York: Farrar, Straus and Giroux. 2011.

Muehlhoff, Tim, and Richard Langer. *Winsome Persuasion*. Downers Grove, IL: IVP Academic, 2017.

Sire, James W. *Why Good Arguments Often Fail*. Downers Grove: IL: InterVarsity Press, 2006.

ON SPIRITUALITY

Calhoun, Adele Ahlberg. *Spiritual Disciplines Handbook*. 2nd ed. Downers Grove, IL: InterVarsity Press, 2015.

Foster, Richard J. *Celebration of Discipline*. 4th ed. New York: HarperOne, 2018.

Mulholland, M. Robert, Jr. *Invitation to a Journey*. 2nd ed. Downers Grove, IL: InterVarsity Press, 2016.

Nouwen, Henri J. M. *The Return of the Prodigal Son*. New York: Doubleday, 1992.

Silf, Margaret. *Inner Compass*. Chicago: Loyola Press, 1999.

Smith, James Bryant. *The Good and Beautiful God*. Downers Grove, IL: InterVarsity Press, 2009.

Warren, Tish Harrison. *Liturgy of the Ordinary*. Downers Grove, IL: InterVarsity Press, 2016.

Willard, Dallas. *Hearing God*. 4th ed. Downers Grove, IL: InterVarsity Press, 2012.

NOTES

1 FINDING AN OPENING

[1]Bill Bryson, *The Lost Continent* (New York: Harper Perennial, 1989), 4, 26.

[2]Inspiration for these thoughts about commas and periods comes from Amor Towles, *A Gentleman in Moscow* (New York: Viking, 2016), 68.

[3]Malcolm Gladwell, *Blink* (New York: Little Brown, 2005), 245-48.

2 KNOWING YOUR AUDIENCE

[1]William Zinsser, *On Writing Well* (New York: Harper Perennial, 2006), 24-25.

[2]Zinsser, *On Writing Well*, 25.

[3]Zinsser, *On Writing Well*, 24.

4 THE CHARACTER OF PERSUASION

[1]Daniel Kahneman, *Thinking, Fast and Slow* (New York: Farrar, Straus and Giroux, 2011), 126. This approach is called anchoring.

[2]David Brooks, *The Social Animal* (New York: Random House, 2012), 181.

[3]Fair use is a complex legal topic. Generally it means writers and artists are allowed to use a limited amount of protected material from others without permission or payment. Nonetheless, using quotation marks for direct quotes and giving credit to such sources are always required even if permission is not. To find out more about fair use, consult copyright.gov/fair-use/more -info.html or copyright.ubc.ca/guidelines-and-resources/faq/basics as well as other sources, your publisher, or an intellectual property lawyer.

[4]Steven D. Levitt and Stephen J. Dubner, *Think Like a Freak* (New York: William Morrow, 2014), 8-9.

[5]Pat Robertson, "Robertson: Natural Disasters Due to Mideast Peace Talks," *700 Club*, July 23, 2013, www.youtube.com/watch?feature=player_embedded &v=0DHm70W5_oU.

[6]See Andy Crouch, *Culture Making* (Downers Grove, IL: InterVarsity Press, 2008), 20-22, 102-4.

[7]Brooks, *Social Animal*, 284-85.

5 THE CRAFT OF PERSUASION

[1]Daniel Kahneman, *Thinking, Fast and Slow* (New York: Farrar, Straus and Giroux, 2011), 63.

[2]"Homer Defined," season 3, episode 5 of *The Simpsons*, quoted in Jay Heinrichs, *Thank You for Arguing*, 3rd ed. (New York: Three Rivers Press, 2017), 120.

[3]Andrew T. Le Peau, *Mark Through Old Testament Eyes* (Grand Rapids: Kregel, 2017), 9.

[4]David Brooks, *The Social Animal* (New York: Random House, 2012), 128.

[5]Kahneman, *Thinking, Fast and Slow*, 63.

[6]Kahneman, *Thinking, Fast and Slow*, 62.

[7]See, for example, Heinrichs, *Thank You for Arguing*, 38-46 and 305-8, upon which much of this subsection is based.

[8]On the importance of admitting when your opponent is right and when your own position may have flaws, see also Steven D. Levitt and Stephen J. Dubner, *Think Like a Freak* (New York: William Morrow, 2014), 167-88.

[9]The following quotations are from Susan Cain, "The Power of Introverts," TED2012, February 2012, www.ted.com/talks/susan_cain_the_power_of _introverts/transcript#t-1115856.

6 CREATING DRAMATIC NONFICTION

[1]Chip Heath and Dan Heath, *Made to Stick* (New York: Random House, 2007), 204-37.

[2]Each October a number of large tents are set up in downtown Jonesborough, Tennessee. A variety of storytellers are scheduled in different time slots throughout the three-day event along with other activities. You can learn more about this annual event at www.storytellingcenter.net/events/national -storytelling-festival.

[3]Orlando Crespo, *Being Latino in Christ* (Downers Grove, IL: InterVarsity Press, 2003), 26.

7 CRACKING OUR WRITER'S BLOCK

[1]Betty S. Flowers, "Madman, Architect, Carpenter, Judge: Roles and the Writing Process," *Language Arts* 58, no. 7 (October 1981): 834-36. It is also found at www.ut-ie.com/b/b_flowers.html.

[2]I owe several of the ideas on personality and writing in this section to Roy

Carlisle's reflections on the challenges that each Myers-Briggs type presents for writers and editors. Roy M. Carlisle, "Working with Writers: How to Understand Creative Temperaments and Edit More Effectively" (lecture, Academy of Christian Editors Annual Retreat, Byfield, MA, September 13-15, 2007).

8 THE NUTS, BOLTS, HAMMERS, AND SAWS OF GOOD REWRITING

[1]William Zinsser, *On Writing Well* (New York: Harper Perennial, 2006), 3-4.

[2]George Orwell, "Politics and the English Language," in *All Art Is Propaganda*, comp. George Packer (New York: Harcourt, 2008), 281.

[3]The six points in quotation marks are from Orwell, "Politics and the English Language," 285.

[4]Gary's teacher was apparently paraphrasing a quote from *With Hemingway: A Year in Key West and Cuba* by Arnold Samuelson: "The way you tell whether you're going good is by what you can throw away. If you can throw away stuff that would make a high point of interest in somebody else's story, you know you're going good." Maria Popova, "Hemingway's Advice on Writing, Ambition, the Art of Revision, and His Reading List of Essential Books for Aspiring Writers," Brainpickings, accessed December 19, 2018, www.brainpickings.org/2016/01/04/with-hemingway-arnold-samuelson-writing.

In chapter nine I say not to end a chapter with a quotation, even one from a famous person. Why did I not follow that advice here? Good question. But I also say, "An exception can be a quote from someone in a story you've told." You can judge if the ending here is a worthy exception.

9 WE REMEMBER ENDINGS FIRST

[1]William Zinsser, *On Writing Well* (New York: Harper Perennial, 2006), 64.

[2]Zinsser, *On Writing Well*, 5.

[3]George Orwell, *1984* (New York: Signet Classic, 1949), 245.

[4]Nora Ephron, "The Assassination Reports," in *The Most of Nora Ephron* (New York: Alfred A. Knopf, 2013), 21.

[5]Ariel Leve, *It Could Be Worse, You Could Be Me* (New York: Harper Perennial, 2009), 10.

[6]Maya Angelou, *Even the Stars Look Lonesome* (New York: Random House, 1997), 22, 24.

[7]Angelou, *Even the Stars Look Lonesome*, 75.

[8]Zinsser, *On Writing Well*, 31.

[9]Andrew T. Le Peau, "Vice President of Looking Out of the Window," *Andy Unedited* (blog), October 9, 2007, andyunedited.com/2007/10/09/vice-president-of-looking-out/

[10]Mitch Albom, *Tuesdays with Morrie* (New York: Doubleday, 1997), 1-2.

[11]This is similar to what Aristotle, in his *Poetics*, calls reversal of the situation and recognition (when some new or startling information is revealed, such as the identity of a character).

[12]Angelou, *Even the Stars Look Lonesome*, 133.

[13]F. Scott Fitzgerald, *The Great Gatsby* (New York: Simon & Schuster, 2004), 180.

[14]James Baldwin, "Faulkner and Desegregation," in *Nobody Knows My Name* (New York: Vintage, 1989), 119, 123.

[15]Baldwin, "Faulkner and Desegregation," 125-26.

[16]Ken Murray, "How Doctors Die," in *The Best American Essays 2012*, ed. David Brooks (Boston: Houghton Mifflin, 2012), 235.

10 TITLES THAT WORK

[1]I owe much of my thinking about code to Ken Peterson.

[2]Kevin Kelly, "Best Magazine Articles Ever," *Cool Tools*, accessed December 19, 2018, kk.org/cooltools/best-magazine-articles-ever.

[3]See John Milliot, "Self-Published ISBNs Hit 786,935 in 2016," *Publishers Weekly*, October 20, 2017, www.publishersweekly.com/pw/by-topic/industry-news/manufacturing/article/75139-self-published-isbns-hit-786-935-in-2016.html.

[4]Chip Heath and Dan Heath, *Made to Stick* (New York: Random House, 2007).

[5]Steve Levitt says that the publisher, HarperCollins, was "scared to death of the title 'Freakonomics' when my sister Linda Jines first thought it up." While it had content, they probably wondered if it was too creative. But it is understandable why they stuck with it because these were some of the others they rejected:

- *Economics Gone Wild* (this has content and creativity, but the creativity side is a bit lame)

- *E-Ray Vision* (creative but no content)

- *Dude, Where's My Rational Expectation? Bend It Like Veblen* (creative but too obscure)

(See Steven D. Levitt and Stephen J. Dubnar, *When to Rob a Bank* [New York: HarperCollins, 2015], 277. Rejected titles from Stephen J. Dubnar and Steve Levitt, "How Did 'Freakonomics' Get Its Name?" *Freakonomics* (blog), January 3, 2013, http://freakonomics.com/2013/01/03/how-did-freakonomics -get-its-name-full-transcript.)

11 CREATIVITY, THE MYSTERIOUS MUSE

[1]"Remote Associates Test," Remote Associates Test, accessed December 20, 2018, www.remote-associates-test.com.

[2]Sarnoff A. Mednick, "The Associative Basis of the Creative Process," *Psychological Review* 69, no. 3 (1962): 221. The notion that associating two separate ideas is core to creativity goes back even further to Scottish philosopher David Hume who, in the eighteenth century wrote, "Thro' this whole book, there are great pretensions to discoveries in philosophy; but if any thing can intitle [*sic*] the author to so glorious a name as that of an *inventor*, 'tis the use he makes of the principle of the association of ideas, which enters into most of his philosophy." David Hume, *Abstract* of *A Treatise of Human Nature* (1740), in *An Enquiry Concerning Human Understanding*, ed. Peter Millican (Oxford: Oxford University Press, 2007), [35] 145.

[3]Thanks to Dave Zimmerman for these last two examples.

[4]Thomas Goetz, "How to Spot the Future," *Wired*, April 24, 2012, www .wired.com/2012/04/ff_spotfuture/all/1.

[5]Goetz, "How to Spot the Future."

[6]Art Markman, "Your Team Is Brainstorming All Wrong," *Harvard Business Review*, May 18, 2017, hbr.org/2017/05/your-team-is-brainstorming -all-wrong.

[7]Markman, "Brainstorming All Wrong."

[8]Melissa Dahl, "How Neuroscientists Explain the Mind-Clearing Magic of Running," *Huffington Post*, April 27, 2016, www.huffpost.com/science-of-us /how-neuroscientists-expla_b_9787466.html. See also Maheedhar Kodali, Tarick Megahed, Vikas Mishra, Bing Shuai, Bharathi Hattiangady, and Ashok K. Shetty, "Voluntary Running Exercise-Mediated Enhanced Neurogenesis Does Not Obliterate Retrograde Spatial Memory," *Journal of Neuroscience* 36, no. 31 (August 2016): 8112-22; doi.org/10.1523/JNEUROSCI.0766-16.2016.

[9]Mathew Honan, "Photo Essay: Unlikely Places Where *Wired* Pioneers Had Their Eureka! Moments," *Wired*, April 24, 2008, www.wired.com/2008/04 /ff-eureka.

[10]Gavin Weightman, "The History of the Bar Cade," *Smithsonian*, September 23, 2015, www.smithsonianmag.com/innovation/history-bar-code-180956704.

[11]For example, see "Improv Games," *Improv Encyclopedia*, accessed December 20, 2018, http://improvencyclopedia.org/games.

[12]You can find many online sources for writing exercises. Here are just a few: "Welcome to Writing Exercises," *Writing Exercises*, accessed December 20, 2018, writingexercises.co.uk/index.php; "9 Creative Writing Exercises," *Authority Pub*, accessed December 20, 2018, authority.pub/creative-writing-exercises; Mary Jaksch, "10 Creative Writing Exercises to Inspire You," *Write to Done*, accessed December 20, 2018, writetodone.com/10-best-creative-writing-exercises.

12 BREAKING THE RULES

[1]"Welcome to the New Words," *Merriam-Webster*, accessed December 21, 2018, www.merriam-webster.com/words-at-play/new-words-in-the-dictionary -sep-2017.

[2]Lynne Truss, *Eats, Shoots & Leaves* (New York: Gotham Books, 2003), 115.

[3]Richard Nordquist, "Why It's Not Wrong to End a Sentence with a Preposition," ThoughtCo, August 15, 2017, accessed January 29, 2018, www .thoughtco.com/is-it-wrong-to-end-a-sentence-with-a-preposition-1691034.

[4]Bryan A. Garner, *Garner's Modern American Usage* (New York: Oxford University Press, 2009), 654.

[5]In homage to Harold Arlen, "Ding, Dong, the Witch Is Dead," *The Wizard of Oz*, who did not split an infinitive.

[6]John F. Kennedy, "Inaugural Address," Washington, DC, January 20, 1961. www.jfklibrary.org/learn/about-jfk/historic-speeches/inaugural-address.

[7]See "Conjunctions to Start Sentences," *Grammarist*, accessed December 21, 2018, grammarist.com/grammar/conjunctions-to-start-sentences.

13 THE KEY TO POWERFUL PROSE—TONE

[1]Donald Miller, *Blue Like Jazz* (Nashville: Thomas Nelson, 2003), 187.

[2]In his *Poetics*, Aristotle, thinking mostly of plays, identifies six elements: plot, character (not just those who act in the plot but their moral makeup), thought (the reasoning of the characters or narrator), diction (speech or language), melody (music), and spectacle (props, costumes, scenery and so forth). Others identify seven prime elements, adding conflict and point of view to the five noted in this chapter. I see conflict as a component of plot, the key to creating tension, drama, and intrigue, which moves the action

forward. Point of view (first-person, second-person, third-person limited, third-person omniscient, and alternating points of view) for me falls into the category of literary devices authors use, like foreshadowing, metaphor, personification, symbol, and so forth. Others will no doubt disagree with my choice here. And that's part of what makes discussing literature so much fun.

[3]Robert Fulghum, *All I Really Need to Know I Learned in Kindergarten,* 15th anniv. ed. (New York: Ballantine, 2003), 2-3.

[4]Al Anderson, *The Shepherd's Adventure* (Enumclaw, WA: Redemption Press, 2001), title page.

[5]D. H. Lawrence, "Benjamin Franklin," in *Studies in Classic American Literature* (London: Penguin, 1977), 15-16.

14 FOR THE LOVE OF METAPHOR

[1]Frederik Backman, *A Man Called Ove* (New York: Atria Books, 2014), 6, 31, 155.

[2]James Geary, *I Is an Other: The Secret Life of Metaphor and How It Shapes the Way We See the World* (New York: Harper Perennial, 2012), 27, 29.

[3]Geary, *I Is an Other,* 174-75.

[4]Geary, *I Is an Other,* 52.

[5]Geary, *I Is an Other,* 163.

[6]J. Robert Oppenheimer quoted in Geary, *I Is an Other,* 176.

[7]"In my mind's eye" (*Hamlet,* act 1, scene 2); "All the world's a stage, and all the men and women merely players" (*As You Like It,* act 2, scene 7); "Now is the winter of our discontent" (*Richard III,* act 1, scene 1); "But love is blind, and lovers cannot see" (*The Merchant of Venice,* act 2, scene 6); "Why, then the world's mine oyster" (*The Merry Wives of Windsor,* act 2, scene 2); "But, for my own part, it was Greek to me" (*Julius Caesar,* act 1, scene 2); "A dish fit for the gods" (*Julius Caesar,* act 2, scene 1); "Yet do I fear thy nature; it is too full o' the milk of human kindness" (*Macbeth,* act 1, scene 5); "Out of the jaws of death" (*The Taming of the Shrew,* act 3, scene 4).

[8]J. R. R. Tolkien, *The Fellowship of the Ring* (New York: Ballantine Books, 1965), 164.

[9]J. R. R. Tolkien, *The Two Towers* (New York: Ballantine Books, 1965), 140.

[10]Both mixed metaphors are found at Geary, *I Is an Other,* 144.

[11]"Week 310: It's Like This," *The Style Invitational,* March 14, 1999, www .washingtonpost.com/wp-dyn/content/article/2007/03/16/AR20070 31600738.html.

15 LESS IS MORE

[1]Paul Harrill is the filmmaker. The quotes reflect my memory of the essence of his comments. My apologies for any inaccuracies. The seminar was "Faith, Doubt, and Cinema," Calvin Festival of Faith and Writing, Grand Rapids, April 14, 2016.

[2]Kathleen Norris, *Dakota* (Boston: Houghton Mifflin, 2001), 1. My apologies for besmirching her wonderful writing with my additions.

[3]Abraham Lincoln, quoted in Ronald C. White Jr., *Lincoln's Greatest Speech* (New York: Simon & Schuster, 2002), 17-19. This source is used for all quotations from the address.

[4]White, *Lincoln's Greatest Speech*, 113.

[5]Anne Farrow, Joel Lang, and Jenifer Frank, *Complicity: How the North Promoted, Prolonged, and Profited from Slavery* (New York: Ballantine, 2005), 3-7.

[6]Claudia D. Goldin and Frank D. Lewis, "The Economic Cost of the American Civil War," *Journal of Economic History* 35, no. 2 (June 1975): 299-326; https://dash.harvard.edu/bitstream/handle/1/2662305/Goldin_EconomicCost.pdf.

[7]White, *Lincoln's Greatest Speech*, 203.

[8]The Gettysburg Address as well as Lincoln's House Divided Speech and Cooper Union Address also use the past-present-future structure. See White, *Lincoln's Greatest Speech*, 51.

16 CALLED TO WRITE

[1]Andrew Purves, *The Crucifixion of Ministry* (Downers Grove, IL: InterVarsity Press, 2007), 138-39.

[2]God did use these bad outcomes for good purposes—saving Joseph's family (Genesis 50:19-21). But we should not assume it was God's will for Joseph to respond in pride and instigate family resentment. Rather, God could have fulfilled the dream without Joseph's wayward reactions, which God was nonetheless able to turn to good results.

17 THE QUEST FOR VOICE

[1]Mark Twain, "Note to the Young People's Society," Greenpoint Presbyterian Church, 1901; *Pudd'nhead Wilson*; "Advice to Youth," April 15, 1882; and "The Czar's Soliloquy."

[2]Dave Barry, "I Slalomly Swear," *Miami Herald*, February 5, 1989, www.miamiherald.com/living/liv-columns-blogs/dave-barry/article1939642.html.

[3]Dave Barry, "A Journey into My Colon—and Yours," *Miami Herald,* February 22, 2008, www.miamiherald.com/living/liv-columns-blogs/dave -barry/article1928847.html.

[4]Dave Barry, "Swamp Goo, Gators and Beef Jerky: Dave Does the Everglades," *Chicago Tribune Magazine,* December 12, 1993, 33.

[5]Noah Berlatsky, "'Voice' Isn't the Point of Writing," *Atlantic,* November 29, 2014, www.theatlantic.com/entertainment/archive/2014/11/finding-your -voice-as-a-writer-overrated/382946.

[6]Anne Lamott, *Bird by Bird* (New York: Anchor Books, 1994), 198-99.

[7]T. S. Eliot, "Tradition and the Individual Talent," in *The Sacred Wood* (New York: Barnes & Noble, 1960), 52.

[8]The tradition regarding goodness, truth, and beauty began with the likes of Plato and Aristotle, and was given significant attention in the medieval era by Aquinas, Ibn Sina, and others. For a contemporary discussion see James Bryan Smith, *The Magnificent Story* (Downers Grove, IL: IVP Books, 2017), 6-16.

18 THE SPIRITUALITY OF WRITING ABOUT YOURSELF

[1]Books on spiritual journaling include Helen Cepero, *Journaling as a Spiritual Practice* (Downers Grove, IL: InterVarsity Press, 2008); Luann Budd, *Journal Keeping* (Downers Grove, IL: InterVarsity Press, 2002); and Ron Klug, *How to Keep a Spiritual Journal* (Minneapolis: Augsburg, 2002).

[2]Adapted from Adele Ahlberg Calhoun, *Spiritual Disciplines Handbook,* 2nd ed. (Downers Grove, IL: InterVarsity Press, 2015), 59.

[3]As to the uniqueness of the *Confessions,* historian Jaroslav Pelikan says, "Its nearest analogy for centuries before it is *The Meditations of Marcus Aurelius,* and if you read the two books side by side, as I did with a group of undergraduates a few years ago, you realize that they are altogether different in their outlook, method and style." Jaroslav Pelikan, "Writing as a Means of Grace," in *Spiritual Quests,* ed. William Zinsser (Boston: Houghton Mifflin, 1988), 87. Sarah Ruden comments, "It's doubtful that the *Meditations* [of Marcus Aurelius], a sort of private intellectual journal, circulated much in antiquity, and even more doubtful that Augustine knew the work." Sarah Ruden, introduction to *Confessions,* trans. Sarah Ruden (New York: Modern Library, 2017), xl.

[4]What about the apostle Paul? Isn't he the progenitor of this genre of spiritual memoir? After all, his Damascus Road story occurs from his own mouth multiple times in Acts and his letters. First, however, while Paul's story of

turning to Christ is mentioned no less than three times in Acts (9:1-19; 22:3-16; 26:9-18), we need to remember that Luke is the author. He is the one who thought it was important. Paul had not set out to produce a memoir that Luke duplicates. Since Luke essentially follows Paul's ministry in the latter half of Acts, it is not surprising that Luke felt he should recount Paul's story initially and then at the key turning point when he was arrested and gave a verbal defense. Second, in his letters, Paul tells his story in even less detail than Luke does, and his main purpose is to defend his authority as an apostle, not to provide a model of Christian conversion, of the Christian life, or the interior Christian life (Galatians 1:11-24; Philippians 3:1-11; 1 Corinthians 9:1; 15:8-9; 2 Corinthians 12:1-9).

[5]Augustine, *Confessions*, 97-98.

[6]Augustine, *Confessions*, 318.

[7]Augustine, *Confessions*, 223.

[8]Andrew T. Le Peau, *Mark Through Old Testament Eyes* (Grand Rapids: Kregel, 2017), 65-66.

[9]Augustine, *Confessions*, 462.

[10]Gordon D. Fee and Douglas Stuart, *How to Read the Bible for All Its Worth*, 3rd ed. (Grand Rapids: Zondervan, 2003), 22.

[11]Matthew does, however, assume that his readers understand the Jewish and Greco-Roman culture of his day. Since we aren't from that time or place, we'll need to fill in our understanding with study of historical, cultural, and Old Testament background.

[12]Augustine, *Confessions*, 230.

[13]Augustine, *Confessions*, 37-38.

[14]Augustine, *Confessions*, 280.

19 SPIRITUAL AUTHORITY AND WRITING

[1]Andy Crouch, "It's Time to Reckon with Celebrity Power," *Gospel Coalition*, March 24, 2018, www.thegospelcoalition.org/article/time-reckon -celebrity-power.

[2]Rodney Stark, *The Triumph of Christianity* (New York: HarperOne, 2011), 247-48.

[3]Andrew T. Le Peau, *Mark Through Old Testament Eyes* (Grand Rapids: Kregel, 2017), 162.

[4]Frederick Buechner, *Wishful Thinking* (New York: Harper & Row, 1973), 95.

20 THE COURAGE TO CREATE AND LET GO

[1]Alan Fadling, personal correspondence with author, July 17, 2018. Used by permission.

[2]C. S. Lewis, *The Screwtape Letters* (New York: HarperOne, 1996), 71.

21 STEWARDS WITH A MESSAGE

[1]Lauren DeStefano (@LaurenDeStefano), "Give someone a book, they'll read for a day," Twitter, January 25, 2015, 8:06 a.m., twitter.com/laurendestefano /status/559381901002407936.

[2]*For the Love of Spock*, directed by Adam Nimoy (Los Angeles: 455 Films, 2016).

[3]Nancy Kerrigan, quoted in Kim Masters, "Kerrigan Off the Ice Doesn't Seem Half as Nice," *Washington Post*, March 4, 1996, www.washingtonpost .com/wp-srv/sports/longterm/olympics1998/history/timeline/articles /time_030494.htm.

[4]John H. Walton, *The Lost World of Genesis One* (Downers Grove, IL: IVP Academic, 2009), 77-85.

[5]G. K. Beale, *The Temple and the Church's Mission*, New Studies in Biblical Theology (Downers Grove, IL: IVP Academic, 2004), 46-47.

APPENDIX A: GET THEE TO A PLATFORM

[1]"Bookstores: Establishments and Sales," Humanities Indicators, September 2016, www.humanitiesindicators.org/content/indicatorDoc.aspx?i=11095.

[2]"Report from Bowker Shows Continuing Growth in Self-Publishing," Bowker, September 7, 2016, www.bowker.com/news/2016/Report-from -Bowker-Shows-Continuing-Growth-in-Self-Publishing.html; and "Self-Publishing ISBNs Climbed 8% Between 2015-2016," Bowker, October 11, 2017, www.bowker.com/news/2017/Self-Publishing-ISBNs-Climbed -8-Between-2015-2016.html.

[3]Al Hsu, "Transcript, Session 3, Platform: Finding and Building Your Audience," ivpress.com, accessed December 26, 2018, www.ivpress.com /Media/Default/Your-Publishing-Playbook/3-platform.pdf.

[4]Al Hsu, "A Theology of Platform," October 25, 2004, unpublished paper.

APPENDIX C: THE COAUTHOR DOTH PROTEST TOO MUCH, METHINKS

[1]Tom Woll, *Publishing for Profit* (Kahtonah, NY: Cross River, 2006), 132.

APPENDIX D: TO SELF-PUBLISH
OR NOT TO SELF-PUBLISH

[1]Amanda Hocking, "A Self-Published Author's $2 Million Cinderella Story," interview by Guy Raz, NPR, January 8, 2012, www.npr.org/templates /transcript/transcript.php?storyId=144804084.

[2]"World Population," *Wikipedia*, accessed December 26, 2018, en.wikipedia .org/wiki/World_population.

[3]Patrick Johnstone, *The Future of the Global Church* (Downers Grove, IL: InterVarsity Press, 2011), 101.

[4]Over 78 percent are published in other languages besides English, according to Sergey Lobachev, "Top languages in global information production," *Partnership* 3, no. 2 (2008), https://doi.org/10.20183/partnership.v3i2.826; and 72 percent are published in languages besides English according to David Graddol, *The Future of English*, (Edinburgh: British Council, 2000), 9, www.teachingenglish.org.uk/sites/teacheng/files/pub_learning-elt -future.pdf.

APPENDIX E: THE COPYRIGHT'S THE THING

[1]Thanks to Ellen Hsu for the analogy of a property manager.

INDEX

academic publishing, 253
academic writing, 253
Achebe, Chinua, 74
active voice, 95, 133
advice from others
  (receiving), 79-80,
  110-11, 174-75, 200-201,
  205-6, 213-14, 232, 234
agents, 233-37, 240, 248
Albom, Mitch, 94
Alcoholics Anonymous, 51
*All I Really Need to Know I
  Learned in Kindergarten*, 20,
  139-41, 143-44
alliteration, 52-53, 101,
  141, 168
American Gods, 161
analogy, analogies, 44, 52,
  146-47, 149-50
Anderson, Al, 140-41, 143
Andy Unedited, 3-4, 253
Angelou, Maya, 91-92, 95
Anna Karenina, 10, 120
Aristotle, 51, 260, 262
art
  African American, 95
  blurred lines and, 168
  breaking rules and, 130
  defined, 2
  phases of, 161
  tradition and, 184-85
  whole person and,
    158-59
associative thinking, 116-21,
  149-50, 261 n. 2
*Astrophysics for People in a
  Hurry*, 101
attention (keeping readers'),
  9, 19, 28, 33, 65-66,
  102-3, 111
audience, 19, 25-29, 92
  persuasion and, 34,
    48-58

story and, 59-60, 63-64
titles and, 102-8, 110
Augustine of Hippo,
  190-97, 265
Austen, Jane, 10, 74
authority
  credentials and, 55, 229
  defined, 199
  institutions,
    organizations, and,
    201-8
  of Scripture, 194
  spiritual, 198-208
autobiography, 33, 159,
  186-97
Backman, Fredrik, 146,
  148
Bailey, Kenneth E., 62
Balderdash, 75-76, 127
Baldwin, James, 12, 96-97
Barry, Dave, 180-81
Bartlett's Familiar Quotations,
  88
Beethoven, Ludwig von,
  74, 81
Being Latino in Christ, 69
Big Brother, 89-90
Big Kahuna, The, 36-37, 47
Birdseye, Clarence, 117
blinding (research tool),
  110
Blink, 18-19, 23-24
Blixen, Karen, 138
blogs, blogging
  author's blog, 3-4,
    92-93, 253
  guidelines for, 253
  ideas for, 74, 127, 211
  platform and, 230-31
  reliable sources and, 40
  spiritual authority and,
    198, 202,
  titles for posts, 100, 105

Blond Crazy, 76
Blue Like Jazz, 136-37
Bohr, Niels, 124
Bolles, Richard, 26
bookstores, 227, 244
Brackin, Ron, 78
Bradbury, Ray, 14
brainstorming, 121-22
Brooks, David, 47
Bruce Almighty, 99
Bryson, Bill, 13, 180
Buechner, Frederick, 208
Cagney, James, 76
Cain, Susan, 56-58
Capon, Robert Farrar,
  20-21
Case for Christ, The, 67
Catcher in the Rye, The, 138
character, 137-38
Christmas Carol, A, 131
chronological structure, 34,
  168, 264
Cicero, 46, 203
City of God, The, 191
clarity, 83-85, 89,
clichés, 52, 83, 151, 153-55
coauthors, coauthoring,
  238-41
code, for a title, 103-8
coercion, 38-39
Collapse, 104
Collins, Suzanne, 26
community, writers and,
  176, 184, 189, 204-05,
  228, 232
confession, 188-90
Confessions, 190-97
conjunctions, beginning
  sentences with, 132-33
content, in a title, 100-106,
  108
convergent thinking,
  116-19, 261 n. 2

copyediting, 85-87
copyright, 43, 247-52
counsel from others. *See*
  advice from others
  (receiving)
courage in writing, 209-16
creativity, 115-27
  four stages of, 125
  in Genesis, 212
  titles and, 103-8
Crespo, Orlando, 69
Crichton, Michael, 26
criticism (receiving), 72-73,
  206, 211-12, 214, 221,
  223-25
Crouch, Blake, 161
Dakota, 138, 159-60
Dalai Lama, 199
Dallas Times Herald, 90-91
Dark Matter, 161
*Day Wall Street Exploded,
  The*, 104
Declaration of
  Independence, 21
DeStefano, Lauren, 217
details
  effectiveness of, 11-12,
    66, 86, 137, 140,
  not including too many,
    151, 159, 163
  writer's block and, 74, 79
Devil in the White City, The,
  138
Diary of a Wimpy Kid, 107
Dick, Philip K., 161
Dickens, Charles, 16-17,
  131
Dillard, Annie, 138
divergent thinking, 116-19
drama
  nonfiction and, 59-71
  openings and, 13
  passive voice and, 85,
    133
  subtitles and, 108-9
dreams, 175-76
Du Bois, W. E. B., 133

Duvall, Robert, 157-58
Eats, Shoots & Leaves, 131
ebooks, 242-44
Ecclesiastes, 17
editors, 82, 100, 181,
  202-3, 233-37
Elegant Universe, The, 109
elements of writing, the
  five, 137-38
Eliot, T. S., 177, 184-85
Ellison, Ralph, 73
"End of Global Warming,
  The," 14
Ephron, Nora, 90-91
Esquivel, Laura, 161
ethos, 34, 54-57
examen, examination of
  conscience, 187-89
exercise
  mental, 147
  physical, 122-25
  spiritual, 187-89
  writing, 74-75, 125,
    127, 253, 262 n. 11
extroverts, extroversion,
  56-58, 64, 78
Ezra, 228
Fahrenheit 451, 14
failure, 72-73, 211, 215
fair use, 257
faith, 157, 192, 215-16
  statement of, 204, 207
Fast-Food Nation, 120
Fatal Grace, A, 13
Faulkner, William, 96, 133,
  181
fear and writing, 211-12,
  214-16
Fellowship of the Ring, The,
  154
Fey, Tina, 180
fiction 3, 65, 137-38
  titles, 101
  trends in, 161
First-Book Syndrome,
  209-11
Fischer, Bobby, 122-24

Fitzgerald, F. Scott, 95, 181
Flowers, Betty, 77
Franklin, Benjamin, 142-43
Freakonomics, 107, 120,
  260-61
Fulghum, Robert, 20,
  139-41, 143-44
Gaiman, Neil, 161
Gandhi (the movie), 70
*Garner's Modern American
  Usage*, 131
Geary, James, 148-49
generosity toward readers,
  221
Genesis, 165, 214, 264
  first chapter of, 17, 195,
    212, 221-22
Getty Museum, 18, 23-24
Gladwell, Malcolm, 18-19,
  23-24
Glass Castle, The, 161,
Go Set a Watchman, 73, 138
goals in writing, 45, 55, 80,
  183, 185, 211, 214,
  218-19
God Behaving Badly, 99, 104,
  108
Graham, Billy, 199,
grammar
  breaking the rules of,
    128-34
  clarity and, 83
  purpose of, 129
  stage to check, 77
  tone and, 141
Grandparenting, 121
Grann, David, 68, 162
Grapes of Wrath, The, 101
gratitude, 3-5, 188-89,
  196-97, 220-21, 223-24,
  234
Great Gatsby, The, 95
Hamlet, 70, 135-36
Harvey, Bob (Robert), 59,
  61, 71
Heart. Soul. Mind. Strength.
  175

Heath, Chip and Dan, 52-53, 106-7, 149
Heidi, 158
Heinrichs, Jay, 44
Help, The, 138
Hemingway, Ernest, 87, 101, 138, 160, 181
Hersey, John, 11-12
Hidden Figures, 138
Hillenbrand, Laura, 161, Hiroshima, 11-12
Hocking, Amanda, 243-44
honesty in persuasion, 36-37, 39-45, 54-55
"How Doctors Die," 96-97
How Stuff Works, 27
Hume, David, 261 n. 2
humility, 199-201, 213, 232
    passion and, 162-68
    persuasion and, 44-45
humor, 29, 159, 180-81
    openings and, 13, 21
    self-deprecating, 64-65, 89, 137, 141, 143, 192
Hunger Games, The, 26
"I Have a Dream," 54
Immortal Life of Henrietta Lacks, The, 67-68, 101, 120, 162
improv, 126-27
in medias res, 69-70
individualism
    authority and, 203-6
    voice and, 184-85
institutions and organizations, 40, 54, 57, 199, 202-6
intellectual property, 43, 245, 247-52
introversion, introverts, 56-58, 64
Invisible Man, 73
Jefferson, Thomas, 21-22
Jesus, 17, 36-37, 50, 58, 172, 176, 207, 215

metaphors of, 151-52
parables of, 70-71
John (Gospel of), 17, 152, 199
journaling, 187-88
Joy Luck Club, The, 138
Jurassic Park, 26
Kahneman, Daniel, 54,
Kennedy, John F., 90-91, 133
King, Martin Luther Jr., 15, 54, 199,
Lamott, Anne, 182-84
Larson, Erik, 138
Last Juror, The, 104
Last Lion: Visions of Glory, The, 13-14
Lawrence, D. H., 142-43
Lee, Harper, 73, 138
Le Peau, Phyllis, 64, 153-54, 175, 201
"Letter from Birmingham Jail," 15-16
Leve, Ariel, 91
Lewis, C. S., 213
Lewis, Michael, 106
Life of Pi, 161
Life, on the Line, 109
Like Water for Chocolate, 161
Lincoln, Abraham, 104, 142, 162-68
listening
    to others, 79-80, 110-11, 174-75, 200-201, 213-14, 232, 234
    in prayer, 176-77
    to stories, 63
logos (in persuasion), 34, 54-55
Lord of the Rings, The, 60, 117, 155
Lost City of Z, The, 68, 104, 162
Lost Continent, The, 13
Made to Stick, 52, 106-7, 147

Making of the Atomic Bomb, The, 124-25
Man Called Ove, A, 146, 148, 150-51
Man in the High Castle, The, 161
Man Who Mistook His Wife for a Hat, The, 120
Manchester, William, 13-14
manipulation, 37-39, 56, 158
Marcus Aurelius, 265
Mark (Gospel of), 52, 71, 152, 173, 214-15
Mark Through Old Testament Eyes, 50, 52, 173
Markman, Art, 121
Martel, Yann, 161
Martian, The, 243
McCullough, David, 161
Mednick, Martha and Sarnoff, 116-17
memoir, 12, 243
    spiritual memoir, 159, 190-97, 265-66
memorability, 50-54, 109, 151
metaphors, 62, 83, 95, 145-56
    associative thinking and, 149-50
    brain research and, 149
    clichés and, 153-55
    defined, 147
    failed, 155-56
    stories in miniature and, 150-53
    titles and, 101-2
Millard, Candice, 161
Miller, Calvin, 212
Miller, Donald, 136-37, 143-44
Moneyball, 107
Mozart, Wolfgang Amadeus, 74, 81, 115-16, 161

Munich Philharmonic Orchestra, 23-24, 162
murder mysteries, 13, 66, 95, 103-4, 150
Murder on the Orient Express, 103
Murray, Ken, 96-97
narrative question, 28, 65-66
narrative. *See* story
Nehemiah (Book of), 228,
Nimoy, Leonard, 220
1984, 83, 89
Nobody Knows My Name, 12
Nordquist, Richard, 131
Norris, Kathleen, 138, 159-60
Offering of Uncles, An, 20-21
Old Man and the Sea, The, 101, 138
Old Yeller, 158
Oliver Twist, 120
Omnivore's Dilemma, The, 11
On Writing Well, 27-29, 82, 89, 92
Oppenheimer, Daniel, 48-49
Oppenheimer, J. Robert, 150
organizations and institutions, 40, 54, 57, 199, 202-6
Orlean, Susan, 105
Orwell, George, 83-85, 89-90, 160
Osborn, Alex, 121
Oswald, Lee Harvey, 90-91
Out of Africa, 138
Outliers, 102, 107
outlines, 30-35
parables, 62, 70-71
parallelism, 52, 85-86, 168
passive voice, 84-85, 94-95, 133-34, 163-64
pathos, 34, 54, 56, 58
Peck, M. Scott, 10
Penny, Louise, 13

People's History of the United States, A, 105
perfectionism, 72, 75, 213
perspective on ourselves, 186-97
persuasion
coercion and, 38-39
defined, 38-39, 45
honesty in, 36-37, 39-45, 54-55
manipulation and, 37-39, 56, 158
memorability and, 50-53
pervasiveness of, 37
principled, 39, 45-46
purpose in, 45, 47
repetition and, 53-54
simplicity and, 48-50
structure and, 34, 54-58
Pilgrim at Tinker Creek, 138
Pilgrim's Progress, 138
plagiarism, 42-43
platform, theology of, 228-29
Plimpton, George, 106
plot, 137-38
Poe, Edgar Allan, 103
Pollan, Michael, 11
post hoc ergo propter hoc fallacy, 43-44
praise (receiving), 219-21, 223-24
prepositions at the end of sentences, 130-31
Presumed Innocent, 104
Pride and Prejudice, 10-11, 120
proposal for a book, 25, 231, 233-37
psychobabble, 49
Publishing for Profit, 240
Purves, Andrew, 172
Quiet, 56
Radiolab, 27-28
RAT test (Remote Associates Test), 116

Red Pony, The, 101
Reese, Harry Burnett (H. B.), 117
repetition, 53-54, 140
reversal of the situation, 95, 260 n. 11
rewriting, revising, 29, 31, 77, 81-87, 212-13
rhetoric, 46, 54
Rhodes, Richard, 124
rhyme, 51-52, 85
rhythm, 52, 86, 109, 132
rights, literary, 244-52
Road Less Traveled, The, 10
Rowling, J. K., 124
Rueff, Roger, 36
Russell, Mary Doria, 15, 70
Sacks, Oliver, 120
Salinger, J. D., 138
Screwtape Letters, The, 213
Scripture, authority of, 194-95, 207
Seabiscuit, 108, 161
Second-Book Syndrome, 211
Second Inaugural Address (Lincoln's), 162-68
Sedaris, David, 180
self-publishing, 227, 242-46
setting (literary), 137-38
1776, 21
Shack, The, 138
Shakespeare, William, 70, 74, 135-36, 152-53
Shepherd's Adventure, The, 140-41, 143
simile, 83, 146-47, 153
simplicity, 48-50, 52, 106-7, 139-40
Simpsons, The, 49
Sire, James W., 5, 44, 211, 235
Skloot, Rebecca, 67-68, 162
slavery, 162-68, 207-8

Smite Me, O Mighty Smiter, 99-100, 104
Smith, Noah, 14
sources (reliable), 39-41
Sparrow, The, 15, 70
specifics. *See* details
spiritual disciplines
  gaining perspective on ourselves, 186-97
  gratitude, 3-5, 188-89, 220-21, 223-24
  paying attention, 172-79, 187-88, 208
  remembering, 188-90
split infinitives, 132
Star Trek, 132, 220
Stein, Joel, 180
Steinbeck, John, 74, 101
Stephenson, Neal, 105
stewards, stewardship, 221-22
Still Life, 104
Stockett, Kathryn, 138
story, 52-53, 55-56, 59-65, 107, 138, 151, 161-62
  metaphor as a, 150-53
  opening with a, 18-19, 23-24
  research as a, 66-68
  structures for a, 33, 68-71, 92-93
storytelling, 61, 63, 258
Stott, John, 190
Strobel, Lee, 67
structure. *See* outlines

Strunk, William Jr., 160
subtitles, 100-101, 104, 108-9
success (effect of), 73, 197, 200, 211, 219-21
Sun Also Rises, The, 101
SuperFreakonomics, 109
Tale of Two Cities, A, 16-17
Talese, Gay, 105
Tan, Amy, 138
Taylor, Dan, 60
Team of Rivals, 104
temple (cosmic), 222
Tender Mercies, 157-58
tennis, 105-6, 123-24
Thank You for Arguing, 44
theme, 33, 136-42
thinking, convergent and divergent, 116-19
This American Life, 27
Thompson, Hunter S., 105
Thurber, James, 180
To Kill a Mockingbird, 73, 101
Tolkien, J. R. R., 117, 154-55
Tolstoy, Leo, 10
tone, 135-44, 181, 262-63
tradition, 184-85, 207-8
"Tradition and the Individual Talent," 184-85
Truss, Lynne, 131
Tuesdays with Morrie, 94-95
Tulsa World, 155
Twain, Mark, 131, 180, 183,
Unbroken, 107-8, 161

Unhurried Life, An, 211
Universe Next Door, The, 5, 211
Up (the movie), 68
vacation, 74, 124-25
vanity publishing, 242
Wall Street Journal, 18
Wallace, David Foster, 105
Wallas, Graham, 125
Walls, Jeannette, 161
Washington Post, 156
Weir, Andy, 243
Wesley, John, 207
What Color Is Your Parachute? 26
What to Expect When You're Expecting, 107
White, E. B., 160
Why Good Arguments Often Fail, 44
Wired magazine, 105, 117-18, 124
Wolf, Virginia, 133
Woll, Tom, 240
word choice, 82-83, 137, 140-41, 181
work for hire, 249
World Is Flat, The, 120
Wozniak, Steve, 57
writer's block, 72-80, 210-11
Zinsser, William, 27-29, 82, 89, 92, 160